SIMON
GARNER

One Last Shot

With Dan Clough and Richard Slater

northpoint™

Published by Northpoint Publishing
East Park Lodge, East Park Road, Blackburn BB1 8DW
info@northpointpublishing.co.uk

Printed by Book Printing UK www.bookprintinguk.com
Remus House, Coltsfoot Drive, Peterborough, PE2 9BF

Printed in Great Britain

ISBN 978-1-3999-7315-1

For Jane.
She knows why.

Acknowledgements

Thanks to Kenny Dalglish for the foreword and all those who gave their stories and memories that appear throughout this book. We are grateful to those who helped connect us to old friends

Thanks to the teams at www.chairboys.co.uk and www.wfchistory.com which provided valuable information, and to Windsor and Eton FC historian Michael Gegg.

Special thanks to Olivia McCaughran.

Picture credits

Thanks to The Lancashire Telegraph for images from my Blackburn career, Clive Lawrence for previously unseen images taken in his student days, Graham Smith for the images of Wealdstone FC including the back cover, Michael Porter for images from the Tony Parkes charity match. Thanks too to those who gave access to private collections.

Internal images featuring West Bromwich Albion and Wycombe Wanderers: PA Images / Alamy Photo Stock

Main cover images: PA Images / Alamy Photo Stock

About the authors

Dan Clough is a writer who worked for five years at the Lancashire Telegraph and now works in communications for the NHS. He also works as a freelance copywriter and ghost writer. A Blackburn Rovers supporter, Dan lives in Lancashire with his wife, two children, two dogs and a cat.

Richard Slater collaborated with Simon on There's Only One Simon Garner, published in 2002, and managed his 2003 testimonial match. Richard began his career as a journalist at the Lancashire Telegraph. He is founder and chairman of media organisation Northpoint which publishes Lancashire Business View.

CONTENTS

FOREWORD

By Kenny Dalglish

I was first asked to write a foreword for Simon's book back in 2002. At the time, Simon was still fondly remembered by the Blackburn Rovers supporters even 10 years after he had left the club – and for good reason. In the 20 years that have passed since then, Blackburn's fortunes have ebbed and flowed, and yet I know for a fact there will always be a special place in the heart of all Rovers fans for the one and only Simon Garner. And I am delighted to provide some words of introduction for this second book.

What stood out about Simon throughout his career was his finishing ability. He was a very natural striker with two good feet and he anticipated the game very well. He was never that quick – there wouldn't be much in it in a race between me and him – but he had it upstairs and knew where the goal was.

Simon was a tremendous servant to Blackburn and a very fine player, but football was changing in the early 1990s when I went to the club. He was never exactly the most disciplined of players. He liked a drink and a smoke and I was never going to change his ways. But that approach to the game was on the way out. Players were becoming increasingly conscious of how they should look after themselves.

Maybe he would have played at a higher level if he had kicked the fags and booze into touch, but I'm not so sure. The way he lived his life probably helped him. He is what he is and lived his life the way he wanted to by enjoying himself on and off the pitch. And I believe he still lives like that to this day.

When I arrived at Blackburn, Simon was coming towards the end of his career and he knew he wasn't going to see much first-team action with the changes that were happening at the club. But he responded well and played an important lesser role as the season went on.

When it came to the play-off final at Wembley in 1992, the club was allowed three non-playing team members to sit on the bench with the staff and substitutes.

The only place for Simon to be that day was with the team. He had given so much to the club and this was one of the most important days in its recent history.

Like Tony Parkes, who I asked to lead out the team, Simon was part of the fabric of the club and had helped create the platform for us to build on. His role had been a crucial one.

He didn't win much during a lean time at the club, but he had been a magnificent servant and I know how much it meant to him to be with the team that day. If you look at the celebration pictures, they say it all.

PREFACE

18 May 2003
Simon Garner testimonial match, Ewood Park, Blackburn
Blackburn Rovers XI 6 Simon Garner XI 3

I place the ball down on the spot and take a few paces back. I turn. Facing me is Irish international goalkeeper Alan Kelly. But in front of a Blackburn End full of blue and white there's only going to be one result. In it goes. My 195th goal for Blackburn Rovers, not that it really counts.

It's a special feeling for me to go back to Ewood Park, pull on that famous shirt one last time and score. The stands look a bit different to the ones I played in front of, but it's the same people chanting my name and taking me into their hearts. I'll be forever grateful to the people of Blackburn. They accepted me as one of their own. And I like to think I paid them back – 194 times to be exact.

To be invited back for a testimonial was an incredible honour. I'd had one back in my playing days when 7,000 turned out for a game against Newcastle. But being asked back eleven years after leaving feels truly special.

I'm part of a team made up of legends from the 1995 Premiership-winning Blackburn team – a team I wasn't part of in the end, although I like to think I played a significant role in the build-up to that memorable season in the club's history – bolstered by some of the kids whose careers are yet to truly take shape. There's Tim Flowers and Bobby Mimms, two fantastic goalkeepers from the glory days, Mike Newell, probably the best player I ever played with, and Stuart Ripley. Even my old mate Mark Atkins, who joined us as a kid and went on to be a crucial part of that title-winning side, has come back and performed in his typical under-stated yet solid manner. And Kenny Dalglish, known as the king to the Rovers faithful thanks to his achievements, is watching on from the sidelines. Even though he ended my Rovers career, he was a manager I feel honoured to have played for.

Among the opposition are some of the current Rovers stars. Tugay –

what a player – along with David Dunn, Dwight Yorke and Damien Duff. It's humbling to think they're here for me. And I am proud to count myself among a privileged group of people who have played for this famous old club.

I prepared for the game in the appropriate manner. Getting drunk with Gordon Taylor at Northcote Manor the night before. It was a bit classier than the boozers I'm used to, but this was a special occasion after all. Gordon was still chief executive of the PFA at the time, and as a fellow ex-Rover we have a lot in common.

I'm 43 now so I don't fancy a full 90 minutes. But at half-time our team of veterans and kids is 3-1 down. It's clear they need something. I come on as a half-time substitute for Welsh legend Mark Hughes – a like-for-like swap I'd say – and five minutes later I get my chance from the spot.

Okay, so maybe the penalty has been engineered deliberately and maybe I already know which way Alan Kelly is going to dive. But it is my testimonial after all.

To hear that roar from the Blackburn End one last time as a player is like music to my ears. My appearance is short-lived however and I hurt my calf after about five minutes, but the standing ovation and reception from the supporters as I leave the field makes the pain in my leg almost worthwhile. My last game of football had been in front of about 70 people for Flackwell Heath, a midtable side in Ryman League Division Three. This was different. This was special.

My professional football career lasted almost twenty years, and I continued playing at an amateur level and in friendly five-a-sides for a few years after that. The game was good to me and I think I made my mark. My dreams were to break goal-scoring records, play at Wembley and perform at the highest level of English football. I certainly went some way to achieving those dreams – and that day at Ewood was just about as perfect a send-off as I could have wished for.

CHAPTER 1

It's been a ball

It's been a long time since I played football. A bloody long time. The best time of my life. I had ups and downs during my playing career and, if truth be told, maybe I didn't fulfil my potential. I scored a lot of goals and played a lot of games. Most of them for one club. Had I moaned a bit more, kicked up more of a fuss, perhaps I'd have played at the top level. Mind you, had we not fallen at the final play-off hurdle quite so many times during my time at Blackburn, I would have got to the First Division. But it wasn't to be and I can honestly say I have no regrets.

I had a knack for scoring goals. And if I had left Blackburn Rovers I wouldn't be the club's all-time leading goal scorer. Nor would I have enjoyed such a relationship with the supporters of the club in that town that I love. The town I called home for almost as long as I spent in my childhood home of Boston.

I was fortunate to play with some great players who were more than happy to do a lot of the hard work and give me the ball to put in the back of the net. They were great players but also great lads. Lads who would become great friends – and great drinking partners. Football isn't a normal job. It paid the bills and kept me in fags and booze, but it also provided me with the lifestyle that only a footballer gets to enjoy. And I loved it.

Sadly, no one can play forever, and I may have got a bit longer at a decent level had it not been for the intervention of Her Majesty's Prison Service. More on that later.

I've been fully retired from football now for twenty years. Twenty bloody years. Two decades. I've been retired from the game I loved to play for almost as long as I was playing it.

With the help of Richard Slater, who was then a journalist starting out in business, I was able to get my story down on paper. There's Only One Simon Garner was published in 2002 and the response was excellent. It was humbling to know that, even a decade after I had left Blackburn Rovers, the supporters still thought so highly of me. And that's something when you consider my departure came in summer 1992, right at the beginning of the Jack Walker-inspired fairy-tale.

The following years saw King Kenny bring in Shearer and Sutton and the rest of the gang. International superstars took my place in the team, but they didn't take my place in the hearts of the Blackburn faithful who continue to remember those years of toil in the Second and Third Divisions of the Football League, when the Rovers barely had a pot to piss in.

Leaving Blackburn was a wrench, but I went on to play for two great clubs in West Brom and Wycombe, reunited with Ossie Ardiles – a World Cup winner and a great friend with whom I shared a love of tobacco and booze – and later worked with Martin O'Neill who was a truly inspirational leader of men. And I had a great time in the years that followed, plying my trade in non-league – working my way down the pyramid playing part-time for pocket money helped me to keep playing for as long as my body would allow. It also brought me my only league winners' medal.

My football earnings peaked at £600 a week, so there was no nest egg tucked away to live on, and so after a few odds and sods, I became a full-time painter and decorator, and I'm still doing that today. Throw in the occasional appearance on TV or a bit of summarising work on BBC Radio Lancashire and I'm doing okay. I did chuck the fags in at one point, but it lasted about half an hour.

So, for all intents and purposes I'm out of the game. At least I'm out of my game, anyway. And I'm pretty sure they don't play my game any more. The game I see on TV today is a far cry from what I used to play.

Football is far less physical than it was. As a striker I would have loved to play in today's game. Defenders are no longer allowed to just kick you from behind. The number of fouls I would have picked up by today's standards would be enormous. Matches when I played tended to be a battle, and some battles would be more ferocious than others. You had to be mentally strong enough to stand up to the verbal and physical abuse. And you had to be prepared to give them a kick back. There were a lot of players who got scared by that. They would get kicked in the first five or 10 minutes and then would go into hiding for the rest of the game. But as a striker going up against these big burly centre-halves who could cut you in half, you just had to be tough.

We had a running ding-dong with Portsmouth when I was at Blackburn – it was like a local derby even though the clubs are more than 250 miles apart. I tended to get a good kicking from their centre halves Billy Gilbert and Noel Blake, and I would give them a good kicking back. But after the game we would all shake hands and have a beer together.

Micky Droy at Chelsea must have been about eight feet tall. At least that's how he seemed on the pitch. He was a big bugger, put it that way. An absolute monster. He just had this presence and a big part of his game was upsetting the opposition players however he could. Intimidate them so they don't want to play. Blackburn played them a few times in the early to mid-80s. The first time I came up against him he kicked me in the first two or three minutes of a game and I didn't say anything to him, but the next time I got near him I kicked him back. He looked at me as if to say, "Oh, okay then. This one's not for being wound up."

Characters like that were commonplace in those days, now they're like hen's teeth.

I'm not saying the lads playing the game now are soft, but they certainly don't have to deal with the level of physicality meted out to me throughout most of my playing career.

The old system of having the reserves in the Central League with all the big local sides involved meant I came across some hard and experienced players when I was young. It was a really good grounding that helped me understand just how tough I needed to be to play the game professionally. I really don't think young players today get the same benefit from the under-23s setup that exists in the modern game.

And there's a lot more protection from the referee now as well. Saying that, refereeing has changed enormously – they're like celebrities nowadays. When I was playing you could talk to the ref and, God forbid, have a laugh and a swear and it wouldn't end up in a 10-match ban. In one game for Blackburn, away at Leicester, it was snowing like mad and the Leicester fans were throwing snowballs at us. One of them clocked me right on the side of the head and I went down. My mum and brother had come for the game – which was a real rarity because I don't remember Mum coming to many games at all – and they were worried I had been hurt because I didn't get straight back up. I was fine. It was the ref who was standing over me.

"Just stay down, let's run the clock down for a bit!"

The biggest difference between 'the good old days' and today is, of course, the astronomical amount of money in the game. The top players are all millionaires but even the squad players who barely get a kick in the Premier League are on anywhere from £30,000 a week and more. As long as they're not stupid with their money, they'll never need to work again. The kids start on big money now as well. My first professional contract at Blackburn was £45 a week, which was doubled to £90 when I was 19. Kids today are earning more than £1,000 a week before their 18th birthday. As Nanny Garner would say, they don't know they're born.

While they might earn a heck of a lot of money and enjoy the freedoms of a game where they don't get kicked for 90 minutes, the lads can't go anywhere without it ending up all over social media. When I was playing, I could be out in a pub having a pint and a fag and, thankfully, nobody could get out a mobile phone and film me. Not that I was up to anything nefarious, but the scrutiny was nothing like it is now. At Blackburn and West Brom I lived locally and drank in the town so I was pretty recognisable. I would love to play nowadays from a financial perspective, but I really wouldn't want all the social media attention the players have to put up with. They just can't go anywhere.

I only used an agent once in my career but they run the game now. Life was much more simple back then, most people were on a year's contract and were either offered a new one or they weren't. The player, or their agent as the case may be, didn't have as much power so in general you would accept what was offered to you. Players don't even talk to the club now when it comes to negotiating contracts, it's all done by their agents. These are people motivated purely by business, driving up the value of their client and earning them, and themselves, as much money as possible in various different ways – salary, bonuses, clauses, add-ons. You name it, they've thought of it, and are making money from it.

And training – flipping heck – a hard training day for Blackburn in the 80s was running round the pitch about 10 times. Half a lap, then a rest, then another half a lap. Bit of work with the ball – how much of that depended on who the gaffer was at the time – and then back to the ground for something to eat. The team would pile back to Ewood Park and have something from the menu in the John Lewis Suite. I used to like a chip butty, but I doubt today's pros would get away with that. I'd hate to see what the diet sheet says now – it's probably all chicken and fish, and my opinion on fish is that it should not be considered food.

There's so much science in it these days. I went down to Wycombe a couple of years ago and the players all had heart monitors on. This was in League One – I couldn't believe it. They had somebody sitting inside watching the numbers on the computer and when a player's heartbeat reached a certain level they could stop training.

The scientists know so much more these days and training is completely different as a result of that. But the knock-on is that in today's game it isn't enough to just be a decent footballer. If you aren't super fit you probably won't make it. You have to be able to run and run and run.

In spite of the earning potential, I don't think I would have enjoyed playing now half as much as I did 30 and 40 years ago. I might not have much to show for it, apart from a couple of medals, a bit of memorabilia and some wonderful memories, but it just isn't the same as it was. The craic isn't there now, not for the lads playing in the top divisions, and I just enjoyed being able to wander down to the local for a beer with the lads.

I got lucky throughout my career that in every team I played we had a tremendous team spirit and everyone got on. That started for me at Blackburn and went right through to my days in non-league. Everywhere I went we had a real bond between the lads and we all looked out for each other and, most importantly, had a good drink together. And that was probably as important to me as the payslip at the end of the week. I couldn't have played at a club where there wasn't a good team spirit. Being a footballer is a dream job, but only when there's a good bunch around you who all get on.

Footballer's books are ten a penny these days, and this is my second. If you read the first you may remember some of these stories. It's great to see some of my old pals putting their own stories out there. Baz Rathbone's published his own sequel and Mark Patterson's book was great. We're all getting older but football is a sport that clings to and cherishes its past.

Some days I feel older than others. And the guys I played with are all getting older, too. I'm at the time of my life where funerals for former colleagues come round quicker than I would like. Lads like Chris Thompson who partnered me up front for three years at Blackburn, and Lenny Johnrose who fought so hard against motor neurone disease. And the great Cyrille Regis who I played with at Wycombe. All top players and fantastic friends.

And of course there are those struggling with their health. At the time of writing the legend that is Tony Parkes has been fighting dementia. A great servant to Blackburn and an incredible coach and man, there's many a footballer who's gone through Blackburn Rovers owing Tony a great deal and it is devastating to see his struggles now.

It's important our stories are remembered of the days when football was so different. Or at least I think it is anyway. And this time around I've had help and I have to thank the former players and managers who have kindly contributed and shared their thoughts and stories.

Thank you for taking the time to pick up this book. I hope you enjoy it.

Dave Garner
Older brother

When Simon was born I went to stay with a relative in Fishtoft, which is a village about three miles outside Boston. I was seven at the time and at school, somebody spun round in the playground and knocked my two front teeth out. As brothers, Simon and I naturally share some traits – not least our dashing good looks – but missing front teeth was never part of the plan.

I never held that against him and we have always been the best of friends. I followed his football career closely and we remain in regular contact.

Growing up there was always quite an age gap. When Simon was five and starting primary school, I was going off to the grammar school and when he started at the grammar school I was getting ready to go off to university.

My overriding memory of Simon is of him playing football. Constantly. Either outside on the large lawn at the side of the house or playing keepy uppy with a balloon in the lounge or on the landing, which would drive our mum mad. But that was what he did. All the bloody time.

In front of where we lived there was a green and he would play on there. You had to be careful because there were privet hedges in front of all the houses and you had to keep the ball down otherwise it was an issue getting it back. We did a lot of tapping the ball about in the back garden because there was a plant nursery behind the house and if the ball went over there the chap who owned it would get quite upset at us trampling all over his plants.

He's never had the most sophisticated of palettes, and it's pretty widely known he was never the model footballer and was partial to a pint and a chip butty, but growing up if he wanted a snack he would get an unsliced loaf of white bread, pull all the inside out and eat that with either cucumber or tomatoes. And when he started school it would be round to Nanny Garner's for his dinner of either bread and gravy or pancakes.

Family holidays would be in sunny Mablethorpe, which is on the coast just under an hour's drive from Boston, and we always went with Mum's sister and her children, so there would be four adults and five children all sharing a house. They were fantastic holidays with massive games of cricket on the beach. And if it rained we would go out there and play golf in a pac a mac. While winning was never important, Dad and our uncle Bill would always end up playing against each other competitively and get into an argument over whether the ball was on the line. They were good times.

Sport was always important in our family. Dad was a goalkeeper for the village team and his two brothers also played. As a long-distance lorry driver he tended to be away most of the week but when he came home he would tell us about games he had been to. He was a bit of a Manchester United fan so he would go to Old Trafford when he could, but he went to lots of other games, like the Old Firm Derby in Glasgow.

By the time I was 16 I had played for my school football team and Dad ran two or three teams. It was a huge part of what we did as a family. Simon picked up on that and developed a real love of football. And you could soon tell there was something there. He clearly had the ability to go on and play the game at a much higher standard than myself or Dad ever had. Lots of kids go through phases and then find other interests, but with Simon he maintained a commitment to playing and to his development.

By the time he was making his way into professional football, I had grown up, gone to university and become a teacher. But I was so proud to see him succeed and when he started going on trials, one of the clubs who looked at him was Leicester City. My wife and I were living in Leicester at this point and he came to see us. You could tell he was loving the fact he was on the verge of being paid to play the game he had been obsessed with since kicking that balloon up and down the living room.

When he made his home debut for Blackburn, which turned out to be against Leicester, he rang me up in the morning to tell me he was playing. We were just on with the Saturday morning chores and I turned to my wife, Janet and told her I really fancied going. We had a ropey Mini at the time so it took ages, but I got there and it was incredible to see my brother wearing that famous blue and white shirt.

Having a brother who was a footballer gave me an insight into other sides of the game. I was at a Blackburn game once when manager Don Mackay was shouting and ranting in his thick Scottish accent and all the players were looking over and nodding as though they had got the message. Don's wife was sitting near us and we asked what he had just said.

"No idea. He always does that and nobody has a clue."

After the game, Simon was able to confirm he had no idea what instructions his boss had been yelling from the sidelines.

The vast majority of the Blackburn games I saw him play were away, often around the Midlands as that's where we lived. After matches he was always the same. Very matter of fact, never upset if they hadn't won, except for after the 1989 play-off final at Crystal Palace when he was absolutely gutted. But I was always quite impressed that despite all the pressure of being the one relied on to score the goals, he could put all that to one side and not let it affect him.

And he was always so amiable with the supporters and other people who wanted to stop him and have a chat about the game or get a photograph or autograph. My wife and I went up to Blackburn one weekend and went for a meal at a new Italian restaurant with Simon and Mandy, his wife at the time.

A woman came over and asked if he would have a photograph with her grandad who was a big Rovers fan and was out to celebrate his birthday.

"Yes, of course."

He went over, had the photograph and a chat with the family for a few minutes and made their evening. It was just so typical of him and the way he is, and the way he always has been.

It was a pleasure watching Simon play football and seeing how his career developed. But perhaps even more important is the way he handled it all. He never let it go to his head and always remained true to his roots. I am proud to call him my brother.

CHAPTER 2

The birth of the Lincolnshire Poacher

1959 to 1976

I was born at Nanny Garner's. November 23, 1959, at Fishtoft, near Boston, sometime between 10 and midnight. Dad was a lorry driver and away working so he missed it. When he was out of town, Mum would sometimes stay at her mother-in-law's and when she was heavily pregnant with me it was insisted on. There was never any question of me being born in the hospital. The reason I know the time is because Dad left my uncle Ivor the name of the club he'd be in that night and he learned about his second son's arrival in a strange town with a bingo card in one hand, a fag in the other and a glass of lemon and lime in front of him. He didn't drink, but he did like bingo.

Some think it's in the genes. A parent, brother or cousin – a distant uncle perhaps – must have been involved at some level of sport and that sparks a domino effect of achievement through successive generations. Not in my family. The highest sporting honour belonged to my dad – and he was a second-rate goalkeeper in a third-rate team in a fourth-rate amateur league. No one was any good at sport. Only me. Just as well, too, because I was never much good at anything else.

If sporting ability doesn't necessarily pass through the generations, perhaps it's a sporting obsession which is transferred. You know the situation – the offspring is transfixed by the bright lights and heady atmosphere of a major sporting event. And once tasted, the ambition is inspired and the obsession reborn.

Nope. Not me. I was brought up in Lincolnshire, and it's not what you'd call a hotbed of sporting prowess. The nearest professional football club was Lincoln City – Boston United at that time competed in the Southern

League, three or four divisions below what was then the Fourth Division and is now called League Two. In the flesh I saw just one professional game before signing apprentice terms at Blackburn Rovers. It was a night match at the City Ground, Nottingham. I have no idea who Forest were playing and I can't remember the score, but I know I was bored. I wanted to be playing footie with my mates.

I would say the first team I supported was Manchester City. Not that I became a dyed in the wool Cityzen. It came about mainly because I really liked Colin Bell. He was the first footballer I ever really noticed. He was such an exciting player to watch and was part of that great City team of the Sixties and Seventies with Franny Lee, Mike Summerbee and the rest. They had a great team in those days.

I was never much of a spectator and I'm still not, though I do the odd bit of punditry with the BBC, mainly when Blackburn are playing down south. There is simply no substitute for kicking a ball around. I played as long as my legs would allow me and was still taking part in the odd five-a-side until I was almost 60. I'd play with anyone, for anyone. Money had nothing to do with it.

In fairness to my Dad, Geoff, he wasn't such a bad player – or so he always told me – but his cartilages packed in. But he was a big sports fan, much more than I could ever be. I think it was because his own ambitions were frustrated by a lack of, well, ability, that he became a once-removed sports addict. He would watch any kind of sport at whatever level and whenever he could. It could be schoolboys playing cricket or it could be some obscure Olympic event on the box – if it was available, he'd be watching.

Football was his favourite though, and I know he'd like to have watched much more but Boston is miles from anywhere. Boston was a quality side for their level, but for professional football it was Lincoln – who were in the Fourth Division – or Forest. In my late teens it was the Brian Clough era, though when they started to romp their way round Europe I was at Blackburn and my dad was more interested in my career than watching anyone else. He never really had allegiance to any particular team, just to watch was the joy of the game for him and he didn't need to be wearing a scarf to prove he was a real fan.

I'm sure that's why he became interested in coaching. It was only at an amateur level, but Dad got quite involved with a number of teams. He was ambitious for his players, though not in that over-bearing way some parents want their children to live out their own unfulfilled dreams. He just wanted to see more kids involved in sport rather than have them hanging around getting into trouble.

David, my brother, is seven years older than me. He says he played football, but all I can remember about him when we were little was that he was mad about model aeroplanes. I could never work it out, to be honest. What was the point in sitting indoors with a tube of glue, 200 bits of grey plastic and an instruction leaflet that read like it had been written by the bloke who sweeps up the factory? What was wrong with going out, kicking a ball, playing a bit of cricket, going swimming? He improved with age though and he did play with my Dad's team when he got older. But he was more academic than me and he definitely cared more for his future. David seemed to have sensible plans while all I wanted was to be playing football professionally. As I've matured, so has my outlook on life. I can now look as far forward as tomorrow, but not much further.

It served him well, too. He went on to university which was as big a deal in my family as me making my debut for Blackburn. It was different 50 years ago, not as many people went to university and certainly not many from council estates around Boston. Dad was a driver and Mum, Peg, was a hairdresser who later worked in a bakery and a dress shop, so David's achievement was a source of genuine pride to them. He taught art and design until he retired, which perhaps explains why he was so obsessive about getting exactly the right colours in those little tin pots to finish off his replica Spitfires or whatever they were. Still, he made a career out of something he always liked doing. And it took him through to retirement on a decent wage. The irony, by the way, isn't lost on me – I've largely scraped a living as a painter and decorator for the past 20-odd years.

We were never close, but that's not to say we've not always been friends – we have – and, with the exception of my Dad, he followed my career as keenly as anyone. But when we were younger we had nothing in common and with seven years between us we had a wholly different set of friends. When I started primary school he was moving into secondary school. When I went to secondary school he left home for university. And when I moved to Blackburn he was taking his first steps into teaching.

I've never considered myself academic because I was always side-tracked by sport, but I did pass my 11-plus and was accepted into Boston Grammar School. So there must have been something there. There was never any pressure on me, though. The achievement was that I had got there and I had always told Mum and Dad I was going to be a footballer. They never once tried to persuade me otherwise.

School was good. I liked it. Not the lessons, of course, I was never much use in class, but school gave me a chance to play more sports. After school I'd get home, throw my bag inside and play football or cricket with the lads in the street. And at school they made it all a bit more formal. I learned how to play tennis and the cricket coaching was excellent – I had county trials but never made the team. I wasn't bothered at all, only football counted.

It was a great childhood and I was allowed to grow up just as I wanted to. I did what I wanted, within reason, and my parents were always supportive. Clifton Road, Fishtoft, was where we lived. We had the top flat in a two-storey house with two bedrooms for the four of us. It was never warm – you had hot and you had cold. Mostly cold. There were coal fires in the kitchen and the living room and no central heating. I'd get out of bed and it was freezing. I'd have to run to the kitchen and sit in front of the fire just to get dressed without contracting hypothermia.

What I really liked about living there was the fact it was on the estate. I knew everybody and, on Clifton Road, I knew everybody very well. Outside the house was a big green. That sounds a bit posh, and it wasn't, but it was a great big grass area. The Wembley of Fishtoft. Or something. Dad's brothers lived close by and a lot of people who worked at the same place as my Dad lived on the estate. I don't want to sound all sentimental, and I know it's a horrible cliché, but you could leave your doors unlocked and let kids play out until it was dark. And that's what we used to do. There would be six or seven of us out every night kicking a ball around and then we'd go down to the chippy round the corner for chips and scraps.

Dad never worked weekends, which was great. When I was very young we would watch local football on a Saturday afternoon, we'd be in the baths for 7.30 on Sundays and in the afternoons it'd be back to the parks for more football. He was often away for three or four nights during the week with his job, so his weekends were special to him. But they always revolved around watching or playing sport. It was the same with holidays. We'd meet up with other families so there would be maybe 20 or 30 of us and it was always football, cricket, tennis, swimming. Anything so long as there was sport involved.

I'd be about 10 when he started coaching. He took on Boston Colts under-16s and under-18s. I've no idea how it all began but he knew a lot from his own playing days and there was no one in Lincolnshire who'd seen more football than my Dad. He'd obviously learned a lot, too, because his teams were incredibly successful – within a couple of years they were winning the league every year and they were always in with a shout of the cups. He managed to attract the best young players around and made them one of the hottest teams in the county.

The first match I remember playing in was for his under-16 side. I was 12. If he ever had a problem with his teams it was that some of the older players started to become attracted to the snooker halls, the pubs and the girls. So occasionally there were gaps on the pitch, despite the fact we'd trawl players' houses on a Sunday morning looking for stragglers. By this point we were also at the football ground two nights a week getting the pitch ready for the first team. Mum was fine about all this. She was a generous, loving woman and was just happy for my Dad to be enjoying himself. I was living and breathing football from then on. I knew all the teams, all the players. I wasn't as obsessive as my Dad, though my collection of magazines and cards was growing nicely. If I'd had doubts before, I knew now there was only one thing I was ever going to do when I finished school. The game, the first I remember, was a Lincolnshire Cup Final. We were a player short, and Dad decided it was time I tested myself against bigger, stronger, meaner boys. Actually, he was desperate, and I had my boots on. I scored and we won. Mum was proud as punch of both of us.

I don't want to give the impression that somehow Mum was left out with Dad and me being so close. It wasn't like that. And it wasn't just my Dad who worked hard in that house. When Mum worked at the bakery, I'd jump on the back of her bike and she'd cycle to Nanny Garner's where

I would stay until it was time to go to school. As soon as the last bell went, she was at the gates, we'd go home, I'd play out and she'd do the housework. And Dad would be on the other side of the country lugging his lorry around. When I got older I'd bike it myself, but the draw of Nanny Garner's never changed. I was very close to Nanny Garner. She was already retired by the time I was going through my childhood and she had really bad arthritis in her hands. I wouldn't say she brought me up but I used to be round her house every day because Mum and Dad would be working. She had to feed me most lunchtimes as well. I had one school dinner and that was it. I didn't like it. So I would get back on the bike and cycle to her house. It was a two-mile round trip which, in the freezing cold depths of a Lincolnshire winter, could be a trial. She'd make me bread and gravy or pancakes, egg and chips. When I was older, she'd slip me 20 fags from her pension money.

In Boston, there was a choice of two schools, or three if you count St Bede's. But nobody went to St Bede's. Unless you were a Catholic. The other choice was Kitwood. Academia was never my strong point and I'm not sure I could spell the word without the aid of a dictionary, but I wasn't daft and I knew the Grammar School, being a grammar school, had better sports facilities. With this insider knowledge, the 11-plus was never going to be anything more than a formality. Unfortunately, once I was in the schoolwork took a tumble. But the football was terrific. By the time I was 14 I was only interested in games lessons and sports matches. The crowning achievement was being selected to play for the school's first team. The school had a sixth form so this meant I was playing with lads – men – who were four years older than me. I was the youngest player to ever get into that team. But best of all I got to miss double history every Wednesday afternoon for matches. It was brilliant – you could see my classroom from the pitch. It was inevitable my schoolwork would suffer, and it did. The facilities were fantastic and I was playing tennis and basketball and I was in the swimming and cricket teams. Strangely, rugby wasn't played. I was pleased about that. I didn't like the game.

Rod Dunn was my sports master and he was superb. He persuaded me to go to county cricket trials and suggested I put myself forward as a wicket-keeper. I ignored the advice, went as a fielder and bowler and never got past the first selection round. I wasn't disappointed at all. In fact, I deliberately contributed to my own failure. When he was telling me I should go, I told him I was really only interested in football.

"You're a good footballer, Simon, but you're a good cricketer, too. You could perhaps make a living in both of them."

Well hang on a minute, Dunny. Thanks for the flattery, but let's get some perspective here. The end of the cricket season overlaps the start of the football season. End of story. Mr Dunn never fell out with me, though. He knew what I really wanted. Unlike Philip Johnston. A man, I am ashamed to admit, that I detested. He was the headmaster and, by an unfortunate twist of bad fate, he later became headmaster at Queen Elizabeth Grammar School in Blackburn. Just to be in the same town as him was enough to make me feel queasy. I got my own back, though. Twice. When I joined Blackburn he had no option but to see me regularly plastered over the pages of the local paper. And I think even he would have to have conceded that I had done all right. The first piece of revenge came much earlier.

I had always swum and for a time I was a member of Boston Swimming Club, which the school seemed to think made me something of a butterfly expert. Granted, I had once swum a competitive length for the school in our own pool. It was 15 metres long and I just about managed to reach the other end without drowning. The next time I was picked was for some inter-school event – off home ground. The pool was 25 metres long and by halfway I was sinking. I hated it.

I happened to be ill on the day of the next gala. I really was ill and it was no fun. Mum and Dad were both at work, Nanny Garner must have been busy, and I was miserable. I knew it was serious, because I couldn't even muster the energy for a kickabout. The phone rang. It was on the floor below.

"Hello?"

"Where are you, Garner?"

"I'm ill sir."

"You're skiving more like, You're a disgrace."

Not for the first time, nor the last, Johnson got it wrong. Then he made a very bad mistake. He rang my Dad at work.

"Mr Garner, this is Simon's headmaster. I am appalled your son is skipping school just to avoid a length of butterfly."

Now Dad, being a lorry driver, knew one or two choice phrases, and Johnson got them full on. He even wrote to Johnson, the only letter I ever remember him writing. It was littered with F words. I don't remember us getting a reply. No matter, I never swam for the school again.

I could never really work Johnson out. I remember him telling me I was just wasting my time, that I should stop thinking I could ever kick a ball around for money. It seemed such a stupid way to deal with a child's ambitions. It wasn't as if he was trying to get me to spread my energies, he just told me I should be thinking of my future, of responsibilities, of getting a proper job, of stopping playing football. I could never understand his attitude. Schools like BGS and QEGS are renowned not just for the academic side of things but for sport as well. And he just didn't seem to like sport at all, other than to bask in the reflected glory of Mr Dunn and the occasional big victory for one of the teams.

I suppose breaking into the first team when I was 14 was when I started to think I really had a chance of making it. The local football scene in Boston was very tightly knit and well connected with the professional game, certainly at the scouting level. I was playing for Dad's teams and it didn't take too long for my name to get around and for the letters to start coming through the door offering trials. I did Scunthorpe, Leicester, Brighton, Forest, Ipswich, Hull, Derby and Blackburn Rovers.

Scunthorpe offered me terms. The conversation with the youth coach makes me laugh even now.

"Keegan started here, lad."

And that was about the extent of their pitch. They offered me £8 a week, which would go up to £10 after a year. I didn't consider it much of a loyalty bonus.

John Blackwell, who was the club secretary at Boston, had recommended me to Blackburn. He was still friendly with boss Jim Smith who had been the Boston manager a few years earlier. John was a family friend who had known Dad for years. He's still part of the furniture at Boston United now. In fact, he's the club president.

Around the same time as the offer from Scunthorpe, Blackburn came in with £16 rising to £18. No contest. It wasn't just the money, though it played a part. Scunthorpe was much closer to home but Blackburn seemed a better opportunity for me. Also, at that time Scunthorpe had the biggest pitch in the football league, so I'm not sure how I'd have got on running around on there for 90 minutes.

My Dad was pretty astute in the negotiations. He always said I should never sign schoolboy forms with anyone because it might tie me up and that I should wait instead for apprentice terms. He was even cagey about Boston United. Howard Wilkinson was manager there when I was in my last year at school and because my Dad knew the club secretary he wangled it for me to train with the club. Howard asked me to sign on as a non-contract player but I didn't want any problems if a league club came in for me.

"No, no, there will be no problems like that."

He was true to his word. I did sign the forms but four weeks later I was a Blackburn Rovers apprentice. No money changed hands, not a penny. I know the families of youngsters now can be offered six-figure sums as sweeteners towards them pledging their sons' futures. Maybe there was some of that knocking about then, but I'm not so sure. I was about to turn 16 and everything I'd ever dreamed of was now in my hands. My family wasn't well off but we were never skint, and Mum and Dad worked hard to make sure it stayed that way. They, like me, were just delighted I had been given the chance. Looking back it was probably naïve, but for me and my parents money always lagged way behind happiness in the important-things-in-life stakes. My view then, as it was throughout my career, was that I had the chance to play football for a living. Cash was always a side issue. Well, nearly always.

I genuinely don't regret that at all. People used to ask me why I didn't go for a transfer and pick up a signing-on fee. But it was simple – I was on a good wage and I was playing football. I never used to look beyond the next season, never even considered retirement. I thought it would never end. I was perfectly happy just to go out and kick a ball.

John Blackwell
Family friend and Boston United club secretary in 1976

While Simon never kicked a ball for the Boston United first team I have always felt very proud that I was able to help him on his way to a very good career.

I became friendly with Simon's parents, Geoff and Peg, while coaching junior football in the Boston area. One of Geoff's teams, Boston FC Youth, were our arch-rivals, and every Sunday I would meet up with him and his football-mad son at the Main Ridge launderette to wash the kits.

We would have a great laugh and chew over the day's football gossip, and Simon was always with him. He went everywhere with his Dad.

I got to know Simon and followed his progress through school, county and local football. He was an incredible talent even then and you could just tell he had that something special and had the potential to make it big in the game.

I even played alongside him for a season in the Lincolnshire Standard Sunday team, with the likes of the editor, deputy editor, photographer and my brother-in-law. Simon was the youngest in the team by many years and scored goals for fun.

He was a great player but he did like his food and so earned the nickname 'Guts Garner'!

I convinced him to come down and play with the Boston United youth team. Not long after that I got in touch with Blackburn manager Jim Smith, who was another friend due to his time as manager of Boston, and persuaded him to give Simon a trial.

Jim immediately saw how good he was and offered him a contract, which made me very proud. When he went down to sign for Blackburn, my wife Maureen and I went along with the Garners to renew our friendship with the Smiths.

On another occasion Simon invited me and the then-chairman of Boston United to a match at Ewood Park. It was a great day and we were very well looked after. They took us into the impressive boardroom with all the oak panels and the plaques from all the other clubs, you could just feel the history there.

In later years whenever Boston was playing at Wycombe he would always come along to watch and find us for a chat and, of course, one or two drinks. He never forgot where he came from and it was lovely that we were able to keep in touch.

I am glad I could play a part in a great career.

CHAPTER 3

From Boston to Blackburn

1976 to 1979

Blackburn was a similar sort of place to Boston, although it was quite a bit bigger. I had already spent a week there on trial with about seven or eight other lads and we were all there for one reason – to try and get a contract as an apprentice. We got on really well and we all went into training every morning and worked hard to impress the coaches.

We spent the week in a terraced house right next to Ewood Park in Nuttall Street. There was a Hovis television advert some years ago with a shot of a football ground and cobbled streets. That was the Blackburn End entrance to Ewood Park on Nuttall Street. When Jack Walker redeveloped the ground the house was demolished. Given the current facilities for young Blackburn players, I doubt if it's missed much. A house full of lads. No adults, except for the lady who came in to make our breakfast and cook our evening meal.

Training finished at about one o'clock every day, so I quickly discovered where I could go and play snooker and have a pint. Yes I was only 16, but this was the Seventies after all. Some of the lads were very dedicated and would spend the afternoon in the house watching TV or just relaxing, preparing for the next day of the trial. But thankfully I was able to find a couple of like-minded lads who were up for going out.

I obviously did enough as they offered me a deal. Perhaps there was a bit of luck there as Jim Smith was the manager and we both had the Boston connection.

I signed in the August as a 16-year-old and that was me leaving home. It was a wrench because I didn't know anyone in Blackburn but I did know I was joining a professional football outfit with a fantastic history. It might not have been Liverpool or Manchester United, but it wasn't Scunthorpe either.

I coped well. My Dad had always been on the road a lot and I had become used to being away from home because of all the trials I was doing, which usually meant two weeks away at a time, but I still missed Mum and Nanny Garner. We were a close family in the sense that we got on well and shared interests, but we were also strong enough for me, like my brother, to move away and for that sense of belonging to remain. And, let's be honest, this was what I had always wanted and to play football I would have to move out earlier than most of my friends and break the family bonds sooner. And that was fine – I was a footballer now.

Dad was so pleased for me to get an apprenticeship. He knew Blackburn wasn't the biggest club in the world, but it wasn't that long since they had been a good First Division side with internationals like Bryan Douglas and Ronnie Clayton. It was a famous old club with a rich history and all the family was proud I'd been taken on.

I was planning a future where I could have my cake and eat it, where I could wake up in the morning and think 'bloody hell, I'm playing football today – and they're paying me to do it!' That was a good feeling.

I wasn't brilliant at school and, if I hadn't got the apprenticeship at Blackburn, I would probably have got an apprenticeship at the firm where my dad worked, Fogarty Quilts and Pillows. It stayed open until about five years ago so that could have been a job for life.

The club put the apprentices up in digs, so it was back to a little terrace in Nuttall Street. Four or five of us lived there and Connie would come in and cook breakfast for us, wash up and then come back and fix us an evening meal. Connie was great. She knew what she was doing and she looked after the lads. Other than that we were left alone. Which is a dangerous thing to do with a bunch of kids under any circumstance, but with a bunch of kids who thought they were going to be the next George Best...

We would spend almost as much time in The Fernhurst pub, just down the road from the ground, as we did on the training pitch. I still love to play snooker now and it was no different back then. There would be six or seven of us in there, some drinking lime and lemonade, some drinking beer. You'll never guess.

Our serious drinking nights were Saturdays at the Cavendish nightclub in the shopping centre. It's shut now but people in Blackburn have long memories. It's been called Romeo and Juliet's, Peppermint Place, Utopia, Heaven and Hell, but it was always known as The Cav by kids who weren't even born when that name died.

We stayed in the digs until the club could find a family willing to take in an apprentice. They would be paid to look after us. After a few weeks I moved up to Darwen to live with Mr and Mrs Watson. They were a lovely old couple but they kept forcing spinach on me. They were very set in their ways. Mondays it was steak and kidney pie. Tuesdays, liver and onions. Sausage and mash on Wednesdays. Week in, week out. And spinach. Every bloody day. Well maybe not every day, but enough to put me off for life. Spinach. Bloody spinach. I bloody hate the stuff.

I started to get to know the locals when I lived in Darwen. I probably (definitely) shouldn't have but I began frequenting The Victoria in Sudell Road. I wanted to mix in. I got to know them and got on well with them. They were my kind of people with a similar background to mine. And although the Watsons were lovely I didn't want to spend every night with them watching Coronation Street, I wanted to get out for a few games of snooker and a drink. I had a life outside football living in the area which lasted throughout my career in Blackburn.

Mr Watson was much older than his wife and sadly had a heart attack while I was there which left him bedridden and me looking for a new place to live.

Next stop was Trevor Close on the Wimberley Estate in Blackburn. A modern well-looked-after council estate, with Harry and Hilda Wilkinson. They were a lot more family-oriented than the Watsons, who had never had children. They had three kids, all a bit older than me, and they were great to live with – easy-going and big Blackburn Rovers fans.

It was hardly glamorous. But then, neither was the club at the time. In fact, football was not the glamorous, star-studded industry it has gone on to become. We had to get to training on the bus once we'd left Nuttall Street. And we had to pay for it out of our own pockets. I was always skint but fortunately there was a tobacconist on the corner at Darwen Circus who sold fags in singles. God knows how else I'd have managed.

As an apprentice you had to get to work early. We would be at the training pitch, which was five miles away in Livingstone Road behind Accrington Stanley's ground, for nine every morning. The routine was fairly monotonous, but we did get to train at the same place as the pros. I was learning and my appetite for improvement never dimmed throughout my career.

We would get the kit ready at Ewood, load it on to the minibus, take it up to Altham, put it out ready for the senior players, clean everything up when they finished at lunch time, put the gear back in the minibus, come back to Ewood and do all the jobs back at the ground.

I was in charge of cleaning the baths and the showers. We did it every day but on a Friday it had to be done properly for the match the following day. In those days there was a massive bath plus two or three individual showers. It was my responsibility to clean them and make sure they were spick and span. After a home game on a Saturday it would be our job to go in and sweep out the Ewood terraces after training on the Monday and Tuesday. We would clean the kit and boots of the first team after they finished training.

I looked after the boots of Gordon Taylor and Ken Beamish. They were great and put their hands in their pockets for a generous tip come Christmas time.

We couldn't leave the ground until the youth team coach, John Pickering, or Pick, had come and inspected everything. It was like the Army. Everything had to be sparkling. I was always desperate to get away to play snooker so I used to hate Fridays. We would finish training at 12 and sometimes we wouldn't get away until three.

It was tough being an apprentice. Thankfully there were no daft initiations or anything like that to put up with. I've heard stories about all sorts of shenanigans during the 80s, and even now they tend to make the new players sing a song in front of everyone or something like that, but that didn't happen for me. But it was still hard going.

When you think about it, using the kids for all those jobs back then must have saved football clubs a fortune. They have so many people working at clubs now that the kids just focus on the training – they don't have all the jobs we had to do.

Yes it was tough but it was great for character building and toughening us up. Young lads nowadays are training and learning all the time. They'll never have to sweep the terraces. It wasn't glamorous and it wasn't particularly fun, but it gave us a good grounding. And if anything it made you work harder because you wanted to sign a professional contract as quickly as possible to put an end to all the bloody chores. Talk about motivation.

Today Blackburn has one of the finest academy setups in the country, if not the world. The facilities at Brockhall are incredible, especially in comparison to what we had. Not long after I joined we stopped training at Altham and spent time at Brockhall (before it was redeveloped) and used some of the public parks in Blackburn. We used the pitches at Pleasington until well into the 90s, even when Kenny Dalglish was the manager. At Brockhall there's a bunch of pitches, all identical in size to the one at Ewood, a swimming pool, an indoor pitch, fantastic catering facilities, accommodation for the youngsters, a gym, physio rooms, everything. The new stadium and silverware are what fans will point to as the lasting legacy of Jack Walker – but for players, those kinds of training facilities mean everything.

It shows just how far one man's passion can take something. In my first autumn at Blackburn, when I had only been there a couple of months, the club was briefly banned from entering the transfer market by the FA because of some payment irregularities. In under 20 years the same club broke the British transfer record twice to buy Alan Shearer and Chris Sutton. Granted, the club's had a bit of a sticky patch this past decade, but without Jack Walker's investment back then, who knows where Blackburn would be today?

A couple of scousers, Billy Riley and Chris Johnson, Mark Stein from Scotland and Winston Small from Leeds were the lads I hung around with in those first few months. We had a good time but there's no question there's a lot of pressure on. It says something that only Mark and I were offered professional terms, and he only lasted a year. That's not unusual. Poor Winston was a great player and the club had big hopes for him. Then he broke his leg and that was the end of his dream. Despite the fun and excitement, it was a fragile existence which could be cruel.

Once we had got all the kit together for the seniors we would start our training, but pretty much on our own, separate from the first team who would work with Jim Smith and Norman Bodell, his assistant. Jim was great and Pick was a superb youth coach, but Norman was just feeble.

"I think you've said it all Jim."

That was his standard response to just about anything Jim ever asked him. We never had much contact with Jim or Norman and, to be honest, I'm not even sure if they knew our names. They would come and watch the odd youth team game on a Saturday morning and ask Pick for reports, but that was about as close as the they got. Norman fancied himself, too. The trouble was that he couldn't keep it to himself – one of the lads found a picture of him modelling underwear in a Grattan catalogue and pinned it to the noticeboard. With the greatest respect, this was a bloke who spent most of his playing career in the Fourth Division with Crewe Alexandra.

I played every Saturday, mostly for the A team, which was the apprentices' side. The games took place at Pleasington playing fields.

Squads were much smaller in those days and there were no under-23s like they have now. It was the A team and if you were good enough and lucky enough as a young lad you'd play in the reserves. That certainly toughened you up because you weren't just playing other 17 and 18-year-olds, these were grown men and often full-time professional footballers. Fairly quickly I was getting the odd game in the reserves and I became a regular after about six months. That was where I really started to play as a striker having started out as a midfielder, a position I also played for a while when I got promoted to the first team.

We played in the Central League, which was the league for reserve teams of north west clubs in the First and Second Divisions, and maybe even the Third Division. I didn't have a problem with the switch from apprentice to reserve level, probably because my time at Boston had served me well. I was used to playing with older, more experienced players from a very young age. A lot of pros who were released by the likes of Grimsby or Scunthorpe would find a home at Boston and I learned a lot from them.

Nowadays a 17-year-old would never get the chance of playing against first-team players who were coming back from injury or squad players trying to break into the first team. Unless they go out on loan, these kids today are stuck playing in their age group. I'm not saying that's a bad thing. Maybe it makes them better players, I don't know, that's just the way the game is played now.

In those days, the reserves played at their club's main ground. So if I was in the Blackburn reserves a home game would be at Ewood Park. This meant that I played at some of the biggest grounds in the country. Everton, Manchester City, even Liverpool. I played at Anfield against the likes of Steve Heighway and Phil Thompson.

Tommy Smith was also in that team and he was the centre half I was up against. Smith was a legend for Liverpool – he played almost 500 games for them during those great years under Bill Shankly in the Sixties and Seventies – and he was a tough bastard, and that's putting it mildly. It made me grow up fast. Just playing at Anfield was an incredible feeling, even if it was a reserve game with about 200 people there. It was still bloody exciting. I was only 17.

It would be easy as a younger player to just stand there and look around gobsmacked. I mean, this is Anfield. But I never used to think like that. Even as a kid I didn't think 'oh my God that's Tommy Smith what am I doing?' I used to get on the field and give it everything I could. I'd blank out who I was playing against, no matter how famous they were, because I just wanted to play football.

Today Blackburn's under-23s play at Leyland and all the other teams play at secondary grounds as well. But I think it was a real benefit to me to play in these huge stadiums at a young age. I played against some better players and in bigger stadiums for the reserves than I did in the first team. We were using those dressing rooms and walking down that tunnel, thinking about the players through the years who had walked down the same tunnel and played on the same grass. I rarely got nervous before games throughout my career and I wonder if playing on those big stages helped me.

Howard Wilkinson was the player-manager at Boston and we would train on Tuesday and Thursday nights for an hour or so. It was running, running and running. It was a treat just to get the ball at your feet. He was renowned for running then and renowned for running when he went into the professional game. When Howard was manager at Leeds they would arrive in Blackburn on the night before the game, get down to Ewood for a session and then he'd make them run twelve laps around the pitch. Bloody running. Why not give 'em a ball? He was right to concentrate on fitness but wrong to leave it at just that.

The main football culture shock involved in moving to Blackburn was the mix of training styles and the fact we were at it most days. It was exhausting.

"To start with you'll get very tired because your body's getting used to training full time."

I liked John Pickering. He was honest and he was right. Training virtually every day and playing at least once a week nearly killed me. I was knackered for a month, but there was a ball at my foot at least some of the time. I never much looked forward to Mondays and Tuesdays though, as they were the physical days, the hard days. The rest of the week was given over to ball work and tactics and this was where Pick really shone – he was one of the main influences on my game. Pick was relatively new to the club as well. He played more than 300 games for Halifax in the old Third Division and then had a couple of years with Barnsley in the Fourth. But it was as a coach where he really made his name and it was great to get the chance to learn from him so early in my career.

After a midweek reserve game, Jim spoke to me in the tunnel.

"Right, I'm going to take you to Southampton on Saturday. Nothing to play for. I'm going to give you your debut."

It was the second to last game of the season. It wasn't exactly out of the blue because I had been playing well and I knew Jim had been saying a few nice things about me. All the same, I was chuffed to bits. Or at least I would have been.

"I can't play boss."

Jim and Pick, who'd been standing with me, looked at each other and then at me. An explanation was required. I think they thought I was taking the Mickey and I wish that had been the case.

In those days to become a professional you signed Football Association forms and to play in the Football League you had to sign an additional Football League form. If you signed FA forms, your club had to give you £250 as a kind of welcoming arrangement. If you signed League forms, it was £500. I was coming up to 17 and they had to offer me some kind of professional deal but, hardly the richest club in those days, I scrawled on the FA's dotted line and not the League's. It meant my pay went up from £18 to £45 a week – which was decent money for a teenager in those days especially when I lived in digs and had all my food and bills paid for – but no one ever gave me the Football League form to sign.

So, no signature, no right to play in the League, no debut. And nobody had told Jim.

I finally did sign the League forms that summer but it was more than a year before I got another chance with the first team, by which time Jim had left and the club was in freefall to the Third Division.

It was terrible. It was the spring of 1978, we were well placed in the league and then Jim upped and offed to Birmingham. He said he was disappointed that the crowd didn't react well to a side that was playing well. There may have been more to it, but I was still young and not party to the gossip around the place. But let's not forget, Birmingham finished the season mid-table in the First Division and Jim had arrived from his first league job at Colchester. For Blackburn it was a disaster but, as a career move for Jim, you could understand it. Norman the yes man took over for a period and then he waltzed off to Birmingham, too. I doubt anyone in Blackburn missed him.

It was a big shock. There was a link through Jim back to Boston but managerial changes were something I, like most players, had to get used to. And Jim had looked after me.

I'd had a bit of trouble when I was an apprentice from Pick because of my smoking.

I started when I was about 12 or 13. Mum and Dad smoked and Dad would bring them home for me. In fact, Dad bought me a cigarette rolling machine when I was 13. None of the other youth team players smoked so I think that's why Pick had a go at me.

"You've got to stop smoking. I'm going to tell the manager."

I thought 'piss off John, I'm not at school'. I carried on smoking and he found out again.

"Go and see the manager."

So I had to go and see Jim. I went up into the Bald Eagle's nest which, like the apprentice accommodation, was in Nuttall Street.

"Come in Simon."

I sat down.

"What's this about you smoking?"

I blabbed something or other and watched him, sitting behind his desk, sucking on a fat cigar.

"Look Simon, Pick wants me to sack you. He's serious. But I'm not going to do that. Just be careful when you're smoking – don't get caught."

Then he offered me a cigar.

The big replacement? Jim Iley. From Barnsley. What a shambles. Jim Smith had taken a newly promoted side, consolidated, and was now pushing for promotion. Rovers were fifth in the Second Division when he left, chasing league leaders Tottenham. Over the course of the final 12 games we got just eight more points – although still finished fifth.

Iley wasn't a big name as a manager – he'd spent his entire career in the Fourth Division with Peterborough and then Barnsley – but he had played at the top level as a left back for Tottenham, Nottingham Forest and Newcastle. This was a big opportunity to make his name in management.

He wasn't built so leniently as his predecessor. He was a very dour, very down-to-earth Yorkshireman with absolutely no sense of humour. Compared to Iley, Howard Wilkinson was like Ken Dodd. His training methods were bizarre and, worse still, he didn't seem to know anyone's name.

One of our big stars at the time was Stuart Metcalfe. He was local, which always helped, he'd been with the club forever and he was a fantastic footballer, one of the best midfielders I have ever been on a pitch with. Rumours regularly used to fly around about Metty being tracked by this, that or the other First Division club, particularly when he was a bit younger. He was one of the older pros who I really got on well with and he took me under his wing. A few of them did. And we had a shared interest in afternoon snooker sessions. And afternoon drinking sessions. And best of all, afternoon drinking sessions in the snooker club.

"Number ten. NUMBER TEN. Get round there now and get it done."

That was how Iley addressed his players – by their tracksuit numbers. Metty was number ten. We'd been running around these two pitches at

Brockhall Hospital in the days before Jack Walker developed some of the grounds into training facilities and there was a hill that Iley made us run up and down. It was more like doing an assault course than football training because we had to go round the pitches, up the hill, back down again, jump some hurdles, stop, do some press-ups and start all over again. The more I think about it the saner Wilkinson's methods seem.

"Send 'em round again."

Bonkers. Bloody bonkers. He just about finished Metty off at Blackburn which was a disgrace. He dropped him to the bench. Another disgrace. Then he upset Dave Wagstaffe who was an absolute hero in the Seventies for Blackburn and he went off to Blackpool. Dave has a place in history. He became the first player to receive a red card – for arguing with the referee in a game against Leyton Orient in 1976.

There were a couple of bright spots, albeit selfish ones. I got a new contract and my pay doubled from £45 to £90. It doesn't sound a lot, but there were win bonuses in there and you could earn a good bit of money if you were in the team and got a result. Unfortunately back then they didn't do goal bonuses which would have come in handy in the years to come.

And while Jim didn't know me from Adam, he gave me my debut.

It was a Tuesday night, 29 August, 1978. We travelled to Exeter for a League Cup match at St James Park. I started the game and played in midfield. We lost 2-1 and I didn't do an awful lot to catch the eye. Exeter's manager was Bobby Saxton, who later managed at Blackburn, and their side featured Vince O'Keefe in goal, who became and a very good friend after he signed for us, as well as Colin Randell, who also moved north to Ewood Park.

Exeter were at least two divisions below us but were the better team that night. There were about 4,000 people watching the game, which was the first meeting of Exeter and Blackburn since the 1928 FA Cup run when Blackburn went on to win the trophy for the sixth and final time.

It's not uncommon among footballers as making your debut can be an emotional time, and it's certainly not uncommon for me, but I remember nothing about the game itself. But to play a proper game alongside people like Derek Fazackerley and Glenn Keeley was huge for me when I was only 18 and I was immensely proud.

My next taste of first-team action also came at St James' Park, albeit a slightly bigger one. Twelve days later, on 9 September, 1978, we played at Newcastle in a Second Division game. We lost 3-1 but I came on as a substitute for John Aston and saw my first four minutes of league action.

Stepping out at St James' Park was crazy. That stadium was huge. Still is. Certainly the biggest ground I'd ever played in. I had come from playing reserve football in front of 200 or 300 people. Granted there were a few more than that at Exeter a couple of weeks before, but the atmosphere at Newcastle was something else.

The noise of those 23,00 people was unbelieveable. But as soon as I walked across that line and on to the pitch, I shut the crowd out and got on with it. On that day I could have walked out in front of all those people and frozen. I could have looked around and thought 'wow, this is an unbelievable atmosphere' and let the occasion get the better of me. But I just used to think about the fact I was there to play a game of football and concentrate on that.

The following week I made my full league debut and my first game for Blackburn at home, when on 16 September we drew 1-1 with Leicester City. I remember absolutely nothing whatsoever about the game.

I was playing well but it wasn't always good enough for barmy Jim Iley. In a game some time that autumn it was 0-0 and there were about five minutes to go before half time. A long ball came over the top. I was chasing it down. It bounced just outside the area and the goalie came charging out. I'm going for it and I'm thinking 'he's going to nail me'. I just stopped. He clattered me anyway but self-preservation kept me from breaking any bones. We got a free kick and scored from it. Iley wouldn't let up in the dressing room at the break.

"You chickened out, you soft bastard!"

There wasn't much I could say, I was a kid. But I'd had a good half and I'd won a free kick in a good position. If I'd kept running I'd have almost certainly picked up a serious injury. More to the point, I didn't chicken out. Aggression has its place in football, but you have to know where the line is. It was as though Jim didn't know the first thing about the game. It didn't take long to realise he wasn't too hot on the second, third and fourth things either. Funny really, considering he'd spent so much time playing at the highest level.

But I was still on a high. I was in the side. Blackburn Rovers, though, were on a big downer and we were heading out of the division.

On 1 November 1978, with the club 20th in the league and on the back of a dour 1-1 draw with Wrexham a couple of days earlier, Jim Iley was sacked. Big sighs of relief from everyone. The campaign in the Lancashire Evening Telegraph by Rovers writer Dave Allin had been vitriolic to say the least. He had lasted just 16 games – a record only broken in 2012 when Henning Berg was sacked after 10. It was clear Iley was disliked by the media and the fans and he was far from popular with the players. Despite the breaks I got under him, I was as happy as anyone to see the back of him.

Pick was put in temporary charge and we travelled to Craven Cottage in south west London for a game against Fulham on the Friday night, 3 November, 1978. Fulham needed to win to go top. We were third from bottom and without a manager. Against all the odds I scored my first two goals for Blackburn Rovers. The opener was a doddle. For some reason, the keeper went flying out of his goal on to the wing. Kevin Hird, who we later sold for £375,000 to Leeds – an enormous sum at the time – went past him and squared the ball. I tapped into an empty net at the open end of the ground from 12 yards. For the second, the ball was clipped over the top and I smacked it in from 20 yards. A fine goal! Even Pick, who picked the team that night, said so. We won the game 2-1.

I had the bug. All I wanted to do from that moment on was score goals. I liked that feeling and I wanted it to carry on. There was nothing better than seeing a shot leave your foot, or your head, and crash into the back of the net. Upsetting the other team's fans, making your own fans happy, and running off to celebrate with your teammates. You cannot replicate that feeling in any part of life. And to have done it against the team at the top end of the league when we were down near the bottom showed me I could do it against anyone. It just gave me confidence.

It was a strange period for me. I had broken into the team but it felt as if a revolving door had been put into the manager's office. Pick was eventually given the job on a full-time basis and, despite the problems over my taste for nicotine, he knew me well enough as a player and as a person because of our time together in the youth team. More to the point, he liked what he saw on the pitch. I don't think we ever really hit it off, but there was a mutual respect – except that I could never see him being a manager. A coach certainly, but not a manager. He called me into his office for something or other soon after getting the job.

"Hiya Pick, what's up?"

"No Simon. You call me boss from now on."

The point he was making was a fair one, but it was like he was talking to a stranger. Sadly, that set the tone for his brief career as manager of the club. The trouble is, it takes something really special to be a football manager, something players really respect. And Pick didn't have it. Brilliant coach, crap manager. Rovers fans saw it when Ray Harford took over from Kenny Dalglish, and when Brian Kidd came in after many successful years as a coach at Manchester United.

John just didn't have the strength of character to release players. To end a youngster's career must be heart-breaking, but it has to be done. And it has to be done by the manager, not the youth team coach. So Pick had gone to a position where he was sacking the kids he had been nurturing. It really didn't work out for him. And despite the fact he wasn't making a particularly good fist of managing the club it was difficult not to have a lot of sympathy for him.

It was a good season for me, though. I played 20 or so games and scored eight goals, which wasn't a bad return for my first season in the first team. Especially when you consider the whole team only scored 41. I felt as though I had proved myself, which at that age was more important than the fact we were struggling. The flip side was the way the name on the manager's door kept on changing. And so I kept having to prove myself again. I was young, though, and I suppose the arrogance of youth kept me going. I never doubted my own abilities and felt that whoever came next would like me as much as the previous boss. As you get older that changes. If you're in your thirties and a new man arrives you start to wonder where you're going to fit into the picture. I know because it eventually did for my professional career when I genuinely thought I could have been useful for another season or so at Wycombe Wanderers. Alan Smith felt differently.

Blackburn were relegated. Five points adrift of safety at the bottom of the league. And that was in spite of winning the final three games of the season. It should have made me miserable, but it didn't. I'd achieved the first stage of my ambitions by being selected regularly at Blackburn. I had also had the chance to play with some of my heroes. Like most clubs, we had a mixture of youth and experience on the books. But some of those older players were legends. John Radford was one, he'd won the double with Arsenal. Duncan McKenzie was another, he was one of the most gifted players of his generation. Unfortunately, it was an era when skill and grace were not the most sought-after attributes for international selection.

Pick once took us to Ireland for a break. I was the youngest there and I was rooming with Raddy. He liked a drink and we stayed up most of the night boozing with John Bailey. When we got back to Blackburn we had a big meeting down at the training ground. Pick wasn't best pleased, he'd obviously heard about the session which, to be honest, was no big deal.

"Garner, I'm fining you two weeks' wages. I'm not standing for that kind of behaviour."

And then Raddy had his two penn'orth. It was like a scene from Spartacus.

"He had a drink but so did I. If you're going to fine him two weeks' wages, you fine me two weeks' wages. It was my idea to stay up!"

And I'm thinking 'go on Raddy, get him told'. It was like my dad sorting out the headmaster all over again. Maybe that's one of the reasons Pick fell out with him. Raddy was a strong character. He said what he wanted to say. He was the union rep as well and I think he felt he owed it to the other players to stand up for them. He certainly wouldn't let me be pushed around because I was a kid. Where Pick went wrong, though, was in not fining either of us. It was, strictly speaking, an offence. He should have stood his ground and carried out the threat. He didn't. He was never going to make a manager.

McKenzie was a great fella. And he liked a cigarette, too, so we had something in common straight away. He cost us £80,000 from Chelsea, which was a club record that stood for years. Before that he'd been one of Brian Clough's signings in his brief spell at Leeds and had played for Everton and Anderlecht in Belgium. Everyone knew he was a fine player, but he was still best known for the fact he had jumped over a Mini. For me though, the fact he smoked was brilliant and he was my lookout on the team bus. No one was going to tell him to put a fag out, but I'd have been dropped on from a large height if I'd been caught. It was like being at school. Duncan, like Raddy, was brilliant to play with. He really helped me along. I played him through for a goal at Wrexham and he spoke to a newspaper afterwards.

"He's the best striker I've seen outside the First Division."

That made me feel fantastic. Duncan was different from the rest of us, basically because he had money. There was no jealousy though, and he was well liked. He was just a bit more polished than the rest of us which, given where he had played, was hardly surprising. As soon as you went into his house near Haydock Park you knew it wasn't like your own. There was all this fantastic furniture which he'd shipped in from abroad and a nice car in the drive.

As the youngest member of the first team I had to focus on retaining my place. We'd had three managers in a 12 months and with each switch there was a period of change and uncertainty. I think that's why I sought security off the field and, at a very young age, got married.

I met Mandy in The Beechwood, a pub on Livesey Branch Road, which is pretty close to Ewood Park. It's a Tesco now, but back then they had a fantastic disco on Mondays which became a big night out for a lot of the younger players. We married soon after in November 1978, a month after I'd scored my first senior goal and just a couple of weeks after Jim Iley was sacked. Ron Greenwood, a somewhat more successful manager, once said he liked his players to be settled down. It was a fair point because I cut back on the boozing and got into the best shape of my life.

We got married at the register office in Blackburn and had a reception at The Kiosk in Sunnyhurst Woods in Darwen. It says something about how football salaries have progressed because we couldn't afford a photographer so my brother, David, took the pictures – or thought he had. After spending what seemed like hours arranging all kinds of different family groupings we found out a couple of days later that he had forgotten to put a film in the camera.

Looking back I sometimes wonder what I thought I was doing. I was

19 and a professional footballer. What on earth made me get married? It was simple really. Nanny Garner was old and I desperately wanted to give her a grandchild and Mandy's family wanted to see a ring on her finger. I think Mary, Mandy's mum, was quite keen on the idea of her daughter marrying a footballer because it gave her some local celebrity status. It was one of her ambitions to see her daughter married to someone rich or famous. I didn't really fit into either category, but I was the closest thing in that part of town.

SIMON GARNER

Derek Fazackerley

Teammate at Blackburn Rovers from 1978 to 1987

When Simon first came in he was a typical young lad. He was probably a little over-awed, as you would be, and he was a little shy and it took him a little bit of time to come to terms with moving away from home. But once he started getting on the football field you could see the potential in him because he was very good at scoring goals. You could tell straight away he wasn't the biggest or the tallest, but he had good feet and his one-touch finishing was excellent.

He was confident in his abilities, or at least he came across that way. Sometimes you find players put on a brave face and while they might look confident, if they are going through a poor spell, then they may doubt themselves. But Simon didn't go for long periods without scoring.

I wouldn't say he led the perfect lifestyle for a professional athlete. But then again how many of us could say that back in those days? He smoked and he drank and he was always up for a night out. I wouldn't say he drank to excess, but if we had a night out we would have a good night out and he would always be at the centre – until his money ran out which never took long. We certainly weren't the best paid players in the league.

He didn't like the running in training. In pre-season we always did a cross-country run and there was a young Polish lad who used to come down to watch training. One day he turned to the manager, Bobby Saxton, and asked if he could join in. Bobby told him if he wanted to then he could. By then we were about 200 yards gone, but he overtook Garns and beat him in. He was not athletic in terms of his running and he would not have been at the front in those training sessions. But his anaerobic fitness and his sharpness around the penalty area was excellent.

Jim Iley gave him his debut and then under Howard Kendall it looked like he might leave. For whatever reason he hadn't done enough to convince Howard that he was the genuine article. But of course he stayed and Howard left after almost achieving back-to-back promotions. When Simon did break into the side he showed he had the ability to be a successful striker at the level we were at. It wasn't long before he was one of the first names on the team sheet.

He was a popular member of the dressing room and we had quite a good social life. The football certainly never got in the way of it, put it that way. There was the 100 Club back then and we would go for a drink afterwards and so would the opposition. We didn't have a players' lounge as they do these days. We would often go out on a Saturday night as a group for a meal and a drink with the wives and the partners. There would be the occasional night out during the week. Often if we were on a bad run we would decide we needed a night out to bring everyone back together. Garns would always be available if we decided we needed to let our hair down.

We had a close group of players. Most of us played with each other for seven or eight years as a settled group. There was nobody in that group that didn't get on. It became a big strength – we didn't want to let each other down. We played for each other and we relied on each other to earn ourselves a decent living.

Every year we would have a Christmas do. All the wives would be invited, as well as the directors and the staff at the club. It used to take place at different venues and on one occasion we chose the Foxfields Hotel near Whalley, which had just been refurbished and was just around the corner from me.

I think on this occasion Simon had a little too much to drink and had a bit of a tiff with his wife who disappeared in a taxi and left him there to make his own way home. It must have been about 4am when my telephone rang - the house phone, we didn't have mobiles back then - and it was Simon's wife asking me where he was. I had no idea, so I set off looking for him and found him asleep on a bench. He had been trying to find my house, got lost and given up.

Simon was certainly a character and a great lad. I used to enjoy his company socially, but you can't take away from the fact that he was an outstanding goal scorer. He was unlucky not to have played at the top level with a bigger club. Back then we didn't have agents who would be off touting us to other clubs, but if Simon was around today, with the way that agents work I am sure he would have had that opportunity.

We were a decent club punching way above our weight. We were competing against clubs like Manchester City, Leeds, Newcastle, Chelsea, Tottenham, Leicester and West Ham at various times. These were big city clubs with far bigger budgets and we were very unlucky not to push on and get promotion to the First Division.

And I think Simon would have been able to play at the top level. He was an excellent one-touch finisher with his head and his feet. He wasn't the quickest, but crosses into the box, anticipating rebounds and knockdowns, he was very good at that. And he was a very calm finisher. You didn't see him lash too many shots over the bar, and his goal record speaks for itself.

Simon was an outstanding striker for the club and he was only pipped in later years by the great Alan Shearer.

CHAPTER 4

You'll never play for Blackburn Rovers again

1979 to 1981

Pick was ousted just after the season finished. It's a shame really. If he had stayed as a coach he could have had a lot longer at Blackburn, where he was liked and respected, but I guess any football coach given the chance to prove themselves in the top job wants to give it a go.

Howard Kendall – one of the great names of football – was hired for his first job in management. It was a real coup to get him and it was a breath of fresh air having him at the club. Unlike the previous couple of managers, Howard had real pedigree. He was a legend at Everton and had also played at Birmingham in the First Division. He was still playing well and he had been coaching at Stoke City, so a move to Blackburn as player-manager looked a good deal for everyone.

It was good to have a boss who still had a foot in the players' camp. He liked a drink and he was always with the boys. If we were socialising, he wanted to socialise with us. And he loved to take us on trips. We'd always had them, but Howard would get us away two or three times a season. Mind you, it mostly seemed like little more than an excuse to arrange a big piss-up for his mates. There was one trip to Jersey and, strangely enough, we played a friendly against Stoke and all his drinking buddies were there. One night in my room me, John Butcher, Noel Brotherston and Mick Rathbone were supping the tax-free vino and getting smashed when there was this incredible crash in the corridor. It sounded like someone had fallen down the stairs. An annihilated Kendall lurched through the door, landed in the corner, opened his mouth and slagged off each one of us in turn. Or so I'm told. I slept through my dressing down and he didn't even notice.

Morecambe was a popular destination with Howard and on one of our many trips we had snuck out after curfew for a night on the tiles. On our way back, late and inebriated, a car parked outside the hotel flashed its lights and we were beckoned across. It was Howard.

"You lot are fined as much as I am."

He'd been out all night as well.

But back home Howard had to be more professional and make that transition from player to manager, which I think he sometimes found tough when he just wanted to be one of the boys. But he had to do things like go and see the press after games, pick the team, and give the bad news to those youth players who weren't quite good enough to make it. On the team bus he had to sit at the front with the chairman and talk about how the game went, but you could see he was desperate to come down the back of the bus and have a beer with the boys.

Having a player-manager was unusual in some respects. And Howard is the only one Blackburn have ever had. When we were on the pitch he was very much a player. It wasn't the same as him being on the touchline. But then in the dressing room at half-time it was a bit odd having the team talk from a man wearing full kit and covered in mud. And he must have found that tough because he wouldn't have been able to see everything that was going on in the game like he would from the side-lines. And having run around for 45 minutes he didn't get much of a break having to come in and rally us all up to go back out for the second half. But he adapted very well and had a fantastic career in management.

He was inspirational on the pitch. He demanded effort and concentration and gradually made us into a team that just wouldn't concede goals. We were like the Arsenal of old and the 1-0 final score was a speciality. It didn't begin brightly though. We only won one of our first ten games – 3-0 at Sheffield Wednesday right at the start of the season – and by October we were way down at the bottom of the table. Brian Clough's Nottingham Forest put six past us at the City Ground on their way to winning the League Cup (they also won the European Cup that season).

We stabilised after that poor start and then in January we went on this incredible run where we got 29 points out of 30 when it was just two points for a win – and we knocked First Division Coventry out of the FA Cup.

At the heart of it all was a superb defence which Howard had developed, despite having to offload some of the best defensive talent in the country. One of the first things he had to do when he came to the club was negotiate the sale of John Bailey to Everton. That meant two of our best players, John and Kevin Hird, both attacking full backs, had been stripped from the team in a few months. He was a canny operator, though, and brought in Jim Branagan from Huddersfield who was solid as a rock. We also had Mick Rathbone, Glenn Keeley and Derek Fazackerley at the back with Jim Arnold in goal. It was a backline which, by and large, stood us in good stead for years. In midfield it was the likes of Howard and Duncan McKenzie, and then there was me, Noel Brotherston and Andy Crawford in contention up front. It was a great team and way too hot for Division Three. We finally got promoted at Bury when Crawford scored twice in a 2-1 win. They beat us at Ewood by the same scoreline a week later which destroyed any hopes we had of winning the division – and Grimsby's 4-0 thumping of Sheffield United secured them the title by a clear three points anyway.

Crawford scored 18 goals that season. He was electric. But what a tosser. Howard bought him early in the season from Derby's reserves for £50,000 around the same time Jim Branagan was signed. Jim had one hell of a tough task in replacing Kevin Hird. He didn't instantly bond with the fans, mainly because he wasn't Kevin, but also due to the fact he wasn't all that quick, didn't have much of a first touch and treated the half-way line like it had been fenced off with electrified barbed wire. But he was a fantastic team man – reliable, honest, determined and passionate. He was underrated yet he did everything Howard asked of him and he eventually became a real fans' favourite. At the end of the day, if a player is committed, he'll win over the supporters.

Crawford on the other hand was a jumped-up prima donna. Nobody knew him at all. He would come into training at 10am, walk through the door, not speak to anybody, get changed next to the door, train, come back, have a shower and leave – all in virtual silence. There were stories going round that after every game he would go back to his Nuttall Street terraced house and write a report of how well he'd done in the game. He wouldn't even have a drink with us – in a bloody Howard Kendall team!

He wasn't a team man at all and as long as he scored he wasn't bothered. I played up front with him and he wouldn't even talk on the pitch. I'd been used to playing with experienced pros like John Radford and Joe Craig, a former Scottish international who had partnered Kenny Dalglish up front at Celtic, and these were players who helped me out, showed me the tricks. Being in their shadows was fine, they'd proved themselves, but I wasn't happy playing second fiddle to an egomaniac.

Raddy had gone by now though and Joe struggled to get a game under Howard. He never really clicked at Ewood but I bled him for knowledge and ways of improving my own game. Still, Joe and I managed to squeeze in a last bit of teamwork. His wife was in the next room to Mandy at Queen's Park Hospital when our babies were due in February 1981. I sat outside, smoking and scared, he was in with his wife throughout. It's the same on the football pitch. If one player's looking a bit out of sorts then another has to make up for it. Or something! Well it wasn't my fault. I would love to have been there, I really would, only I can't stand the sight of blood. So next door there's all this screaming coming from Joe's wife and I've got Mandy twitching about with only a trainee nurse for company. I wanted to be in the pub. Or anywhere but where the action was.

"Right Mr Garner, put one leg up on your shoulder, I'll have the other leg."

"No, sorry love. I can't stomach blood. I'm not stopping here. You'll have to get someone else to hold that leg. I'm feeling a bit faint."

That's when I left Mandy to give birth to John. While she did all the work, I rolled down the corridor, bounced off the walls, found the waiting room, collapsed in a corner, smoked twenty John Player Specials and became a dad. Strangely, blood and injuries never bothered me in a game. Too much adrenaline to notice maybe, or too focused on the game. But real blood in real life is a wholly different matter. Even the thought of real blood in real life is enough to make my stomach turn. I was at the snooker club one afternoon when some bloke was talking about an operation he was going to have on his eye, about having a needle pushed into it. The next thing I remember is being woken up in the toilet. I hadn't had a single drink – I just passed out thinking about the operation. All of which, perhaps, contributes to my swift exit from the delivery suite. It was the same when Mandy had James, though I did manage to stay upright

– and in the delivery suite – when Suzy, my second wife, gave birth to Thomas and Martha in 2001 and 2005.

I was only young – just 21 – but I really took to being a dad. I'd wanted to be a dad for so long and it didn't disappoint me. Football's a good job for fatherhood because you don't start work until ten in the morning and get most afternoons off, so I probably saw more of my boys as babies than most fathers could dream of. I'd play with John in the mornings before training and take him on long walks in the afternoons, usually just the two of us. I never really had anywhere special to amble to, it was just doing it that mattered. And I didn't really miss the snooker sessions or whatever other diversion the players had planned. I'd sometimes show my face at the snooker club, but not every day like it used to be. As a family we were strong and we lived in a new house just opposite the Shadsworth council estate. That house cost £14,500 and I was so proud to be on the property ladder at such a young age. Mandy wasn't working so we saw a lot of each other, and her parents visited a lot and helped us out. It was a very settled period of my life. I missed my own folks, but it was virtually impossible for me to visit them because they were both working, so I spoke to them every night without fail.

I saw Dad most often as he tended to come to the away games with a mate and a couple of my uncles. He would occasionally stay over at the house for a few days and if we were playing at home he would come to Ewood, but he really loved the away days. All the lads would get two tickets for away games, so I'd have to pinch the extra tickets from one of the others who didn't need them. Everyone got to know Dad as he would be waiting for the bus at the ground when it arrived and would be having the craic. The lads loved him. And he would be there at full time for a chat before we got on the bus back to Blackburn. He would always give me very honest feedback. He was proud that I had made it, but he never minced his words and he was always my harshest critic. After a game at Portsmouth when I scored a hat-trick he said: "You missed a sitter for a fourth." Thanks Dad. But I know it came from a place of love.

Strikers seemed to come and go at Ewood Park and most of them made very little impression, but there were some stalwarts in other positions who, like me, became part of the fixtures and fittings. Mick Rathbone, who is John's godfather, was one of them. There was no reason why we should get on, but we did.

We shared some real laughs. Not least on a trip to Belfast when we were put up in 'the most bombed hotel in Ireland'. Brilliant. Mick and I got to our room and there was a briefcase in there. Mick's face was a picture.

"It's a bloody bomb. I'm not staying in this room."

We moved, although if it was a bomb I'm not sure we were far enough away to keep us safe.

While I roomed with Mick for six or seven years, his absolute devotion to ultimate fitness never rubbed off on me at all. On away trips he would get up early and go for a jog or do some stretching while I would have a lie in and look forward to a bacon butty. For Mick, a lot of it was nervous energy. On Sundays he'd get up at the crack of dawn, get down to the railway station and pick up the first edition of the Sunday People. If they'd given him a mark under six he'd be in a state of depression until the next game. His dark periods weren't as bad as John Butcher's though. John wasn't a bad keeper, but he had no consistency. And he was trying to fill Paul Bradshaw's boots after Paul had to be sold to Wolves because the club was in a financial hole. Some people blamed John for us not going up in 1978 but that's way too harsh and some of the stick he got from the fans was awful. It can be soul destroying for a player and the feeling runs through the team because while everyone wants to help, nobody wants to appear a patronising git.

Howard knew how to help, though, in all sorts of ways. He understood players and what they needed. I think we could have had any set of players that season and Howard would have taken us up. He injected a new life into Blackburn Rovers. He even got me to enjoy training. For a start, there was no more of this bloody running round in circles.

"Right. That's it. I'm knackered."

Howard had run about 400 yards and was breathless. It was the longest training run we did all season. Instead of having us yomp up and down hills, he put the ball at our feet and drilled into us the defensive approach to winning football matches. It left the strikers with few chances and we had to do our share of defending – or some of us did because Crawford didn't want to get involved in all that rough tackling nonsense, he just wanted to stand up front and score goals. So he did, the bastard. Oh, and Duncan never really liked that sort of negative play either. But that was different – I liked Duncan and he was getting on a bit. And of course there's the small fact of what Duncan could offer us in terms of tricks and turns, his flair and the killer pass he could pluck from nowhere. If promotion back to Division Two was never a formality, it wasn't far off, and I wish I could remember the party we had after finally clinching it. I can't even remember where the trip was, except that we bought the cerveza with pesetas and drank ourselves stupid for a whole week. Except Crawford, who always found a reason to stay at the hotel.

It wasn't the biggest surprise when he asked for a transfer during pre-season, despite the fact the fans loved him. Scoring eighteen goals in a debut season, one every other game, is going to make you popular. But he thought he was better than Blackburn Rovers and his dad made no secret of it either. When Howard told him 'no', he didn't bother turning up for pre-season. He went on strike and went off to train somewhere else on his own. He sat in the reserves for most of the next season and eventually got a move to Bournemouth. Fourth Division Bournemouth. Well done Andy. He went on to scrape a living at places like Stockport, Torquay and Poole. Bless him.

I thought I was following him out of Ewood Park, too, but not out of choice. Howard was trying to impose himself more on the side in his second season. And it worked. In the first nine games of the season we won seven and drew two which would have been an achievement for any club, but we'd only just been promoted. We were top of the league come early October. I wasn't a regular, but I was knocking on the door. Or so I thought. Part of the rebuilding involved Duncan leaving and a permanently sun-tanned Viv Busby – a striker who had played in the First Division but had most recently been with Tulsa in the North American Soccer League – coming in. And, it seemed, me going to Halifax.

"You'll never play for this club again."

Howard had a way with words. He wanted to sign somebody from Chesterfield, a big centre forward. They wanted something like £40,000 for him, but Howard didn't have that kind of money available. Maybe £10,000, maybe £20,000, but nothing like £40,000. Howard then got a bid of £30,000 from Halifax for me – problem solved for Howard. If he can get me out. He told me about the offer on the phone.

"No thanks, boss."

I simply didn't want to leave Blackburn. I was settled with a home, a wife and a new baby. More to the point, Halifax was the sort of team that was always near the bottom of the league with the threat of being booted out hanging over them. I went over for a look, though, because Howard hadn't given me much option. According to him, I was never going to play for Blackburn again. Funny how things work out.

The pitch at Halifax was magnificent, one of the best I'd ever seen, but the stadium was teetering on collapse. George Kirby was the manager. I went into his so-called office, which was about the size of a kitchen table, and squeezed into a chair to hear his pitch.

"I want you to sign, Simon. I want you in the side for Saturday."

"I'll think about it."

"Well think quickly Simon. I need you to sign by 2pm and then you can go straight into the first team."

It was noon.

"No, I need to speak to my wife about this."

"Well call her then."

"She's out shopping."

She wasn't, but it seemed gentler than telling him the truth – that I thought Halifax were crap and there was as much chance of me signing for George as there was of me signing for Burnley. Halifax ended the 1980/81 season in 23rd place in the Fourth Division. I knew I was better than that.

"Well call the police to go and find her."

He was desperate.

"Look, if you want to sign me you can wait for another game. I want to think about this."

I drove back to Ewood and I had to go and see Howard. The coaching staff used to get changed in the referee's room and when I walked in Howard was in the bath.

"How did you go on?"

"I'm not happy about it. I'm not going."

Howard was desperate. He really wanted this giant from Chesterfield.

"How much do you want from the transfer fee?"

Oh, bloody hell.

"Halifax have offered me a good deal, boss.".

They had. It was a £10,000 signing-on fee – which was an enormous sum – on top of a similar wage to what I was earning at Blackburn.

"You'll have to give me another £10,000 as well. Then I'll think about it."

"I don't know, Simon. Get out."

I was at home when the phone went. Howard was offering me £5,000 to go. Add that to the £10,000 from Halifax and the company car and the free use of an apartment and it was adding up to an attractive offer, but Howard was missing the point. The money really wasn't the issue and I'd only given him the £10,000 figure because I knew there was no way he could have managed it. Short term, of course, it was a very good deal. Long term I'd be a non-league player driving a Skoda within a couple of seasons. And when you consider we were genuinely pushing for promotion to the First Division, it really was no contest.

"I mean it, Simon. You'll never play for Blackburn Rovers again."

And you're not going to be here forever, I thought. So I'll bide my time. Which, as is the way in football, I didn't have to do for long because Noel Brotherston, our left-footed genius and Northern Ireland international, broke his leg just after deadline day and the squad was already stretched. Howard had no choice but to pick me. While as a player you'd never wish injury on a colleague, you have to take whatever opportunities are put your way – and I did. It gave me another chance, and I even played wide on the left at first in Noel's position. There's no doubt that losing Noel cost us promotion. We'd looked like making it into the top flight, but Noel was central to what we did.

If Noel was the specific reason for us missing out, the more general cause was the fact we had virtually no money and a tiny squad. Tony Parkes was another broken leg casualty that season and while he was never a match-winner in the Brotherston mould, he was supremely reliable and a fine ball-winner. But Noel missed the last nine matches of the campaign and we drew five of them 0-0. We only lost one, and that was at Swansea who finished above us on goal difference and took the final promotion spot.

It was sickening. We were within touching distance of playing Liverpool, Arsenal and Manchester United. Whatever problems I'd had with Howard were nothing compared to the feeling of losing this chance. I was distraught. We all were. And then it went from bad to worse. The rumours about Howard had started earlier in the season. There was a lot of talk about him taking the Crystal Palace job and I think they even came in with a formal offer, but there was no way he could turn down Everton. He was still a legend at Goodison – he captained them to the 1970 First Division title and played almost 300 games for the club. Within a week of the season finishing he was gone. A superb manager, despite his poor taste in strikers, and our best player. Although I'm a natural optimist, I thought we might never recover from a loss like that.

Mick 'Baz' Rathbone
Teammate at Blackburn from 1979 to 1987

I remember it like it was yesterday. Standing ankle deep in mud in the freezing cold at Witton Park. This is a place I have visited pretty much every day since for the past four decades. It was March 1979 and it was my very first training session having joined Blackburn from my boyhood club Birmingham. Temporary manager John Pickering yelled 'mount'! And so I jumped on the back of the lad stood next to me. It turned out to be a 19-year-old Simon Garner, who would go on to spend the next eight years of his career on my back!

From that day on we just connected. We were a similar age and both had moved to this small northern town, leaving our families hundreds of miles away. It was brilliant to just hit it off with somebody, be able to have a laugh with him, a drink with him, I even lit his bloody fags for him. We could even just sit quietly together – and that's the mark of a true friendship, sharing a silence like that.

I was a fantastic runner – I always have been a strong runner – and Garns was just terrible. We used to have cross country runs every pre-season. And it wasn't like in today's game where they have the heart monitors on and all that. These were races.

"Three, two, one... go!".

Everyone would set off sprinting and by the time you got to Preston New Road you'd be strung out, then you'd have to go up the hill past the cemetery and finish at the bottom. I won every race. Garns would invariably come in last. I remember once I was lying face down by the blue bridge in the park, gasping for breath having sprinted my arse off for another first-place finish. A minute and a half later, Garns came sauntering over, hardly touched by it.

"It's all right for you, you're a good runner!"

That was just Garns all over.

There was a big drinking culture in football at the time. There was an even bigger drinking culture at Blackburn Rovers. Wednesdays would be our day off, so Tuesday was the big night out for the boys. After training on a Tuesday, Bobby Saxton would call us together.

"Right, it's your day off tomorrow and I know you'll be out tonight, so I'm going to get to the bottom of you now."

What he meant was: "I'm going to run the bollocks off you before your day off."

I had a German shepherd in those days called Max and I wanted him to be on the park getting some exercise while we were training. So because I wanted to drive the dog up there, I ended up being a taxi driver for Garns and Kevin Stonehouse. They got a free lift out of me every bloody day. I was driving a black Ford Capri with the registration plate SBG 333T. One day someone said: "Look, SBG – Stoney, Baz and Garns!" I can still see it now, looking in my rear-view mirror, Max sat at the back choking on Garns's fag.

We roomed together on away trips for many years and I remember we often used to have a carvery on a Friday night, especially in London. This was in the days before dieticians ruined everyone's fun, and you used to see how much food you could stuff in, which probably wasn't the best idea with it being the day before a game. And then we'd get some sweets and some cans of beer and head off to the room. I'd be sitting on the bed and Garns would be there with his fag in his mouth, drifting off to sleep. I used to have to stay awake so I could put it out so he didn't burn the bloody room down. I can see him now, fag in, eyes half shut, distended belly full of carvery hanging over his boxers. I don't know if he ever thanked me for saving his life on those away trips. But you know what, he would get up the next day and do the business.

We had a standing joke. I suffered with real pre-match anxiety, worse when I played for my hometown team Birmingham before joining Blackburn, but it was really crippling. Before a game, just as the ref was about to blow his whistle, Garns would turn to me.

"Bloody hell, my legs are like jelly!"

We would both start laughing and it would really lighten the mood.

Another favourite would be us shouting to the ref.

"Ref, how much longer? Come on ref, how much longer?"

Eventually the referee would get fed up.

"Four minutes played, 86 minutes to go."

It sounds daft now but it made us laugh.

But my gosh what a player he was. He was the epitome of football in a different era. He was so clever. Left foot, right foot, he could use both.

We had pretty much the same team for eight years and we became such a tight-knit group. We had so many laughs together between the two of us and as a group. We had something special that you just can't relate to in today's game because players move on a lot more now.

People today laugh at our era. I hear fitness coaches saying how the players are fitter now. But I'm telling you, Ian Miller was as quick as any player is today. I'm in my mid-60s and I can still hold my own with the lads I'm working with, no problem. This idea that we couldn't move or couldn't run, or that we were less skilful, is nonsense. We were just as good and we were doing it while running through ankle deep mud on uneven surfaces. We had a belly full of carvery and ale and we trained in a public park that was strewn with dog shit.

Simon could have played at the top level but he just didn't get that break. It was harder to move around back then. By today's standard, with the Bosman rule and bigger wages, Simon could have run his contract down when he was 26 or 27 and gone to a decent First Division side for nothing. And there's no doubt in my mind he would have scored goals at that level. But for Blackburn Rovers and their fans it's great that didn't happen and it is almost certain that his goals record for the club will never be matched.

CHAPTER 5

Bobby dazzler

1981 to 1985

It wasn't a shock when Howard left. He was an Everton legend and - at about 35 - a young up-and-coming manager developing a reputation within the game. He had obvious ambitions to manage higher up the leagues and, having just missed out on promotion, this was his chance to make his mark on football.

Despite the club's success, I have to say I was pleased he left. Purely because he had tried to sell me and so, under Howard, I knew my days were numbered at the club. But I thought I was doing well and wanted to stay.

Whenever a manager leaves, whether you're pleased to see the back of them or not, you're always wondering how things are going to be with the new man. It's always a worry. What am I going to do for the new manager? Will I be playing? You can't live off your reputation. Fair enough I was scoring goals, but what if the new manager feels the same way as Howard Kendall?

This was the first time I felt particularly affected by a managerial change. The Jims (Smith and Iley) had gone while I was still establishing myself. Now I knew I would have to prove myself to the new manager to make sure I stayed at the club. I wasn't the best trainer in the world, which doesn't always help, but I would do the business on a Saturday. This had always been enough for managers I had worked under before.

In today's game, you often know who the new manager is going to be from quite an early stage – well before they are officially appointed. There are odds from the bookies all over Sky, social media chit chat and masses of media speculation. But back then there was none of that. So when the new man came in, it really was out of the blue.

Nobody, and I mean nobody, had heard of Bobby Saxton. Howard was one of the most famous names in the game and then in steps a complete unknown. For most of the players there was the worry that things were about to slow down again at the club after Howard's achievements. With him at the helm and Mick Heaton, who also left for Goodison Park as his coach, we had been an excellent side and one that was knocking on the golden gates of the First Division.

Bobby arrived from Plymouth Argyle where he had just secured a seventh place finish in the Third Division – Plymouth's best league performance since relegation in 1977. He filled the backroom with half of bloody Devon, or so it seemed. Jim Bodell came as his assistant along with chief scout Howard Jarman and physio Tony Long. Pleasingly it was then that Tony Parkes was promoted to the coaching staff, where he would remain in various positions – including six stints as caretaker manager – until 2004. The promotion was great news for Tony. The injury he sustained at, I think, Notts County was dreadful and ended his playing career. He was getting on a bit as a player, but that was cruel. But Tony was smart and he'd had his eye on a coaching role for a while and, like Derek Fazackerley, you always felt he'd do well at it.

But what a job for Bobby to come into. With Howard's profile it was always going to be a tough act to follow. It didn't help his cause that he really didn't like talking to the media. He wasn't being ignorant, it just wasn't in his nature to be the centre of attention except in the company of his players.

As soon as I met the man I discovered he was a down to earth Yorkshireman who said it how it was. He was football mad. So keen and eager to prove himself as a manager having made the step up from Plymouth. For me he was a breath of fresh air. And that's in spite of him getting us running in training again. Howard hated running so we hardly did any. But Bobby was an intelligent coach and understood the sensitivities of the players, so the work was varied from the start. And he was also dedicated. He worked hard on tactics, explained himself well and always set up good shooting workouts for the strikers to go through at the end of a session. He wasn't a bad judge of players either, and he soon got to work building a team which pretty much stuck together during his time at Ewood.

We really gelled as a team during his training sessions and I developed an understanding with those players I knew would supply the ammunition for me to score goals. Players like Noel Brotherston who were already at the club, as well as others Bobby brought in, just knew what I needed and provided it.

We had a set piece routine that worked wonders and nobody ever worked it out. I scored so many goals just by standing at the back post for a corner. I would stand holding on to the post and in those days they would have defenders on the line. I would start talking to them. "Nice day isn't it?" or "Bloody hell what a crap game." Just as they let their guard down, Noel would send over the perfect cross with such pace on the ball, the big centre half would flick it on and I would just step forward and volley it into the net.

Bobby soon brought in another winger in Ian Miller for £60,000, which was serious money considering how little Howard was prepared to let me go for. He was the first of many from the south west and Bobby's connections in that area were clearly very solid, as were his reports on Dusty. Lightning quick and a very direct wing player, he improved the team straight away. He wasn't particularly skilful and he could be somewhat predictable. He hardly ever tried to beat a player on the inside as his left foot was useless, but for a striker predictability is an asset – knowing what he was going to do next put me one step ahead of a defence which might not have done its homework.

I'd like to think a player like Ian could have seen us promoted the previous season because while we were very solid at the back, we too rarely broke free as an attacking force. He was also a grafter and worked well coming back, and he and Jim Branagan were an excellent combination on the right.

But while Bobby was calling on his old pals in the south west, Howard was up to the same on Merseyside. He poached Jim Arnold, our keeper, which gave John Butcher another chance before Bobby stepped in for Terry Gennoe from Southampton. He was another player no one had heard of with no real history, but he became a superb long-term buy.

Terry was incredibly dedicated. It was unheard of to have a keeper who would gladly stay behind to do extra training to help the strikers out, but there was an instant rapport and respect and it was a two-way street because it was no chore for me if Terry wanted to do some additional goalkeeping work. It paid off, too. Terry's enthusiasm rubbed off on his back four who trusted him enormously, giving him the opportunity to command the box without having to resort to the kind of screaming and bawling of the likes of Jordan Pickford.

He was another great addition to the dressing room as well. Never a big drinker – he tended to fall asleep after he'd had a few – but he was always happy to join in with the social side of the team at the time, which was one of the big factors in our relative success during those years under Bobby.

Obviously with Bobby doing some spending, it wasn't long before the attacking line would welcome a new player and Norman Bell, who had been known as the Wolves super-sub, was signed. He was great for me. A big, strong bloke who took a lot of pressure off and gave me the room to get the goals. He didn't score many himself though and the fans were on his back which was unfair. I don't think they realised how hard he worked and how much effort he put into creating space for others to exploit by dragging defenders out of position. It had been a long time since I'd played with a big centre forward and I liked it. He helped me to 14 goals that season.

Other signings Bobby made included Mickey Speight, a player in the Kendall mould, and Kevin Arnott, who came on loan from Sunderland. Kevin was an exceptional talent and had real vision. The only problem was that we just couldn't afford to buy him. What Bobby was looking for was a replacement for Howard, someone who could influence a game from the middle of the park. Because Howard was a genuinely class act, even though he was getting on, it meant we could build a team of grafters and battlers around him. Without him we didn't have anyone to unpick an opposition when it really mattered, though Kevin, for the all-too-brief period he was with us, managed it. We had a dream start to the season and a pretty solid middle period as well. After the initial shock of getting another unknown manager, it took virtually no time to realise how good he really was, regardless of what the media thought. As an attacking force we were creating plenty of chances and that was largely down to Dusty, who would present us with four or five solid opportunities a game which was unheard of with Howard, whose strategy was less direct. But because we had pretty much the same defence, we were still strong at the back.

And then the wheels came off. We were third in the table – very much in a promotion position – well into the spring but we fell to pieces when Kevin went back to Sunderland. It wasn't all down to him going but losing him and a couple of games soon after rattled our confidence. We lost six of the last 10 games, only winning two, including a 4-1 hammering of Newcastle at Ewood. We finished the season tenth, which was hardly a disaster, but we knew we'd let ourselves down after the start we'd had. The atmosphere around the place never dipped though. Bobby just had this aura about him that inspired players and created a fantastic team spirit. There's nothing better than feeling you're an important cog in a well-oiled machine and that spreads a positive attitude throughout the team. Under Bobby we worked hard as a team and played hard as a team. There were no factions or unsettling influences and we stuck together through what had the potential to be a very tricky time.

That's not to say we didn't have our share of lads prepared to speak their mind and upset people here and there, but that was about trying to make things better. It was a professional and not a personal issue. Glenn Keeley definitely fell into this category. Hard as nails on the pitch, hard as nails off it. If he argued white was black, I'd agree with him. Then and now.

If Bobby's first season at Blackburn was a partial success, 1982-83 was almost utterly forgettable as a team event. However I did get my best-ever scoring record of 22 league goals – just four short of the league's top scorer, who was some bloke called Lineker.

Despite the goals the season pretty much passed me by. We picked up a couple of players cheaply – Colin Randell, a midfielder from Plymouth who was never going to set the world alight, and Vince O'Keefe as goalkeeping back-up to Terry.

Those signings told their own story and there was never much chance of us doing anything more than consolidating. In fact, it was the only season of my career when I felt we were only ever capable of achieving a mediocre mid-table position. There was no excitement of any kind because we were never in danger of either pushing for promotion or trying to avoid relegation. We finished eleventh, we were utterly inconsistent and we were boring the pants off the few supporters who could be bothered to turn up. We never played to more than about 8,000 all season.

From a personal perspective, it could have been much worse because at least the fans liked me. Others weren't so lucky. A lot of the players didn't used to like playing next to the old Riverside Stand because they could pick out the voices slagging them off. Jim Branagan would get absolutely slaughtered sometimes and the crowd was so small you'd hear Jim screaming about the whingers during the game.

"It was him. That bastard in the hat. I'll bloody have him if he doesn't shut it."

To be honest Jim did have quite a short fuse and he was the sort of bloke that would pick them out and punch them if they weren't careful.

I know we are all professionals and supposed to be able to take some stick, but it really affected the performance of some players like Norman Bell and, later on, Jimmy Quinn. But for the others, they just got on with the job and tried not to laugh because it was the same old voices with the same old whinges week after bloody week. The club was hardly well off in those days, which is one of the reasons I admire Bobby so much, and he somehow managed to keep spirits high.

Colin and Vince were hardly going to sell more season tickets, so Bobby was under a lot of pressure to get success on the pitch to attract the crowds. Bill Fox, the chairman, had said in the summer that money for transfers would be based only on the number of people coming through the turnstiles. But you can hardly blame the fans for not falling for the bribe, they're not daft and we weren't giving them much to cheer. We were solid but dull to the point of tedium.

We did get good value from Vince though. He was a lovely man but on one trip back from an away game we were playing cards and the lads were rigging it so Vince would lose. The loser had to buy a load of drinks and down the lot. He couldn't believe how unlucky he was but he had no idea the game had been fixed. Poor Vinny ended up plastered, but we got a good laugh out of it.

The one positive note of the season that gave the fans a bit of excitement was the visit of the First Division's reigning champions on a cold Saturday afternoon in early January. We were drawn against Liverpool in the third round of the FA Cup and we had almost 22,000 on to see the likes of Dalglish, Souness and Rush. I scored, smashing it past Bruce Grobbelaar from our tried and tested corner routine. I was on the back stick for Noel Brotherston's corner and in it went. In all honesty my recollection of the game is very limited. But I do know we only led for about four minutes. David Hodgson grabbing an equaliser before Ian Rush put Liverpool ahead on the stroke of half-time.

So we were beating the best team in the country. For a few minutes. At least that was something for the Rovers fans to cheer.

As well as being popular on the terraces, I could take some comfort from the fact I was improving as a player under Bobby. He made me realise I didn't have to run round the pitch like a headless chicken all afternoon. He slowed me down and made me much more aware of positioning and timing.

"Just save your energy a bit, Simon, and get in the box more."

Which was pretty easy. Noel Brotherston and Ian Miller were dreadfully inconsistent but both, on their day, were fantastic. Noel was incredible and had the ability to turn good players inside out and make them look stupid. He wasn't quick, like Dusty who'd knock the ball past his marker and start running, but he really knew how to get round players. And he stuck at it. If it wasn't his day, he'd just keep on trying, always looking for the killer pass. Dusty, though, could let his head drop for the rest of the game if his first cross wasn't half decent.

In truth, none of us got going that season. We did manage a two-month unbeaten run from November to the end of December, our last win of the run coming at Turf Moor. But after Christmas we were really inconsistent. We just couldn't get a run together.

The visit of our old friends Burnley towards the end of the season proved dramatic. I doubt if I need to say this, but the atmosphere in those East Lancashire fixtures was nothing short of poisonous. People talk about Merseyside and Manchester, but I can't imagine a derby in England that has so much local honour at stake. Blackburn and Burnley are only ten miles apart but the people are proud of their own identities. The accents are different, the attitudes are different and there's no question of divided loyalties – it's one team per town. There's no choice to be made about who you support like there is in Liverpool, Manchester or London. Here you're born with it.

Burnley came to Ewood on their way out of the Second Division. They had come up as champions of Division Three but couldn't do enough to stay in the league. The last time we had played Burnley prior to this season was during my first season, when we were relegated, and they beat us twice. Funny to think that the game on 4 April 1983 at Ewood would be the last time I'd play them in blue and white. In a league game anyway. We did occasionally meet in the Isle of Man tournaments that took place in pre-season.

You can imagine the response of the Burnley fans when I missed a penalty. And then their response when I was invited to retake it. I could feel the hate. And the hate felt good!

I know it was only a minority who tried to prevent the retake but a number of Burnley fans had climbed into the eaves of the Darwen End roof and started flinging slates on to the pitch. I've known some pretty stupid and pretty hairy things go on at games, but nothing compared to this – most of the missiles were raining down on their fellow supporters at the front. It was disgraceful.

The players were taken off the field by the referee and Frank Casper, the Burnley manager, appealed for calm. Eventually matters settled and I stepped up for a second bite of the cherry. I scored. That was a sweet moment. We won the game 2-1 and Burnley went down the following month. Within four years they were just one game from going out of the league altogether and, possibly, out of business altogether when they found themselves rock bottom of the Fourth Division.

That has turned around in recent years, but I look forward to renewed hostilities between these rivals. The atmosphere is like nothing else. Mind you some fans can get a bit carried away. After one game for Blackburn at Turf Moor I walked out of the players' entrance and there was a local lad brandishing a carving knife.

"Where's that Simon Garner? I'm gonna knife him."

"He'll be out in a minute pal."

I didn't hang around.

Towards the end of the season rumours about me and the club started to spread. Neither was helpful or true. Regarding me, a freelance journalist who I'd prefer not to name, came up with a story about me hitting the bottle and smashing up my house. It was based on the fact there was a pile of empty bottles outside my home and the windows had been removed. I've always had a good relationship with the media – national and local – and have always been happy to give an opinion or take part in an interview. I'd go so far as to say I enjoy it. But this story made me wary and I never again dealt with this operator. All he had to do was check a few facts. He knew me well enough to ask, but he just wrote the story up and fired it across the sports pages of the national press. Mandy and I had thrown a party – that was why there were so many bottles. And we were having double-glazing installed – which accounts for the windows being out. For the sake of a few quid, we were subjected to some appalling stories.

The other rumour was that the club didn't want to get promotion because it didn't have the finance to support a season in Division One. This story popped up a few times over the years and I have to say I think it was absolute rubbish. Yes the club was poor but under the likes of Bill Fox, who had recently become chairman, we had very ambitious men who wanted nothing but the best for the club. In fact, without people like Bill, who I considered a friend, we might have joined the Lancashire freefall. Blackpool, Preston, Burnley and Bolton were once, like Blackburn, among the soccer superpowers. The prudence and vision of the board in that era at Blackburn ensured, against all the odds, that we never followed them to the brink of ruin and extinction. They all fell to the bottom divisions and took some time to restabilise. We never lacked the desire to be promoted, we simply weren't up to the job.

Bobby liked to keep us entertained. On trips he made sure we got the best hotels and did everything he could to make sure we enjoyed ourselves. We'd compete most years in the Lancashire Manx Cup, a pre-season tournament involving clubs from across the county sponsored by the Isle of Man tourism board. The winners would be invited to go back the following year for the Isle of Man Football Festival. We always stayed in the

Palace Hotel on the bay in Douglas, where there was a casino and a cabaret.

Alan Price – from the band The Animals – was performing and the audience had been a bit rowdy, which we didn't help by standing at the back of the hall singing along.

"This is my show and if you want to sing, that's fine, but I'll go home and leave you to it!"

I really thought he meant it. But we were young and we were drunk, so when he started the next tune we joined in again and, true to his word, he stopped the performance. There were some hard looks directed at us from the rest of the audience but then he broke into a smile and insisted that if we thought we could hack it, we should join him on stage. I don't for a minute think he expected us to do it but, one by one, we trooped to the front of the auditorium, climbed the steps, and acted as his backing singers for the next song.

Chris Thompson joined us in the summer of 1983 from Bolton. He was another of those players people didn't know much about and he was never really that popular with the fans, but I liked him. He worked hard during the game without scoring many, but opened plenty of doors for me with the running he did off the ball. He was pretty much thrown straight into the fray as well, which I think made his performances even more impressive.

His chance came after Norman Bell was injured in the first game of the season, a 2-2 draw with Huddersfield. Norman's knee was mangled and his professional career was over. He went on to be player-manager for Darwen in non-league. Another loss. He was never a big socialiser but he was a great professional to work with and an honest, down-to-earth player who never shirked on the training field or in a game. Even when we played together a few times for the veterans, he still hated being substituted. So that was another striker I'd seen off, but not in the way I would have liked.

I learned from these guys, Thommo included, and we formed a good partnership, despite the fact we had similar styles. In fact, with the single exception of Andy Crawford, all my partners helped me in my game in some way or other. It wasn't an obvious thing, but as I got older and more established I got to understand the game better and how other strikers worked. I nicked their best tricks and later on they nicked mine.

No doubt about it, apart from our sloppy finale, this was a good season for Blackburn Rovers and served as justification of Bobby's appointment. I was an ever-present, which I only managed twice in my career, and I scored nineteen goals which is just short of one every other game – a pretty solid indicator of my form under Bobby. Mind you, five of the goals came in a single afternoon.

Saturday September 10, 1983, at home to Derby County. Final score: Blackburn Rovers 5-1 Derby County.

My first came from a long ball over the top. Paul Futcher let it roll for the goalkeeper but he just stood there, rooted to the spot, and it was easy enough to take it round him and tap in. The second was a right foot shot and the fifth a penalty. I whacked it and it went in. The other two? No idea, I just can't remember them at all. So what – the record books tell me I got all five and I'll settle for that. I'll never forget that afternoon and neither will Paul Futcher. Every time I played against him after that he seemed to set out with the intention of kicking me. Derby were a good side, too. Archie Gemmill and John Robertson were still top-class players and Peter Taylor was a great manager.

Naturally I expected to be grabbing a few headlines in the Sunday papers so I went and bought them all. The only problem was Tony Caldwell got five for Bolton as well so it all got a bit diluted. Still, I got the one and only freebie of my career that night when the boss at the Bull's Head, a pub and restaurant at the Whalley end of Blackburn, picked up my tab for dinner. Nice one.

After I retired and while living down in Berkshire I used to enjoy a five-a-side on Thursday nights with a few local lads. One night a new chap came to join in and he came to the pub afterwards.

"You don't remember me do you?"

I didn't.

"I was marking you the day you scored five against Derby."

That's probably why I didn't remember poor Glenn Skivington. He was a great lad but I don't think I did his career any favours that day. We became good pals.

I can't deny that it was in my head around that time that a move to

Division One must have been on the cards. I was on great form and very sharp. I was never the fastest player but I could shield the ball well and make space – not unlike Kenny Dalglish, I used to persuade myself. Five against a good side like Derby who were close to the top of Division Two and playing consistently well. I must have been in the frame. There were a few stories in the papers saying I was being watched by some of the big clubs but they were holding off for another season to see if I was the real deal. I never had any idea if there was any truth in what they were saying and it was before the days when agents would tout players around. The club said they would be open with me and let me know if there was a top flight club in for me. It was only during the development of this book that I discovered Bobby Saxton did turn down an offer for me but never told me. And from what people have said, it could well have been Joe Fagan at Liverpool. If I'm honest, had I been told about interest from a club like Liverpool, I would have wanted to go. I wouldn't be able to say no to that and I would have pushed the club to let me at least talk to them. As things turned out, it was kept quiet. It could be something that upset me looking back but there really isn't any point living in the past, and I loved playing at Blackburn. Like any footballer I had the ambition to play against the best week in and week out but I always thought eventually I'd do it with Blackburn. I just never imagined when we did make it to the top flight I'd be leaving before the first ball had been kicked.

So back with my feet on the floor, the club struggled along on the meagre resources it had available. Fortunately we were getting some good young players through the ranks and that was the only reason we managed to sustain a decent challenge in 1983/84. Simon Barker was a superb prospect from the first time I saw him play. He'd been doing well in the reserves and though he wasn't the finished article, Bobby threw him into the first team. From his debut onwards he never looked out of place or out of his depth and he had a bag of tricks as big as the one he carried his confidence in. While Simon was never a bighead he had that assured presence which marked him out as a special player. He scored goals from midfield, he was quick to help out in defence, he passed the ball superbly and could run all day. In many respects, he was the player who gave us back what we had been missing since Howard left, a gap we could only fill temporarily with the likes of Kevin Arnott. It was obvious he would play at the highest level and eventually had a great career with Queen's Park Rangers. He wasn't much of a tackler though, and he'd get stick from the crowd if he shirked a big challenge, but he was still young and later in his career he added that element to his game.

He was a good lad off the pitch who joined in with the socialising but knew what it took to be a professional. I spent some time sharing a room with Simon during away trips when he had just broken into the side. I had to teach him about some of the facts of life, such as the importance of smoking in the room and things like that. We got on really well, although he hated my habit of falling asleep with the telly on. He was trying to make his way in the game and he would always get himself off to bed early after the team meal. I would stay downstairs a bit longer and head up later, trying not to wake him up as I made a cup of coffee, had a fag and put the telly on before nodding off. He would go mad when he woke up early to find the telly on with a blank screen going 'beeeeep'.

Mark Patterson started to emerge around the same time as Simon. He lacked the speed of Dusty and the skills of Noel but he could get a cross in from anywhere. The coaching he got from Bobby helped him exploit a more limited game to the best effect. Mark never had the ability of Simon Barker – very few players did – but he had a powerful aggression which, most of the time, he kept just in check. It was the same in training where he was never too worried about letting off a few ripe challenges and I wasn't alone in learning to keep out of his way. He was a typical hard-working player who was never going to set the world on fire but would always get a move if he needed one. Which is why he played for such a lot of clubs and, with Sheffield United, even made it to the Premiership.

The season turned out to be another false dawn though, and we were undone by our usual dismal patch, this time coming towards the end of the season, which made it even more disappointing. We'd had a sixteen-match unbeaten run and we were bursting with confidence. The chances were falling well and we were scoring goals but we just gummed up from April, dropped out of contention and finished sixth. Too many draws. Just like under Kendall.

If it was a disappointing end to the season professionally, at home John got a baby brother, James, and life was rosy. We moved to Cherry Tree, a nice end of town and near to Pleasington. Now I had two lads to take out on my rambles.

There's just no way you can afford to relax as a player, as I'd been constantly reminded throughout my career, and despite having had another excellent season on a personal level my position was back under threat with the signing of another striker. It was clear I was never going to have an easy life in football.

Jimmy Quinn came from Swindon. I'm pretty sure he scored against us in an FA Cup match with a big header. The trouble with Quinny was that he could never keep his concentration for a full match and, what made it worse, the fans knew it. He was a great header of the ball, had a potent right foot and for 20 minutes a game he was a fabulous player. But the rest of the time he'd just wander off into his own little world and it was like communicating with a Martian.

We'd become a very tight unit under Bobby and while there wasn't much flair in the side, we played to our strengths and understood our weaknesses. We had no loners or superstars who stood apart from anyone else. With Blackburn Rovers there were no airs or graces during that era, everyone worked together and Bobby led by example. Though it has to be said he possibly took it a bit far sometimes. I'm sure he was just trying to be part of the team and show he could muck in with the lads – and demonstrate just how tight cash was at the time – but I thought he was going to drown at Pleasington during training one morning. A miscued shot cleared everyone's head and flew into the River Darwen, which runs through Blackburn and cuts through the playing fields. Anyone who knows it will agree that this is a particularly revolting section of the waterways of Lancashire. It's filthy, strewn with rubbish and home to more rats and other vermin than I'd like to dwell on. Even the pub players who use the pitches are reluctant to rescue a ball from those murky waters. Not Bobby. He scampered off in pursuit, got downstream of the ball and crouched on the bank to grab the ball as it passed him. It was inevitable what would follow and it was one of those 'wish I had a camcorder' moments as he lost his footing and then toppled forwards into the blackness. He started screaming for help and someone – not me – jumped in to rescue him. His dog, a Yorkshire terrier, also dived in to offer canine assistance. And all for a bloody knackered old ball. Still, we got the rest of the day off – we were laughing too hard to carry on training.

Up until Christmas we were in pretty unstoppable form, having reversed the fortunes of the end of the previous season. We played at Carlisle and Derek Fazackerley scored a penalty to put us four points clear at the top. It was some position to be in and we strengthened it with a 2-1 win over Leeds on Boxing Day. But then it started to go horribly wrong. Again. Huddersfield beat us at home and then we lost at home against Manchester United in the FA Cup in front of a sold-out Ewood. The pitch was rock solid that day – it was like playing on the plastic at Loftus Road. We had our chances, me included, but United keeper Gary Bailey just wouldn't let anything past him that day. It had started badly when an uncharacteristic mistake from the ever-dependable Baz Rathbone let in Gordon Strachan early on. They scored again in the second half and that was that. In fairness, United were one of the best clubs in the country at the time under Ron Atkinson and they went on to win the cup.

It's hard to place blame for the slip-up and I really don't know what else Bobby could have done.

There wasn't money to strengthen the squad and while the fans may have thought otherwise, we certainly didn't need a star name – the dressing room atmosphere was magnificent and to have upset that would have made a big signing almost pointless and probably counter-productive. It also seemed to me that it was impossible to find players at a reasonable price who might have improved the squad we had. All of which left us lacking a bit of sparkle and by the end of the season that finally took its toll. We needed to win three or four of our last six games to go up but we blew it. We drew too many games on the road and lost 1-0 for three consecutive matches right at the end of the season. Just one result in any of those games and we'd have been promoted. Even on the last day of the season we still had a mathematical chance of going up when we played Wolves. Tommy Docherty, their manager at the time, came into our dressing room just before kick-off and sat in on Bobby's team talk. Something I'd never seen before and certainly never saw again. In fact, I've no idea why Bobby let him in.

"Don't worry about our lot. We're crap."

He was probably right. They were bottom of the league and we beat them 3-0 for the second time that season. He'd just got the sack and his glittering managerial career was coming to its end. We also needed Manchester City and Portsmouth to lose but, inevitably, it didn't work out. We finished fifth. It was a nightmare. Each season we were getting better and up until Christmas we would be something like 10 games from promotion and doing fine. Come the end of the season, we were still stuck in Division Two. I still refused to accept that it was beyond us. I was young and though it was heart-breaking I always felt there would be another chance around the corner.

I'm an optimist by nature, which is why I've always been happy and secure in myself even when I was in prison. I'm optimistic about everything and I always think there will be an answer to any tricky situation. I think it's a footballer thing because whatever else is going on in the world or in your life, your mind is locked into a brief period on a Saturday afternoon. You might be in debt, your marriage might be breaking down, you might have lost someone close. It doesn't matter. Because for those 90 minutes you're in front of 3,000 or 30,000 or any number of people and your job is to give them a lift, give them their week's pleasure. They are with you all the way and you can help their problems evaporate for a few minutes. And you do this week in, week out. If you weren't an optimist, you'd realise how daft it all is.

Bobby Saxton
Manager at Blackburn from 1981 to 1986

"Have we got a goal scorer?"

That was my first question when I arrived at Blackburn.

"Yes we have. Simon Garner."

That was good news for me because it meant I didn't have to buy one, and that saved me a lot of money. And boy were they right.

It was a long way to go from Plymouth to Blackburn and, I'll be honest, I didn't know a great deal about the players I was inheriting. So when I started coaching them I had to quickly get to know who we had and what they were about.

Simon was a fantastic goal scorer. Such an instinctive finisher. He had such an incredible ability to read the balls coming into the box. If a cross came in, Garns would be there. If a pass came in, Garns would be there. He wouldn't tend to take the keeper on and try to go round him. That wasn't his strength. He had the gift of timing his run to get on to the pass or the cross, one or two touches at most, and then, bang, it was in the back of the net. That's why I played with wingers. You just knew he was going to be there. I don't think he ever scored a goal from outside the box. But in and around the box there was no one more lethal than Garns.

He had the knack of being in the right place at the right time and could definitely have played at the highest level and scored goals there. I did have a couple of teams come in for Garns at one time or another. On one occasion a club was really pressing and pressing. I thought to myself, "Should I tell him or not?" Back then things were done differently and if a player was under contract that was it. The club held all the cards. In the end I didn't tell him. How could I sell my goal scorer? There was absolutely no way I was letting him go.

He wasn't the best trainer in the world and when we did any running he would always be at the back – by about a street! I knew he liked a pint and a fag, but that never bothered me. As long as he did his job on a Saturday that was all that mattered. When the referee blows that whistle at 3pm, that's when you needed him to do the job. And he did.

In the dressing room he was a class lad. Top drawer. He was a great character to have around and really epitomised that fantastic bond the players had in the dressing room back then. We had a small squad but they were all pals and they all worked hard.

CHAPTER 6

The end for Bobby

1985 to 1986

After missing out on promotion by just a point, we managed to go from being one of the top teams in the division to almost being relegated. The money had clearly dried up again because there was no incoming movement on the transfer front of any note pre-season.

Christmas came early in 1985. Not that that was good news for Blackburn Rovers, it simply meant our annual run of rubbish football started sooner than anticipated. Halfway through October we were second in the league and flying once again, and then we started to stutter. From the New Year to mid-April we won twice. I had no doubt we were going down. That wasn't a lack of optimism, it was good old-fashioned honesty. It was getting desperate. And then in true bizarre Rovers fashion we battered Sheffield United 6-1 at Ewood. I got the first after about 30 seconds. Dusty got into the box, pulled it back and I stuffed it in from the edge of the area. It was that game even more than the last of the season at Grimsby that kept us up. Our confidence was in ribbons, though none of us could believe we were playing so poorly, and to score six gave us a chance. Against Grimsby I scored early again, after about forty seconds, and we scraped through to win 3-1 and stay up. That was my hundredth goal as a professional and one of the most important of my career. Quite honestly at the time I had no idea. I know it's a cliché but there was only one thing on my mind – win and we stay up. As it happened, Carlisle lost at Oldham, and with a goal difference of -24 they had fared much worse than us, and so we would have survived by the skin of our teeth whatever happened to us. But to ensure a three-point cushion was an additional relief.

The trouble is I can't get close to explaining why it all went so wrong.

Our team was ageing so perhaps there wasn't the same consistency in team selection, but we had good younger players coming through and we were pretty fit. It wasn't as if we were getting bored with Bobby's style, we weren't. Everyone stuck together and we did our best. It just wasn't good enough and we weren't good enough. But the loyalty the team showed Bobby never faltered. He had a great way with players and knew how everyone ticked as individuals as well as a team.

On one occasion I was having a lean spell and I couldn't score goals. I wasn't playing badly but I was missing chances that I would usually put in the back of the net. Bobby called me into his office and said he was going to leave me out for a couple of games. Obviously that's not something any footballer wants to hear. You just want to be playing. But the way Bobby said it left me feeling like I'd just had a pay rise. It's testament to his man management that he could leave me out and I was, not happy, but not angry either.

"I'm going to leave you out for a couple of games, but I will bring you back. I'm not dropping you. Just keep doing it in training, score a few goals."

Quite often I would go through a lean spell around Christmas. Whether Bobby leaving me out of the team had a big impact on me in terms of turning it around or not I don't know. I have always been a positive person. I was always confident things were going to get better and they did. I started scoring goals again and so I got back in the team.

It never got to me when I missed a chance. I wouldn't get my head down and worry about it. I would just wait for the next one and was always confident that one would go in. I always used to go in there and try to put it in the back of the net. It wouldn't make me shy away from putting myself in the box and trying. I would just keep going and eventually one would go in.

Bobby was true to his word and I was soon back in the team. That management of footballers as individuals really marked him out for me as a special boss and I don't think he ever got enough credit for that. Certainly the fans never saw that side of him. Bobby was a reserved and shy man in public. He said his piece in the dressing room and at the training ground. But put a microphone in front of him and he didn't want to know. He could have done with someone to talk to the media for him because it was his only real weakness.

It was a simple philosophy Bobby put in place, it had to be. We were skint so he had to have players who could slot in and out of a hard-working unit. In football you can function reasonably well if eight of the starting line-up are on top of their game – the other three can be carried. Bobby's line was that if those three gave 100 per cent in terms of effort then he was satisfied. Any less than that and he would make his feelings known. In private. Always in private. That's how the loyalty developed.

It was around that time I saw another approach to man-management in the game, or rather boy-management. John, who was about five or six by now, was playing for Blue Star FC in Blackburn. I was a bit of a local celebrity which made it difficult for me watching the games because I could never really shout encouragement in case I was seen to be a smart arse. But the other dads?

"Come on Kevin, use it, USE IT, oh bloody hell ref, REF!"

And on and on and on. All the frustrations of these dads – who would have loved to have been in my shoes – just pouring out from the touchline. Bloody hell, they were worse than the moaners on the Riverside.

At least it gave me the chance to meet people from the area who weren't directly connected with football. People like Bob Dickinson, a car dealer, Andy McKie, who I later went into business with, and Big Jim Kelly from Darwen. They were mostly fans as well, so these guys became regular drinking buddies in the 100 Club after games. In those days most of the players would socialise with fans. Some would leave after a quick half if they had distances to travel but me, I'd stay until the world had been put to rights. It was usually about closing time.

At the end of the 1985/86 season we played in a testimonial game at Plymouth for the manager's old groundsman, George Robertson. He was a legend down there having played 350-odd times in the Fifties and Sixties before joining the non-playing staff. This was his second testimonial game, so it was quite an honour for him and an honour for us to be asked to take part. It was also a demonstration of how popular Bobby still was in Devon despite having left five years earlier.

But what happened after the game was bizarre. As was the custom, we had a few beers at the ground and then went out to a nightclub and then back to the hotel. There was only a porter on at that time of night but he carried on serving us drinks. Somehow while he was serving us, he managed to spill a tray of drinks all over the computer and it took down the whole system.

The next day, when we came back to Blackburn, I walked through my front door and five minutes later there was a knock on the door. It was a reporter from the Lancashire Evening Telegraph who wanted to know about the big party in Plymouth the night before. "You know the one with all the women, where you wrecked the place?"

I couldn't believe it. Firstly, how the hell had this guy found out about it? And secondly, there were no bloody women and it wasn't us that wrecked the place, it was the porter. The lad had obviously tried to deflect the blame and said it was us, and with me being one of the bigger drinkers in the team I inevitably got the blame.

The summer of 1986 saw Bobby make two of the best signings in my time at Blackburn, not that it did us much good. Chris Price came from Hereford and Scott Sellars from Leeds, where he had been struggling to make an impression. Chris gave us a new dimension because he was always keen to get forward from his right back position. He also added a new dimension to my social life because he liked a drink. Chris was another typical Bobby signing in that nobody had ever heard of him, but he settled in straight away. And the fans loved him because his work and scoring rate was unbelievable. Jim Branagan, who Chris effectively replaced, was a fine, steady footballer, but never went over the halfway line, whereas Chris was a throw-back to the Kevin Hird days – a full back who was adventurous and gave the fans something to cheer.

As for Scott, he had the best left foot I have ever had the pleasure to be on the park with. His right foot was useless, mind. But that left was so sweet. Scott was light as a feather and wasn't exactly blessed with great pace but he could walk past a player and cross brilliantly. With Simon Barker inside him in the midfield we had the making of a phenomenal team. The best thing about Scott was that he was always a team player. He had won some England under-23 caps but was nothing other than absolutely down to earth. He was also first to put his hand in the air at the suggestion of a beer and he was a glorious piss-taker and wind-up merchant. Anyone who tried it on with him was quickly cut down to size. The trouble was, you could never really get him back because he was too quick with his mouth and too clever with the ball, which was fine on match day but infuriating in training.

Unfortunately the qualities Chris and Scott brought didn't really help much, certainly not in terms of the league. The fans were really on our backs and Quinny caught most of it which, again, got me off the hook. What fans want to see is players giving one hundred per cent all the time. They'll forgive you if things aren't working out if it looks like you're breaking your back for the cause but Jimmy never even looked enthusiastic enough to break wind, never mind sweat. The fans got to him and he became increasingly withdrawn and depressed by the situation. Even if he'd scored six goals in a game the fans would have booed him for missing a half chance. Rather than trying to nurture him and help him out of the hole, Bobby decided to let Jimmy go back to Swindon in an effort to let him rescue his career. It worked, but it was a first sign that Bobby's judgement was becoming suspect. The signing of Paul McKinnon, a non-league player from Sutton, just before Christmas was the second and effectively sealed the manager's fate. Paul was an odd signing who managed just five games for Blackburn and had a very unusual career flitting backwards and forwards between England and a number of clubs in Sweden. It was a desperate move to try and counter a desperate situation.

With one awful season behind us, another was now staring us in the face and we were heading for the drop again. If the fans thought McKinnon was a surprise signing, imagine how we felt. For the first time players were losing confidence in Bobby's decisions – not Bobby himself, just his response to a difficult time. his judgement was being swayed by panic. Yes, we were dying a death in the league, but Paul was not the answer. He worked hard and did his best but he just wasn't up to the job.

We actually started the season well, winning our first three games, and I scored four against a decent Sunderland side when we hammered them 6-1 at Ewood. But we went off the boil immediately after, failing to win any of our next 10 league matches. By the time we next played Sunderland, when Paul made his debut, the train was off the rails and we were thumped 3-0. On Boxing Day we lost to Huddersfield when Duncan Shearer – a player who would go on to join Blackburn under Kenny Dalglish – scored. We were second from bottom in the table, just one point ahead of Barnsley, and we had won just one more game since the start of the season.

And then Bobby was sacked. The fans were happy but despite everything the players were devastated, and we felt he deserved more time. in fact, we felt he'd earned a right to it. Jim Branagan was club captain at the time and before the board meeting which saw Bobby fired he organised a petition among the players to tell the directors how strongly we felt about keeping him as manager. Not a single player refused to sign. We'd had a great run under Bobby. He had spent something like £350,000 on players during his time at Ewood and recouped around half a million. He kept us happy on fairly modest wages and by and large we had done well. He stood by us when we were getting stick and never once blamed a player in public for the problems.

Jim pushed the petition under the door at the meeting but it made no difference. He was gone. We had a dinner for him at the Red House Motel on the boundary between Blackburn and Darwen and every player attended and drank his health.

In retrospect Bobby made some mistakes towards the end. We were an ageing team and he stuck by players he maybe should have let go earlier. That said, how was he going to replace them? There was still no sign of any cash to strengthen the squad. And anyway, it wasn't Bobby who was on the pitch playing crap – that was us. Me included, though not for the first time my 'man of the people' image shielded me from the more vociferous supporters who diverted their attentions elsewhere. I was viewed as someone from the terraces who'd come good, and I never had any problems being with fans. I loved it and still like being recognised and talked to. After a game we would go in the old Hundred Club, win or lose. People would always want to come and talk to you and it was never a problem for me. I'd be happy to give them my opinion on why we had lost. I know it was never my fault. I came from a working-class background so I understood they had saved up all week to come and watch a football match on a Saturday. I didn't tend to drink in the posh places, I would go in the pubs in town where the fans were in Darwen or Blackburn and I really enjoyed being able to do that with very little stick, even when we were struggling on the pitch.

I'd autograph anything for anybody and try to help out wherever possible. At away games you'd get fans who'd travelled hundreds of miles and they'd be on the scrounge for our complimentary tickets.

"Too right. Here you go sunshine."

They were paying my wages and if they wanted an autograph or my help with a ticket then it was the least I could do. As for wages, we didn't do too badly, despite the fact we were neither a rich nor a particularly successful club in those days. I'd be a liar if I said I wouldn't have minded being better paid, and I can only guess what my salary would be if I'd been in my prime these days, but I have no real gripes. At my earnings peak, which coincided with me leaving the club, I was making a basic of £600 a week, which translates to something like £30,000 a year – certainly not to be sniffed at. During Bobby's time I reached about £450 plus bonuses and, at Blackburn, there was an excellent system which was worth about £40 a point, or £120 a win. In comparison to our wages, it was a good top-up, and it didn't matter where we were in the league.

At a lot of clubs you had to be in a certain position in the league for the payments to kick in. with others it was an accumulating scheme so, for example, you'd get £50 for the first win, £100 for the second, £200 for the third and so on. But as soon as you lost a game you went back to the £50. Chris Woods, the ex-England keeper, had been a friend of mine since school days when we played together at the junior football club in Wyberton, and when he was at Norwich they used this scheme. They played us after winning seven consecutive games, the eighth would have provided a massive amount of cash. I scored twice and we beat them easily. Strangely enough, the drinks were on me that night.

The Bobby Saxton era was over. Seeing his name removed from the manager's door was like losing a close relative. It was a big blow to the whole squad. And not just the first team players, the fringe players as well. All the players at the club liked Bobby Saxton and liked playing for him. We wanted him to stay and we really felt sorry for him.

Bobby had accepted a chalice of fire in taking over from Howard

One Last Shot

Kendall and had twice taken us to the brink of promotion. But in his final few weeks, when things were going horribly wrong for us again in the league, and to be frank, the transfer market, he sowed the seeds for one of the great days of an otherwise barren era.

We'd started to make progress in the Full Members Cup. It was a something-or-nothing tournament which we hadn't even bothered to enter the previous season. About a dozen people turned up for the first match of this campaign and though it was vilified, I loved it. It was a mid-week game, which meant we didn't have to train too hard on a Tuesday morning. Instead of running round a field in the name of getting fit without a ball in sight, we could go and play for real. But once the new manager was in position, it became very serious indeed and effectively rescued the season.

Simon Barker
Teammate at Blackburn from 1983 to 1988

Everyone used to confuse me with Simon Garner because our names were so similar, but sadly I never had his natural instinct for hitting the back of the net.

I signed for Rovers as an apprentice when I was 16 and made my debut against Swansea in October 1983. By that time Garns was an established first-team player and I was just 18. It was a settled side with pretty much the same keeper and back four for several years, Terry Gennoe, Jim Branagan, Glen Keeley, Derek Fazackerley and Mick Rathbone. Mark Patterson and I were the young players who broke into the side around the same time.

It was a very small, tight-knit club back in those days and as apprentices we would look after the pros and clean their boots for a little bit of extra cash. I used to look after Jim Branagan and Noel Brotherston's boots. The older pros were great at Blackburn and made me feel part of the group from the moment I made it into the first team.

My overriding memory and image of Garns at that time is of him with a fag in one hand and a pint of bitter in the other. He was a funny lad. He'd had his teeth knocked out and one of his party pieces was to take his front dentures out and gurn.

I loved playing with Garns. He had good pace and a natural ability to run in behind the defenders. We used to have this little understanding between us where he would come short a couple of yards and then spin in behind the defender and then all I had to do was play it in behind and he was through on goal. Many goals he scored in that time we played together was because of that.

He always used to get his shots off very quickly and he was able to use either his left foot or his right foot equally well. Most of his goals went in close to the goalkeeper. As he had such quick feet he used to get his shot off really quickly before the keeper was set.

He was greedy, as you have to be if you are goal scorer, but he was also a great team player and character to have in and around the dressing room. Back then most of the lads lived in the Blackburn area and we would go out two or three times in a week, but it wasn't particularly about the drinking, it was about the togetherness.

We came so close to promotion on more than one occasion and it was gutting that we never quite made it. We had a good side full of experience with some younger players coming in like Scott Sellars and Mark Patterson. And Garns was always up there as one of the top scorers in the division. When you have a player like that in your team you've always got a chance.

Garns was a great goal scorer who finished with an unbelievable record for Blackburn. I think if he was in today's era, with all the information players have access to and sports science, he would have looked after himself much better and been a success.

That was the reason I left Blackburn for QPR when I was 23, because I wanted to play in the First Division and prove myself, and Garns unfortunately didn't get that chance. It would have been interesting to see if he could have scored goals at that level. I don't doubt it.

CHAPTER 7

Wembley winners

1987

Tony Parkes took control after Bobby left, which was a tough assignment. The players had been right behind Bobby and it didn't matter who took over because there was always going to be something of an atmosphere as the new man – even in a caretaker role – would have to make changes to stop what was becoming a serious downward spiral. What Tony had in his favour was the fact the players had a great deal of respect for him. There was always an air about him that marked him out for a managerial or coaching position and, just like when he was a player, he always put all his energies into his job.

At the heart of it, Tony was one of the boys. He had been at the club for 16 years already and was part of the furniture even by then. It's unbelievable to think he would stay at the club for almost another two decades.

He was a very down-to-earth man. He was the king of one-liners – he could pick you up or knock you down in an instant. And he was just the same when he was caretaker manager. If he wanted to do something in training and you didn't agree with it, he would knock you back with a one-liner. And I think you need that to become a manager or a coach. If you are going to be successful you need something in you that says: "I'm going to do things my way and that's it. If it works it works, if it doesn't then it doesn't." And every time Tony Parkes took over as caretaker manager, it worked!

He did a good job and they always kept him on, which I was really pleased about. I could never see Tony being a full-time manager at Blackburn Rovers – he wouldn't have stayed as long as he did if he had become the manager – but he did a great job as caretaker manager every time he did it. He deserves a lot of praise.

It is devastating to hear about his recent struggles with dementia and my thoughts really do go out to Tony and his family. After everything he has given to the football club and the town itself, it is such an awful shame to see what has happened.

We hadn't won in six games when Tony took over, but we beat Portsmouth at Ewood in his first game at the turn of the new year. He was in charge for about a month while the board searched for Bobby's replacement. Portsmouth got their revenge and knocked us out of the FA Cup a week later, but that was Tony's only defeat before the new manager took charge in early February.

As a group of players we knew we had let ourselves and Bobby down and we knew we had to reverse what was a critical situation. We also knew that a new full-time manager would be in place soon and we would have to impress on him that we were up for the fight or we might be on our way out.

Finally we were introduced to our new manager, Don Mackay. At risk of repeating myself – Don who? He came from a backroom job at Glasgow Rangers and he'd worked in Dundee and for Coventry, which was the sum total of our knowledge. He walked in the dressing room and he sat us all down. You could see straight away he was a very confident man. He stood there, did his speech, told us how he was going to do things and that's what he did.

Almost immediately we noticed the key difference between Don and Bobby. Where Bobby was calm, relaxed and shy in public, Don was brash, loud and confident almost to the point of being overwhelming. We learned quickly that no matter how wrong he was about something, he was still right. Training changed again and, particularly in the early days, it was very long and laborious work. His training sessions were very different from what we did under Bobby. They became very tactical, and some players weren't keen. We were used to training for 90 minutes a day but with Don he could drag it out trying new systems. He could talk all day – he loved to talk about football.

He was in many ways quite arrogant about his approach to the game and would insist on doing things his way. Don't get me wrong, that's the job of a manager, but usually you expect some kind of input from the players. Not with Don.

He wanted to be involved in everything. He wanted all the bibs to be the right colour and he wanted to have the exact right number of balls and that was the way he worked. He even told the tea lady how many bags you needed for the perfect brew and the kitman which soap powder should be used. You get managers like that, but he got his point across. I never had a problem with Don, even though he did like to hear the sound of his own voice. I didn't fall out with him, but quite often I would find myself rolling my eyes and giggling quietly when he was issuing some micromanagement instructions to pretty much anyone in the football club. I'd be sat there thinking: "I mustn't let him see me laughing."

Whether we agreed or not as players we went along with it and it worked for him. So you couldn't really fault what he was trying to do.

And we did get a good team bonding trip to Benidorm out of him. I'm not sure which season it was, but we had been knocked out of the FA Cup and we had a free weekend. On the plane out there Don told us we would be playing a match.

"Yeah, yeah, very funny."

We didn't believe him. We thought it was a jolly to get our spirits back up for the season. We just went straight on the piss and had a great time. We were sunbathing and drinking on the beach. We dug a big hole and stuck Mick Rathbone in it and buried him so only his head was poking out, then I proceeded to fill all his holes with cigarettes – his ears, his nose, his mouth. They weren't lit, he'd have killed me if they were. Someone took a photo. I wish I still had it.

I don't know if it was the same day or not, but all of a sudden, while we were mid-session on the beach, Don turned up with a minibus.

"Come on lads, we're going to play a game of football."

Bloody hell. He wasn't joking after all. Is there even a team in Benidorm? Apparently so. We played a game against a team of waiters or something on a pitch that was as solid as concrete. We were all drunk. Baz fell asleep at left back. I was just walking around a bit. By the 85th minute or so it was 3-3 when Terry Gennoe, for some reason, ventured up the pitch and scored a winner for us right at the death.

We thought this was meant to be a team bonding exercise and we ended up nearly losing a game against a team of bloody waiters! Don had given us permission to relax and enjoy the weekend, and he didn't give us any bother for being a bit worse for wear. He probably didn't think there was any point. We all piled back on the minibus after the game and went back to the bar.

There would be a few trips like this under Don and they usually helped us come together as a team and we often went on a good run straight after.

Don's changes brought results and we started to dig ourselves out of trouble in the league and, with the Full Members Cup as a good diversion, we started to achieve some kind of shape. Under Bobby we had crept past Huddersfield in this most minor of cup contests and we had done so by fielding a strong side. It was the same situation against Sheffield United and it was only after beating Oxford 4-3, when we'd been forced to come from behind, that people started to sit up and notice, not least the players.

Beating Chelsea in the quarter-final was a big deal. I was on the scoresheet and Sean Curry, who Tony had signed from Liverpool's reserves, got one. Then it was Ipswich in the semis.

Just before the game, Glenn Keeley was ruled out for some reason and Don bolstered the defence with a pair of Scottish signings – Colin Hendry, who he picked up for £30,000 from Dundee, and Chris Sulley. The Full Members Cup was the making of Colin and turned him into a Blackburn legend. If Bobby knew the south west, Scotland was definitely Don's patch. He really knew the scene. Despite the fact he was a complete unknown and little more than a fresh-faced kid, Colin walked in like he owned the place. He had a presence which could be recognised instantly. Not quite cocky, but brimming with confidence about his abilities which, to be frank, were modest to begin with. His attitude reminded me of John Radford, but John had a League and FA Cup winner's medals whereas Colin just had a posture, an attitude and a memorable haircut. He was always confident he would go on to bigger and better things and, to be fair to him, he did.

In the dressing room, right from day one, he had plenty to say. Even Glenn was a bit taken aback, and he had the biggest mouth of anyone. A few of the more experienced players found him a pain in the arse. After all, he'd come for a few pennies from Dundee United but talked as though he was a regular in a European Cup-winning side. And he always fancied himself more as a striker than a defender, which wasn't something I wanted to dwell on too much – Blackburn had bought and sold enough strikers to man a picket line since my debut. But Colin was Colin and as he matured he became one of Don's and the club's greatest assets. As a defender.

That certainly took a while to get into his head. He was forever getting forward, regardless of the holes he left at the back, and his only objective in every game, or so it seemed, was to break forward and score. The fans loved it, but it left us exposed and made us vulnerable to counter-attacks. He'd try to dribble past three or four players from the edge of our box and while it must have been exciting to watch, it left the rest of us a bag of nerves. It took the team a while to adjust to his style but Don obviously – and rightly as it turned out – saw the potential. It didn't seem like it when he first arrived, but Colin was a very intelligent player. He'd go on these runs and leave his position, but we very rarely suffered from his actions. He timed things well and never more so than at Wembley for the final.

First though, we had to get past Ipswich in the semi – another home draw. The players, fans and local media were now really up for the tournament. How we had got this far is still a mystery to me. We had been struggling to pick up results in the league but we just kept winning these games and making it through the rounds. We tended to put a strong team out because we didn't have lots of players to rotate. And Don had decided he wanted to win it. This was his chance to win something and prove himself as a top manager. So this wasn't the time to try to blood kids from the youth team.

I'd like to say we were taking each match as it came but that would be a lie. Under Don we had got ourselves out of trouble in the league, which was an enormous relief, and found some breathing space. The only thing I was thinking about was the possibility of appearing at Wembley and there's no doubt we coasted through the odd league match. This might have been a once-in-a-lifetime opportunity.

That night against Ipswich went by in a blur. We won 3-0 in front of just over 12,000 people, the second highest attendance at Ewood that season - and that's saying something for a Wednesday night game. It was quite a contrast from the first home game we played in the competition that season when around 2,000 came out to see us beat Sheffield United 1-0. I scored the goal in that game. My only memories of the Ipswich game are of winning a penalty and being accused of diving, which I didn't, and scoring a goal from open play. The ball came to me from the right wing and I blasted it inside the near post from about 12 yards. It was a sweet shot but there was a late blocking challenge as I struck it and I cracked the bottom of the defender's boot. I was in agony but there was no way I wasn't going to celebrate this one, either on the pitch or over a pint or dozen afterwards.

The final was fewer than three weeks away. A first Wembley appearance for Blackburn in almost three decades, and it never left the back of my mind. I don't care what anyone says but when there was a fifty-fifty challenge in those games leading up to the final, I was a bit wary. Nobody wanted to miss out and I wasn't going to put my place at Wembley at risk by gambling on a tackle in a meaningless league game. It's the only time in my career when I deliberately under-performed.

And even so, we won three of the four games we played between the semi-final and final. We had a new-found confidence that had been sadly lacking earlier in the season and our improved form had seen us up to midtable.

Don was certainly no fool. This game was as important to him as it was to us and he knew his reputation and standing could be bolstered forever if we won. Training eased off and we concentrated as much on staying calm and killing the nerves as organising tactics. It wasn't easy. Regardless of all the promotion close calls and regardless of the fact there was no European place at stake, this was still the biggest game of our careers and we might never get another shot at something so exciting. In the grand scheme of things, very few players get the chance to play at Wembley. I'd never even been there as a spectator.

We got to our base a couple of days before the game and it was very, very boring. There was so little to do and we certainly couldn't have a drink to numb the tension. Under a different manager that may not have been the case, but even I felt it was the right thing to do. We'd train in the mornings and use the gym or the pool to while away the afternoons. Or some of the lads did: I ended up spending most of my time in the snooker room. We'd have a communal dinner in the evening and by ten o'clock there was nothing to do but get into bed and try to get some sleep. That wasn't easy either.

The nerves really started to build when we left the hotel on the day of the game. We had a police escort, which made us feel like real stars, and as we started to see the fans as we got closer to the stadium the butterflies turned into rampant eagles. I don't get unsettled easily and I had always been relaxed going into games but this was different. This was scary.

And here's the thing. You get on to the pitch and it all looks wonderful. The changing rooms were fantastic, the stands look superb, but the pitch itself? Dreadful. On the television it always looked so good with its crisp lawnmower lines, but underfoot it was terrible. The turf was patchy, uneven and pitted. Who says the camera never lies?

"This game isn't going to pass me by. This game isn't going to pass me by. This game …"

The game passed me by.

I know it was a poor match, all stop-start, and that we had very few shots. I know that Vince O'Keefe emerged from the shadows, overcame his awful nerves and played a blinder in goal. I know our fans outnumbered the Charlton fans massively – we had about 30,000 there.

I remember the centre back who was marking me was Steve Thompson, who had played for my hometown team Boston at the start of his career and went on to play for and manage nearby Lincoln City. We were chatting all game and talking about his time in Lincolnshire. He kicked me up in the air a few times and I kicked him back a few times.

Perhaps it's a good thing I don't remember the game as I put one over from about six yards early on and then in the second half ran more than half the length of the pitch but then got a poor contact on the ball and it went straight to the keeper. It would have been the cherry on top of a perfect footballing day for me to score in that game.

The only other thing I really remember is there were about five minutes to go when Alan Ainscow played Ian Miller in on the right wing. He beat a defender and I was screaming for a ball to the near post. I don't know why I ran to the near post as Dusty's crosses always went to the back post. He knocked it straight over my head. Charlton's keeper Bob Bolder got a touch on it but it fell for Colin, who was partnering me up front, and he smacked it in off the post. No wonder he fancied himself as a striker, it was a superb effort.

In the end the feeling was incredible. I can't imagine what it's like to lose at Wembley after all the sweat that goes into getting there. Nobody remembers the team that comes second. I played there another three times and was never on the losing side. You just don't want to leave the pitch.

If you talk to people now and say you've won the Full Members Cup, they might say it's a Mickey Mouse cup. But it's not if you've played at Wembley. That meant so much to our group. To play at Wembley is the dream of any footballer. It was brilliant.

And it was the first of my three ambitions in football fulfilled – I'd played at Wembley.

That's what being a professional footballer is all about – going to the spiritual home of the game and winning. It's what the years of perseverance and disappointments are all for. You do a lap of honour and you want to do it again. And again. And again. Throughout my career I had always been first off the pitch at the final whistle, straight into the bath and then off to the bar for a pint and a fag. Not at Wembley. That's how good it was.

Don was ecstatic. It was the pinnacle of his career. And though I think a lot of the players had thoughts of Bobby in the backs of their minds, who knows what might have happened if Bobby had stayed? It certainly looked like we might go down and I suspect the Full Members Cup would have been given a lesser priority. And in fairness to Don, he picked the team and his player scored the goal. I know a lot of fans would have liked Bobby to have been at Wembley in some capacity, but that's not the way football is or should be – you have to look forward, not backwards. They say you're only as good as your last game, but in reality it's the next that really counts.

Playing at Wembley was utterly exhausting. It wasn't the size of the pitch, which wasn't that big anyway, and it wasn't the fact the turf was so mediocre. It was simply the occasion. The build-up and the tension eventually get to you and to hear the final whistle – having won – was an immense relief.

"You didn't play very well, did you?"

Then he burst out laughing. My dad was absolutely made up about us winning. He was right, I didn't play well, but I'd won a cup. And I'd won at Wembley. We celebrated in fine fashion. In the players' bar at Wembley I just drank everything in front of me. The journey home was even more of a blur than the game. And the civic reception, which was a brilliant occasion, was really only remembered through photographs! It looked like the same 30,000 who'd been with us to Wembley the day before had descended on the town hall in Blackburn. I was drunk with beer and emotion and I know there were thousands of others who shared the hangover.

The rest of the season came and went. We were battered at Sheffield United in the following game and then it was back to playing in front of the usual seven and a half thousand or so hardy souls for our first home game after the cup final – a 4-2 win against Barnsley. We did beat Derby, who would go on to win the league, 3-1 at Ewood in front of more than 13,000 – our biggest crowd that season.

But we could never beat the feeling of Wembley and I think we were glad when the summer break came. Safe in the middle of the table but, judging by our efforts in the Full Members Cup, plenty to look forward to.

Don Mackay
Manager at Blackburn from 1987 to 1991

After I left Fulham as manager in 1994 I went into scouting, initially with Arsenal. This taught me a big lesson. What amazed me was that a lot of scouts would leave a game with 10 minutes to go. And when you are watching a player or want to see how a team plays, that is often the most important time in the game.

Tony Collins, who was the chief scout at Bristol City at the time, showed me how to do it – get to the game early, watch them warm up and watch them for the whole game. It may seem obvious to some, but that's the only way to really learn what a player is all about.

And I still believe this is part of the problem Simon Garner had. Scouts would watch him at the wrong times. They would often come around the Christmas period when Simon, for some reason, would always have a dry spell.

If they had done their jobs properly and watched him over a bigger number of games and a longer period, they would have seen just how good a player he was and how instinctive a finisher he was.

He was a fantastic goal scorer. That day when he broke the goalscoring record for Blackburn against Manchester City just about summed it up. We got in the play-offs that year but City were pushing for automatic promotion and we absolutely battered them. Simon scored a hattrick and put in an outstanding performance. But that was the sort of player he was. On his day he could score goals against anyone for fun.

He could score with both feet, his head, sometimes his backside! He could just get in those positions to put the football in the back of the net. That was his main asset and Blackburn reaped the benefits over and over again.

And other teams knew it as well. He got kicked to death sometimes because teams knew if you wanted to get a result against Blackburn Rovers, you had to keep Simon Garner quiet.

Simon should have played at a better level. Whether that's down to him working a bit harder or the coaching staff making sure he was working a bit harder, that's neither here nor there. But I guarantee with a bit more work he had the ability to play at a higher level. If that had happened I think Blackburn could have got a lot of money for him. And back then they would definitely have taken it.

But he liked his cigarette and he liked his pint. He thought I didn't know about it and maybe I should have hammered him for it, but I didn't. That was who Simon was and it was a big part of his personality. He was a likeable rogue, always happy. He enjoyed his life and he enjoyed playing football. He was content at Blackburn. Perhaps that was the problem.

And he was loved. If I dropped Simon I would have been shot. He was the be all and end all to Blackburn supporters and that was fair enough because he scored a lot of goals. And it is right that he is remembered so fondly by the fans because he was very loyal to the club. He could have come knocking on my door saying he wanted to move on but he never did.

Winning the Full Members Cup was unbelievable. It was an incredible day.

I took the boys down two days early and took them to Wembley the day before the game. Many of them had never been to Wembley before, far less played there, and it was important they had time to get to grips with the size of the stadium and how many people would be there. I knew this would have an effect on the players if they were going in there for the very first time.

We were amazed when we saw the crowd on the day. The gate was about 45,000 and we were used to playing in front of around seven or eight thousand most weeks. And there were only about 7,000 Charlton fans there, despite them being a London club. To see all those Blackburn fans in and around the stadium was fantastic and it made us even more determined to bring the trophy back.

Simon was outstanding that day. Yes, it was Colin who scored the goal, but people forget the work Simon did to create that. It was possibly Simon who created the space that allowed the goal to be scored.

Things began to change when Jack Walker got involved. All of a sudden the club had money and I was able to bring in players like Frank Stapleton and Kevin Moran. The highest-profile players I had brought in up to that point were Steve Archibald and Ossie Ardiles, and that was the start of the way the club wanted to move forward and improve.

But even with the new money coming in I wanted to build a team around Simon because I knew how important he was to Blackburn Rovers and to the supporters. I never thought he was an out and out number nine and felt he needed a good striker to play off. That's why I initially brought in Colin Hendry, although the two of them didn't really hit it off as a strike partnership and we quickly realised Colin would be much better at centre half.

I had a list of players I wanted to sign to improve that team and push for promotion. I tried to bring in Teddy Sheringham from Millwall. I even flew back from a holiday with my wife to meet him and I wanted him to play up front with Simon, but when Brian Clough came calling he was only ever going to sign for Nottingham Forest. I tried to sign Mike Newell as well but that didn't happen, and that's when I went in for David Speedie. Speedie caused opposition teams all sorts of problems and I thought that would really open things up for Simon to score goals as well.

Sadly I lost my job not long after that and I didn't get the opportunity to see that partnership through.

Kenny came in and, all credit to him, he did a great job bringing in some exceptional talent and getting the club into the Premiership. And of course the rest is history. But I felt sorry for Simon that he wasn't really involved and wasn't given an opportunity to play for Blackburn in the top flight. It was sad in some ways because I had always intended to use Simon and I would have kept him at the club after the promotion.

CHAPTER 8

Record breaking

1987 to 1989

The Full Members Cup was a great achievement despite it having virtually no prestige attached to it, but it was the league where we needed to perform. Don was settling in and starting to shape the team. He brought Ally Dawson down from Rangers and he slotted straight in. While he wasn't well known he was an international player and we didn't have too many of those at Blackburn. If he was a steady, solid player, the same could hardly be said of Howard Gayle.

Don signed him from Stoke but Howard had seen the bright lights at Birmingham and during his time with Liverpool. He had a reputation for being a big-time Charlie and an equally big drinker. He wound up some of the players because he had an opinion about everything and liked the sound of his own voice, but I got on well enough with him. He was good to have around the place. But the tales of his excessive drinking habits seemed way off the mark – he was a lightweight! Importantly though, the fans loved him even if his form was erratic to say the least. It didn't matter how he was playing, he'd try and gee the crowd up like some kind of cheerleader.

Even so, it was a risky signing. And a brave one. If you're from the school of thought that says you only buy to improve what you already have, then you have to wonder if it was a good deal.

Nicky Reid on the other hand was a sure-fire good bit of business. He was just the sort of player Don liked because he would run for 120 minutes a game – I mean it. He'd be running before kick-off non-stop and he'd be running on the spot in the dressing room after the final whistle. I roomed with Nicky for a while which made for an interesting mix. He was a fitness fanatic and I … wasn't. On away trips he'd be up at half seven cleaning his shoes before stretching and going for a walk. I'd be up at half seven having a fag and watching him. I would roll into the dining room for breakfast as late as I could possibly get away with. Taking this into consideration I guess it is surprising that it was Nicky who would go on to run a pub in Chorley.

Nicky wasn't the best footballer in the world but he was brought in to do a job and he played that midfield holding role extremely well. He was never a fans' favourite – steady players rarely are – but he would get stuck in, get the ball and give it to someone who could play a bit. Don made him club captain and he was a good choice. He'd played most of his career at Manchester City and the players had a lot of respect for his achievements. He was also a natural leader, something we needed to help steady our nerve and steel our resolve.

We had another slow start. By the end of September we were down in 16th in the league but we then went on a fantastic run of 23 league games unbeaten and, for the hundredth time in my career, or so it seemed, we were top of Division Two and in the driving seat for promotion. Our defence of the Full Members Cup didn't get past the first round though. We were beaten 2-1 at Ewood by Swindon in what was now called the Simod Cup.

In the League Cup we were given a chance to test ourselves against the would-be champions Liverpool. The likes of Bruce Grobbelaar, Alan Hansen, Peter Beardsley, Mark Lawrenson and John Barnes were among the stars in their line-up as they came to Ewood in September for the first leg. Ewood was packed and the noise was fantastic. We were losing at half-time but Scott Sellars scored an equaliser. Obviously their defenders were too busy keeping an eye on yours truly.

Then Don pulled off two of the most remarkable signings in the history of the club. First he brought in Steve Archibald from Barcelona and then trumped that with the unveiling of Ossie Ardiles, a World Cup winner with Argentina and a world-class player. Not to mention a movie star who'd shared time on screen with Sylvester Stallone, Michael Caine, Pele and Bobby Moore in Escape to Victory. Who says Blackburn isn't a hotbed of Hollywood glamour?

Bloody hell's bells was the general response to Steve's signing. The attendances nearly doubled and suddenly great things were expected of us. We'd known absolutely nothing about it but we did know that he must have been on a fair old wedge. We didn't mind that – he was a massive name and put bums on seats. I think, in part, it suited the image Don wanted to give of himself – as a major operator who could claim credit for these amazing signings.

Steve was under a lot of pressure. He'd done everything at Tottenham and done reasonably at Barcelona. Not only did he have to perform to the level of his reputation, but he also had to put himself in the shop window at a lower league club. This was a loan signing that gave Steve the chance of first team football and time to sort out his next big move. His attitude was similar to that of a lot of modern players – he'd play the game then get straight home. He didn't really mix with the others and just got in with his job. That was difficult for me because here was someone, like John Radford, I felt I could learn from but because he said so little it was hard to get close enough.

We didn't get off to the best start because he wanted the number 10 shirt. Don picked him to play up front with me at Swindon and he announced he wanted to be number 10. The only problem was that was my number and it had been for years. I hated the number nine – I can't say why, it was just a superstition I suppose after all those years – and I wasn't about to change now. Don wasn't strong enough to make a decision either way and so we ended up tossing a coin – and I won! So Steve had to settle for being the number nine.

Ossie became a good friend, partly I'm sure because he was a smoker and card player. As a player he was superb but he picked up a nasty knock from future Rover Nicky Marker so Blackburn fans only saw him play half a dozen games. Playing with him was an unbelievable experience. Bloody hell, this fella's a World Cup winner!

But he was so down to earth. He even stayed at my house once. We were travelling back from Millwall and Steve and Ossie were both on the coach. Steve sat by himself, like he always did, until about 20 minutes before we got back to Blackburn when he came down to the back of the bus to where we were playing cards.

"Right, let's play three card brag!"

We all agreed, he played with us for 20 minutes and then off he went. For some reason he came all the way back from London, got in his car at the ground, drove to Manchester Airport and got on a plane back to London. Why he didn't just stay down there I don't know. Ossie on the other hand was staying locally in a hotel. When we got off the coach I could see he was working out what to do and I invited him back to mine. We had a few drinks – he drank wine, not beer – into the night to celebrate getting in the play-offs. We didn't go to bed until the early morning.

Towards the end of the season the club was invited to take part in the Football League Centenary Tournament at Wembley. This was a mini football festival of sorts to celebrate 100 years since the League was founded in 1888. Apparently they wanted to have a six-a-side affair with all 92 teams in the League, but in the end there were only 16 teams involved and the games were 11-a-side with 20 minutes each half.

The tournament was played over a weekend in April so we had a weekend off from the play-off push and Don told us we were treating it as a piss-up. It wasn't to be taken seriously. Go down, enjoy a couple of days of team bonding before the last four games of the season.

We drew 0-0 with Aston Villa in the opener and lost on penalties. It wasn't a disaster. Steve Archibald took us to Annabel's, a private members club in the posh part of London, where we had VIP access. This was worlds away from the lifestyle we were used to. I paid Steve back by taking him to Sooty's in the Mill Hill area of Blackburn on a Tuesday night. I told him it was just as good. I'm not sure how impressed he was.

Despite the stars around the club, the wheels started to come off in March and we were skidding down the hill by Easter. We'd now slipped out of contention for automatic promotion and we were clinging to the hope of the play-offs. Throughout it all we retained our composure and while results were poor the tension rarely showed. It was never more so than when we had to visit Millwall in the final game of the season and, to be sure of the play-offs, we needed to win. It was a tricky game to call in advance because they had already been promoted and so it could either turn out to be their season's swansong or, with any luck, they would ease off the gas. Either way, it would still be a difficult night because the Den was a frightening place to play due to some incredibly aggressive fans.

The old Den was a nightmare. You used to come out from behind the goal where the Millwall fans were and the home end was all caged in in those days. And for good reason. This wasn't young kids, this was grown men and they would be swearing at you, abusing you, threatening you and spitting at you. It was just a horrible place. If you weren't able to shut it out of your mind then it could get to you. Luckily for me I was strong enough to ignore it and not let it affect me. If anything it spurred me on.

I used to love getting stick from the opposition fans, especially Burnley of course because they really hated me. But on any away ground I used to love it. Let's face it, if you're rubbish they won't bother you.

Derby used to be a good one. At their old stadium, the Baseball Ground, the fans would be right on top of you. It was a bit like QPR's ground is now, you could hear everything they were saying to you. If you went to the touchline you would only be a couple of yards at the most away from them and I used to love it. I would turn round and say something back to them and it would make me more determined. Whenever I got the opportunity I would go and celebrate in front of them as well, with my trademark arms up in the air. You could get away with a lot more in those days. You could give them the middle finger and everything and just get on with it. If you did that nowadays you'd get banned. To be honest I can't see the problem with it. Players have to be so well behaved these days. If two or three thousand fans are giving you stick for the whole game, telling you to eff off and calling you every name under the sun, what is wrong with giving them a bit back if you then score a goal? It's the least they deserve.

It was always fun scoring goals away from home. At Burnley's Turf Moor the away fans used to stand along the Longsight End back then which was split in half with home fans at one end and away fans at the other. It felt like I always scored in front of the Burnley fans and so running back to the halfway line I would start with the fingers up to the Burnley fans and then the hands up to the Blackburn fans who would be going mad down the other end. Sadly I only got to play against Burnley four times in a Blackburn shirt as they were relegated to the Third Division, bless them. Although our friendship was rekindled when I went there with West Brom.

On that final day at the Den we stuffed them 4-1. I scored twice. There was a pitch invasion as soon as the game finished and things got a little bit hairy. When the final whistle went we were attacking in the furthest place on the pitch from the tunnel and I simply legged it off the park. That must be the fastest I ever ran off – or on – a football field. Nicky Reid was the last to appear in the dressing room – he'd been carried off by two policemen after being swallowed up by this mass of Londoners – and the only item of clothing he had left on was his jockstrap. Thank God they'd already been promoted. The invasion was as near to a friendly atmosphere as you're likely to get at Millwall.

We were now in a four-way tussle but we crumbled at the first hurdle. Chelsea, who had finished bottom of Division One and were obliged to take part, took us to pieces and showed that while we had a decent enough team to compete in Division Two, we didn't have the class to get beyond the worst side in the top flight. I've never considered the play-offs a just means of deciding promotion, but that didn't mean I wasn't going to give my all to help us through them. But it counted for nothing. They beat us 2-0 at Ewood and 4-1 at Stamford Bridge. In reality they gave us a good pasting and killed what was a promising and, for a while, a rather glamorous season.

Being my testimonial season, it's a shame we couldn't cap it off with promotion. You get to wonder if it was some kind of subconscious complacency – we knew we were good enough to be promoted but we also knew there was the safety net of the play-offs. It was a feeling we were going to get used to.

I enjoyed the testimonial which was offered in recognition of ten years' service at the club. It was enormously important to me financially because while I was earning what would be considered a good salary, it would be nothing compared to the riches available these days. From my perspective, I saw it as a kind of compensation for the fact I was never transferred and so never made anything from signing-on fees.

My testimonial committee was a great bunch and included Richard Matthewman, who would spend a few years as the club's vice-chairman. Alan Cotton, who I knew from the 100 Club and had run a testimonial season before was my committee chairman. It was good to have him on board. Paul Schofield, a solicitor and another of the 100 Club crowd, was secretary, and Andy McKie, who became a business associate with me with the Rococo shop, partly funded by the proceeds of the year, was also in the team.

While the main event was the testimonial game, there were other occasions like a golf day and dinner dances where a few quid could be made, and then there were pool and darts nights in the pubs, which I really enjoyed – free beer and fags, and I got paid at the end of it.

My game was against Newcastle, who had approached the club about a pre-season friendly, and the attendance was excellent – around 7,000, which was about the size of crowds we were pulling for league games then. When it's your testimonial you have to give the opposition team a present for turning up. I had a friend in Blackburn who supplied hotels with dressing gowns and so I asked him to do me a load of them with the players' initials embroidered. Newcastle's manager at the time was Willie McFaul – and they got the bloody initials wrong! That's about the only thing I remember about that game.

Over the season I made £32,000, which doesn't seem a lot now but to me it was good money. More to the point, it had been a lot of fun.

We lost a lot of players that summer. The loan spells for Ossie and Steve had run their course. Ossie signed for Queen's Park Rangers while Steve went back to Scotland with Hibernian. Chris Price went to Villa, Simon Barker joined Ossie at QPR where he became a successful First Division player. And it wasn't as if these guys were bit part players, they were all first team regulars and major contributors to the cause. I can imagine the fans thinking we were going back to the bad old days when we sold to survive.

That summer's influx hardly inspired. Tony Finnigan was brought from relative obscurity at Crystal Palace. He never really settled at Blackburn, mainly because he was a London boy, a Flash Harry and always a wheeler dealer. He was a good laugh who showed good promise on the pitch but faded quickly.

Ronnie Hildersley was a big boost in the dressing room, even though he was the smallest player in the league at the time. If we lost a game 4-0, Ronnie could have us giggling and relaxed enough for the next game. And he was a good player, too. He never ducked a challenge, played a good passing game and scored a few goals.

Mark Atkins also came in as a replacement for Chris Price and he became one of the most under-rated performers I've ever played with. He was an intelligent, industrious player who understood his strengths. The fans were too quick to see his shortcomings but when Blackburn won the title in 1995 he was a key man in the campaign.

And then there was Andy Kennedy – a legend in his own trousers. No one knew how to take to him. He walked into the dressing room expecting us to ooh and aah and offer to clean his boots. It's just as well he knew how ridiculous he seemed to other people. He liked to have a good time and it was infectious. The sad thing about Andy is that he never got close to fulfilling his potential. He could have been a massive star but never had the discipline to make the most of his talents. He was very quick, though never looked it, and could hit a ball with incredible power and accuracy. But because he would never put the extra mile in, he was utterly inconsistent. Women loved him and he was consistent enough about that area of his life. He dated Maria Whittaker when she was the hot Page Three model of the time, but he was a lad who was never going to settle down and he lived up to the reputation of being a professional footballer.

And he cost me a fiver. Don was another coach who loved to get us running and in training he would pair us up and send us on 400m races – 200m out then 200m back. On one occasion he paired up Andy with Colin Hendry. Colin was a real fit lad and Andy was a lazy bugger in training. Don turned to me.

"I bet you a fiver that Andy beats Colin in this race."

"You're on!"

So off they went and as they got to the 200m mark, Colin was at least 20 metres ahead and I was rubbing my hands thinking my bet was coming in, but as they turned back, Andy just put his foot out and took Colin out. He strode past him and won the race. Don had worked with him at Rangers so he knew all about him.

I'd never seen Andy run like that and I slaughtered him.

"Why don't you do that in a game? Do a bit of my running for me!"

Rooming with Andy was always fun. Very different to Nicky Reid the fitness fanatic. We would be up late at night ordering room service. We used to like a drink on a Friday night if we could get away with it. The rules were no drinking for 48 hours before a game, but I got round that by drinking at home before a home game or taking a few cans on an away game.

It might sound bad but it was necessary if I was going to get any sleep before a game. We would always have a meal together and then be expected to go to our rooms and get a good night's rest, but I could never get to sleep unless I was able to have a couple of drinks. I would be better prepared for the game that way, as daft as it might sound to today's sports psychologists and nutritionists.

There used to be a lot of pranks during those overnight stays but not usually throughout the season. If we were away in pre-season we'd go in and wreck other people's rooms. You'd turn the bed upside down, do whatever needed to be done. We'd be fast asleep in our room pretending it wasn't us.

Despite losing some of our best players, we nonetheless had a strong season as the team began to gel. And on day one we made a big statement. Having knocked us out of the play-offs at the end of the last season, Chelsea had ended up losing to Middlesbrough in the final and being relegated. Our first game of the season just so happened to be at Stamford Bridge, where just a couple of months earlier they had hammered us 4-1. This time we beat them 2-1 to set up a six-game unbeaten start to the season.

Near the end of that season I had the biggest day of my career, which also turned out to be one of the worst in the history of the game. April 15, 1989 is rightly remembered for one thing – the Hillsborough disaster. We knew on the pitch something had happened but we had no concept of how awful it was. My mind had been concentrated on the fact I was close to breaking the all-time scoring record at Blackburn, held by Tommy Briggs. I hadn't scored for ages but I knew I only needed two goals to break the record. The match was against Manchester City, who were top of the table, and we beat them 4-0. I scored a lucky goal in the first half. Howard Gayle had a shot from outside the box which came back off the post for a tap-in. The second was a belter. I cracked it left footed at the Blackburn End into the far corner past Paul Cooper. That was the record-breaker. The hat-trick goal wasn't bad either – I turned into the area and scored off the post. I don't think the record will ever be broken, not the way players move on so much these days, and it's something I am immensely proud of. I'm not ashamed to say I was quietly pleased when Alan Shearer left for Newcastle – he was catching up quick!

So there I was, the greatest scorer in the history of the club. So I never got a big money move to Manchester United or Liverpool, but I did something good at Blackburn Rovers that people will always remember. That's important to me. Even at the time I knew I was trying to give something to the fans to remember me by – not just the drinking and the fags – but the goals.

I think it was Gary Newbon from ITV who collared me at the side of the pitch for an interview.

"How did it feel to break the record?"

It should have felt incredible. I was the record-breaker I'd always dreamed I'd be.

"I'm knackered!"

That's all I could say because it's exactly how I felt.

We finished a creditable fifth in the league and squared up to Watford in the first leg of the play-off semi-final. It was a scrappy game which finished 0-0 and I had a running battle with their centre-half Paul Miller. I never considered myself a dirty player and I never got into too much trouble on the pitch, but enough was enough and he'd been mouthing off through the whole game. They got a goal-kick and as we jogged back to the middle of the pitch together I took a look at the referee and the linesmen, saw they were looking the other way, and whacked him. I caught him right across the face and he went down like a sack of spuds. Then I jogged away looking the picture of innocence.

In the second leg at Watford I scored with my first touch of the game and we drew 1-1 to go through thanks to the away goals rule. As the game wore on they were getting more and more frustrated. I was chasing a long ball over the top with Miller as my marker and he got his revenge for the Ewood spat when he turned round and smacked me one. But I had the last laugh. He was spotted and sent off.

We had been in the play-offs before and we felt good about the home and away final against Crystal Palace. We hadn't lost to them in either of the regular league games that season and fancied our chances. The first leg at Ewood was a strange game. Howard Gayle scored two and then missed a penalty. They came back with one and I scored a late goal.

A 3-1 lead should have been enough for a team as well organised and disciplined as ours. I was rooming with Scott Sellars on the night before the away game and I don't think either of us slept a wink. We just kept spinning it round our heads and talking about how this was the best chance we'd ever get.

The Selhurst Park leg was a disaster. With the exception of the Full Members Cup final, it was the only time in my career that I felt genuinely nervous before a game. Every Blackburn fan knows, and I'm pretty sure most Palace fans would admit, that referee George bloody Courtney had a nightmare. There was definitely a foul by Colin Hendry but it was definitely outside the box. And the penalty definitely cost us a place in the top flight. When we were 2-0 down I hit this shot from twenty yards, the sweetest volley of my life, and I could see it flying into the top corner and I could see me running out at Old Trafford and then I could see the keeper make the most incredible save. And I think I knew then that it wasn't our day. We conceded a third in extra time, most of which we played with thousands of Palace fans encroaching on to the pitch. Courtney should have stopped the game and insisted they move back.

When the whistle went and I had finally fought my way to the tunnel I just sat down and started crying. I really thought we were there this time, that we'd finally laid to rest the hoodoo. Ian Wright, who partnered Mark Bright in an awesome Palace forward line, put an arm round me.

"Hard luck."

He meant it and it meant a lot to me. He was a class act who deserved what he got out of the game. Wright was a brilliant player who put so much work into his game. I know he's remembered for his goals, particularly when he was at Arsenal, but his off-the-ball work was excellent as well. I'd love to have played with him because he was so generous. Years later, when I was at Wycombe, we watched an Ian Wright video on the way to the play-off final for inspiration. I'd have paid to watch him, though obviously not when he moved to Burnley.

Howard Gayle
Teammate at Blackburn Rovers from 1987 to 1992

I played with some top players and I would say, as a specialist striker, Simon Garner was the best. I came through the ranks at Liverpool with the likes of Ian Rush and I had a good working relationship with Rushy, but when you look at Garns's record, it really speaks for itself. He wasn't at a top club but he consistently scored goals.

Football is like a bubble and if you're in the game and someone is doing well, you hear about it. So I knew all about Garns before I signed for Blackburn from Stoke. Anything in that box that bounced around him, it was in. That's how good he was.

There was a saying at the club that nobody was allowed to score a hat-trick other than Simon Garner. They were right. In the 1989 play-off against Crystal Palace I scored two and then got a penalty but missed it.

He was a phenomenal player and I cannot believe he didn't get a chance to play at a higher level. I think at one stage Liverpool were looking at him and Scott Sellars, but obviously that never materialised. He would have fitted into Liverpool's way of playing because he was good at holding the ball up. His movement was very good. I don't feel he got the recognition he deserved.

If he'd had an opportunity at the top level, who knows, he could have been in with a chance of making the national team. Sometimes strikers have to ad lib in the box, but he didn't. He always knew what he wanted to do.

It was a pleasure to play with him. And he is perhaps done an injustice when people talk about his work in the box and his goalscoring because his link-up play outside the box and his switch play was very good as well.

During my time at Blackburn we did well. Of the five seasons I spent at the club, we got to the play-offs in four and we were unlucky not to get promoted. That success was largely down to the relationship we had as a group. The camaraderie that we had really helped us on the pitch. And Garns was a big part of that. We were playing for each other and for the manager, Don Mackay, who had a habit of getting a tune out of players who had failed at other clubs, me included.

Garns wasn't a lad who was out every night with the lads. He was married and he lived locally so he had his life and his friends outside football. He would come out and have a couple of drinks with the team but I wouldn't say he was out three or four times a week like some lads can be. The Woodlands on Preston Old Road was our regular haunt and we would stop off when we were coming back in from an away game and Garns would be part of that crowd.

But he was very humble and down to earth. He didn't go round town telling everyone he was Simon Garner, top scorer for Rovers, and giving it the big 'I am'. Someone in his position could have done that, but he didn't.

He was respected so much within the team. He was our talisman and everyone knew how important he was. Garns is a legend who deserves the utmost recognition from Blackburn Rovers.

Dad, Mum and Nanny Garner.

Posing for pictures in the Ewood Park boardroom with my brother, David, and my two oldest sons, John and James.

With Jim Smith's first team squad in 1977.

The youth team heads off for a tour of Holland in 1978.

A classic pose throughout the 1980s at Ewood.

You don't scare me! Vinnie Jones was a tough opponent for Leeds.

One of the five I scored against Derby County.

Speaking to John Motson for the BBC.

Another one goes in for Blackburn.

Winning the Full Members Cup at Wembley in 1987 was one of the proudest
moments of my career. What a day. And what a party afterwards.

Celebrating at Wembley with WBA teammates Kevin Donovan and Ian Hamilton in the 1993 Division Two play-off final.

Scoring for Wycombe against Carlise in the Division Three play-off semi final in 1994.

I had a great time at Wealdstone where we enjoyed two promotions and a league title.

A spot of commentary with another former Rovers striker Kevin Gallacher, and Andy Bayes from BBC Radio Lancashire.

Take a ride with me in the Simon Garner bus.

With David Dunn and referee Eddie Wolstenholme before kick off and with my son Thomas at Ewood Park in 2003 for my Testimonial match.

Spotting a familiar face on the revamped Ewood Park.

With my old mate Howard Gayle at an event at Ewood.

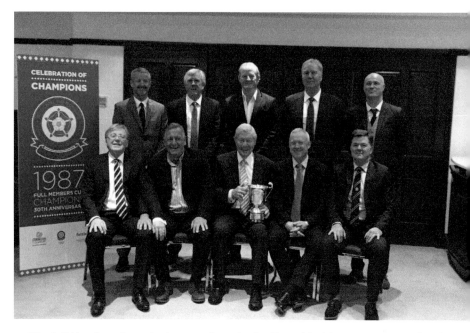

The Full Members Cup-winning squad reunited at Ewood Park in 2017, 30 years after that brilliant day at Wembley.

Enjoying a drink with Simon Barker at the Full Members Cup winners reunion.

Inducted into the Blackburn Hall of Fame with Alan Shearer.

With Mike Newell at a Tony Parkes fundraiser in Clitheroe, 2023.

Top left, with son James, daughter-in-law Charlotte and granddaughter Harriet. Top right, with Jane. Bottom left, my youngest children Thomas and Martha. Bottom right, Jane's children Will, Ollie and Rosie.

CHAPTER 9

Play-off pain

1989 to 1991

It was back to the drawing board again. Don worked hard in the transfer market and picked up Frank Stapleton from Le Havre and Kevin Moran from Sporting Gijon. These guys were legends. They were both coming towards the ends of their careers but there's no doubting the boost it gave us after the disappointment of the play-offs – and the fact Colin Hendry left for Manchester City.

Frank had a big reputation. He'd done everything at Manchester United and Arsenal and was a class act. But there were no pretensions at all. He always had time to talk and his advice was devoured, and he was brilliant to play with because he was a team player who always gave his all. He was dedicated, looked after his body, didn't do anything wrong. He wasn't a drinker. He concentrated, trained hard every day, put everything into his game. You could tell why he'd had such a good career. He was dedicated to improving himself, even when he came to Blackburn. He was another player I looked at and thought he would go off into coaching or management when he finished playing. He was a bit like Tony Parkes in a way, but a bigger name.

Kevin on the other hand was an absolute warrior. He had cuts, bruises and scars all over the place and never shirked a challenge. He and Frank would travel to games together and Frank nearly always drove because Kevin's reputation for liking a beer after the game was well-earned. Like Frank, Kevin also put everything into training and into matches, but he liked a drink. And bloody hell he could drink. He had been at Manchester United and I assumed things would have been a bit stricter at a club like that, but no, he came from a proper drinking school with the likes of Norman Whiteside and Bryan Robson. Work hard, play hard. That certainly suited me. He was a brilliant man who always had a smile on his face. He had the most scarred face I think I've ever seen in football but he was always smiling. He would play a game, kick someone up in the air, and then smile at them afterwards. When he got up in the morning he had a smile on his face and when he went to bed at night he'd have a smile on his face. He was the happiest man I met in football.

Losing Colin was a blow, certainly from a playing perspective. It seemed to us that his dad, who'd been a driving instructor I think, had effectively become his agent and saw better things ahead. Not everyone in the dressing room was upset, though, far from it in fact. He was a good player and clearly ambitious but there was a feeling he was getting too big for his boots and that Blackburn was somehow not good enough for him. When he left a second time for Glasgow Rangers in 1998 I couldn't help feeling a sense of déjà vu. The days of loyalty are over. No further comment required.

On the positive side we had Keith Hill and David May coming through the ranks in defensive positions. They were both very promising and it's a compliment to the club's youth system that they were strong enough to be considered ready to break into the first team. It's always been an impressive setup, especially when you think about the competition within 30 or 40 miles of Blackburn. The Merseyside and Manchester clubs are all looking for the best young talent, too.

My judgement has never been the best but I think most people expected Keith to emerge as the better player. After Blackburn they both had good careers but for Keith it was with the likes of Plymouth and Rochdale while David played a part in winning the Champions League for Manchester United.

Frankly it wasn't a vintage season. We had good young players like Lenny Johnrose, Craig Skinner and Darren Collier to call on, but they didn't seem to offer us much depth. And here's another example of my famous talent-spotting abilities. Later, when I was at West Brom, we played Plymouth and Peter Shilton was player-manager. We went up for a ball together and he smacked two of my teeth out. He rang me up the next day and I thought it was to apologise. It wasn't. But I had the last laugh, even if it was by accident.

"I've been looking at a couple of your former teammates and I wonder if you could give me your thoughts on Jason Wilcox and Craig Skinner."

"Well if it was me, I'd go for Craig."

I genuinely felt he was the better prospect. He seemed to have a better all-round game and awareness. And so Shilts bought him. Craig moved sideways in the lower leagues while Jason played for England and lifted the title with Blackburn before playing for Leeds. And people still ask me why I didn't go into coaching or management.

This was around the time Don took us on a few pre-season trips to Sweden, which was a bit more exotic than our jaunts to the Isle of Man in previous years. We got a ferry the first time and it took about 24 hours to get there. When Don told us about the first trip we all thought we'd have a nice relaxing flight over to Scandinavia but no, it was a boat from Hull.

A coach took us from Blackburn to the ferry and then we were stuck right on the bottom of the boat, not up in the luxury suites. Once again, players today, they don't know they're born. When we got to Sweden we didn't stay in a hotel, we stayed in a block of flats and were pretty much left to our own devices. We got pissed. We would play a few games against some local part-time teams and tended to win most of them comfortably. But the trips were more about team bonding than results.

Being Sweden, it was expensive to go out drinking, so we used to go to the off licence and buy a load of cans. We had a great time. It was more like a holiday than a pre-season trip.

On the last trip in 1989 we had to play six games in 14 days. This time we went posh and stayed in a grand hotel. Not a hostel in the middle of nowhere. We took full advantage of the facilities and those of the rest of the town by being out every night until two, three, four o'clock in the morning – even if we had a game the next day. It was a good trip because there was a really good bunch around, people like Andy Kennedy, Ally Dawson and Scott Sellars, who could all hold their own in the drinking stakes. Don seemed to have no idea what we were up to until the day before the final fixture. The weather was terrific and we were taking a breather during training in the sunshine. Don sat us all down for what we thought was going to be a routine tactics talk.

"I've just found out what you lot have been up to and it's a disgrace. You're here representing Blackburn Rovers, we've a new season around the corner and you lot are pissing training up a wall."

It was about as strong as he ever got and he couldn't even bring himself to raise his voice. It was like being at school with a soppy teacher who never checked your homework. Then he rounded on Scott. He droned on and on about Scott being a pivotal member of the side, someone who could turn games for us, someone who he would be relying on in the coming season.

"You've got one chance to prove yourself, Scott, and that's tomorrow. Back to work."

The others got up to go and I was just catching up when he pushed me over and jumped on me – literally. I was on the floor with the manager sitting on me. He spoke quietly.

"Simon, I'm excluding you from that discussion."

"What do you mean?"

"Look, you've scored eight goals already on this tour and you can do it – you can go out, drink what you want and play a good game, but them…"

I was flattered.

Scott and I were sharing a room on the trip and that night – an early night – we joked about what Don had said but clearly Scott felt he had a point to prove. After about 20 minutes of the game, Scott nearly ripped the spleen out of his marker. It was an awful challenge and totally out of character. We watched him troop down the tunnel after the red card was flashed. I giggled. He really did prove his point.

When the 1989/90 season came around, we never really got into our stride. We drew far too many games and every time we looked like getting a run together we would lose. Despite taking just two points from the last three games, we managed to hang on and make the play-offs. For the third season in succession.

Ossie Ardiles was by now the manager at Swindon, who we played in the semi-final. We lost the first leg 2-1 at home and Don dropped me for the away match to play Frank up front on his own. I didn't understand that idea at all, we needed to score goals. It was the only time I got really upset with Don during his time at the club. I saw Ossie before the game for a natter. He reached into the fridge and grabbed a can of beer.

"Drink Simon?"

"I can't, Ossie, I'm on the bench."

"Go on, share a can with me."

"Yeah, go on."

It was only half a can, but maybe I should have had a crate. We lost 2-1 again and I barely had a touch for the time I was on. Swindon eventually got promoted but didn't kick a ball in the top flight because they were stung for financial irregularities before Ossie's time. There was an argument, mainly coming from the supporters, that we should be allowed a second chance because Swindon, by the due process of fan logic, should not have taken part in the play-offs. Despite the fact we'd missed out three times in the play-offs, it wasn't a view I held. We didn't go up because we weren't good enough. End of story. And while it was devastating to have come so close again I can barely imagine how the Swindon players felt after thinking they'd made it.

It was around this time that the media started talking about us being the 'nearly men' of football. It was fair comment, of course, having come so close on so many occasions in the past decade. We were also getting a name for being every fan's second favourite club – Burnley excepted. It was because of the club's history I suppose, and the romance attached to having won the FA Cup six times. They might have been well-meant words and intentions but the players hated it. We didn't want to be nearly men and we didn't care about being liked by other fans. We wanted to win. We wanted to prove that we could do it. But we didn't realise how soon that was going to happen and how much things were about to change.

Mark Atkins
Teammate at Blackburn from 1988 to 1992

I almost never got to play with Simon as I was supposed to go to Barnsley, not Blackburn. My first manager at Scunthorpe United was Allan Clarke, who signed me as a 14-year-old. Four years later as my contract was running out he was the manager at Barnsley and wanted me to go there. So one Wednesday in the summer I went to have a chat with him and was told I would have a four-year contract and spend the first year in the reserves to get used to playing at a higher level. I was told to go back the following Monday to sign the deal and sort everything out.

That night, Tony Parkes rang and asked if I would go to Blackburn for a chat the following day. So I drove over to Blackburn and spoke with Don and Parkesy, they showed us round the club and we had scampi and chips in the John Lewis Suite – you can't beat that! They said I was going straight into the first team and I signed there and then.

I didn't know anything about the club or the players before I signed. The first time I met Simon was on the first day of pre-season. We went for a run up Livesey Branch Road. No doubt Garns was somewhere at the back. It's a well-known thing in football that you don't want to be beaten in a race by a goalkeeper but Garns couldn't care less. He was quite happy plodding along at the back.

He was a really great guy. He didn't earn the money he should have done if he had played a few years later. He really enjoyed his football and took it very seriously. The technical side of his game was spot on. Crossing and shooting drills in training were fine. He just hated all the physical aspects.

As a young lad just starting out in my career and having made quite a big move up two divisions to Blackburn, Garns was great. He kept himself to himself away from the club but in the changing room he was always around to support and always had something to say.

I shared a car with him to training for a couple of years as we had to get from the changing rooms at Ewood up to the training pitches at Pleasington. I think Scott Sellars was in there as well. It was great being given a lift and Garns wanted to drive up there himself most days so he could wind the window down and light a fag.

On the pitch, you just knew if he was one-on-one with the keeper, nine times out of ten it would be in the back of the net. Some of the goals he scored were unbelievable. Strikes from the edge of the box. Left foot. Right foot. He just came to life when the ball was there. That's what he lived for and he was superb at it. In normal play he didn't really get involved. But when he got the ball anywhere around the box his eyes lit up.

We used to say if you're on the halfway line don't pass it to Garns because it would come straight back to you. He couldn't care less about the ball when it was there but as soon as he got into the final third he loved every bit of it.

It was great to be part of his team because if you have that player who can score goals so instinctively you know you've got a chance in every game. There are probably four players I played with who you can say were like that. Steve Bull at Wolves, who was very similar to Garns in a lot of ways, Alan Shearer, obviously, and Chris Sutton in that one season I played with him after he signed. I'd put Garns right up there with those guys.

He was probably the best striker of the ball I played with. I mean, Shearer could hit a ball but Garns would very rarely mishit it. He knew where he wanted it and where it was going.

His pace would probably have let him down at the highest level and he might have found it difficult because of the fags and the booze. But that's what players did in those days. People say, 'what if he didn't smoke' and 'what if he didn't drink', but he did and so did lots of others.

In the old changing rooms was one of those big baths which would be full after a game ready for the players to get in. I used to sit near the door to the shower and the bath area and the number of times I was still in my kit and Garns was out of the bath, dressed and propping the bar up in the 100 Club with a pint was unreal. He wasn't the quickest on the pitch but he was bloody quick getting out for a beer at the end. If there were matches where the manager wanted to talk to the players at the end of a game or there was a bit of discussion, you could see him edging closer to the door, itching to get to the bar.

We all liked to go out and have a drink. Garns often did his own thing. He had his own place where he lived in Blackburn and his own pubs but we did go out as a group and one thing you did learn was don't leave your pint unattended unless you wanted his false teeth in it.

The second time we went to Sweden, Don said he was taking us somewhere different. The previous year we'd been out every night and things had gone a bit mad. Now we were promised the quietest place in Sweden with nothing much to do. We were gutted. We drove four hours from the airport and we got to this place and it turned out there was a festival on. There were about 15,000 people there.

Everywhere had come to life, there were bars everywhere, and we ended up having a few good nights out. We would travel to games and the lads would be asleep on the bus laid across the seats because we had been out until two or three in the morning and it was now 9am and we were on our way to a game. Don said one morning: "The lads are taking it seriously, they're getting their rest." We had been out all night.

We were there for two weeks and Benfica were there at the same time playing in a tournament. They had played on the Friday night and we were playing on the Saturday. We didn't want to miss out on a Friday night session so we waited for the gaffer to go to bed and then went out. We were in this nightclub a few hours later and these lads from Benfica walked in. Benfica at the time had an unbelievable team with players like Ricardo Gomes and Paolo Sousa and they were managed by Sven Goran Eriksson. One of them walked up to Garns, who was stood there half cut holding on to his pint with a fag, and said: "You have a game today?" And Garns gave him a big thumbs up and said: "No mate. Tomorrow!" This guy couldn't believe it. He just walked off.

CHAPTER 10

A sign of things to come

1990 to 1991

Don's last full season was a let-down in playing terms for all involved, not least for me as it was the first time in my career that I picked up a serious injury – a double hernia caused, more than likely, by general wear and tear. Don tried to bolster the squad and Lee Richardson was a good signing. He came to us from Watford in a swap deal for Andy Kennedy. He was a classy player and a cheeky bugger. He'd call me 'Dad' on away trips, especially when we were pissed, which was probably a little too often. The way the deal worked meant he was valued at £60,000, which was an absolute bargain. He had a lot of skill but did more in games than the fans gave him credit for and even if the magic wasn't there, he'd still put the effort in.

Mick Duxbury came in, too. He was another Manchester United veteran but not from the same mould as Kevin Moran. Mick was a quiet bloke who'd get back to his allotment to tend to his vegetable patch as soon as training was finished.

For most of the season I was a spectator. The club specialist told me my hernia problem was probably not worth operating on because I was coming to the end of my career. Scott Sellars had a similar problem at the same time and he was told he didn't need an operation at all. We both decided to get second opinions – I felt, at thirty, that I had a lot more football left in me and retirement was the last thing I wanted to contemplate, while Scott thought he had a serious problem that needed sorting out.

We took the right decisions in insisting on second opinions, but the pain was only just worth it. We went to a private clinic in Yorkshire and were given hernia tests where the doctor pushed a finger right into the groin. The agony was indescribable and when he told me he was going to test the other side as well I was ready to jump off the couch and run home. Not that I'd have got very far. Sadly the fact I could only hobble wrecked this plan. We'd taken the initiative ourselves for the second opinion but reported back to Bill Fox, the chairman, telling him we needed operations. There was some dispute over our results and Jack Cunningham, the club physio, was backing the club specialist's opinion. But Bill over-ruled and stumped up the cash.

We went together, Scott and I, to a private hospital in Manchester and had a week of being pampered. But it was hard work, especially when you needed to laugh. I had 22 staples on each side of my groin which, as you can imagine, was not comfortable. We were watching LA Law from our beds one night and it was painfully funny, in the most literal sense. We eventually had to turn it off. On the sixth day they wanted to know if we'd managed, as they put it, to open our bowels. No problem for Scott, but I'd been somewhat reluctant.

"So you haven't been at all then Simon?"

"Erm, no. Sorry."

"Well, we'll have to give you a suppository then."

That was not a pleasant experience and nor was our rehabilitation, which was ridiculously drawn out. At the time, players at other clubs who were being seen by sports specialists were getting back into action within a few weeks, but we were more or less planning our own programmes. And that involved lots and lots of cycling. The only benefit of this solitary struggle for fitness was that it took me past, or rather into, some of East Lancashire's more out-of-the-way hostelries.

By the time I returned we were down at the bottom of the table and struggling.

I had only played a handful of games when we came up against Liverpool at Ewood in the FA Cup. We'd only won one game out of the last nine. Liverpool, managed by my boyhood hero Kenny Dalglish and with the likes of Rush and Barnes in their side, were reigning champions. But anything can happen in the FA Cup, can't it?

It was blowing a gale at a packed Ewood, more than 18,000 came out to see the First Division side's visit to town. At our last home game, a 3-1 loss to Oxford, we'd had a few hundred more than 6,000. But we were able to hold our own and took Liverpool by surprise creating quite a few chances in the first half.

And then right at the start of the second half, David May got a throw-in not too far from the corner flag. He had a brilliant throw on him and he didn't disappoint. I was in the middle of the box about ten yards from goal, totally unmarked, and was able to smash the ball past Bruce Grobbelaar with my right foot. It was a sweet strike if I do say so myself. And the roar from that sold-out Blackburn End was magical.

Liverpool hit us with a sucker punch right in the last minute. A teasing cross from Ray Houghton was accidentally poked home by Mark Atkins and the game ended in a draw. I was gutted. So close to being the hero who put Liverpool out and gave little old Blackburn a major scalp. I let rip in the changing rooms after the game and gave Atko both barrels, but it wasn't his fault. If that wasn't bad enough, Jimmy Hill immortalised the incident on Match of the Day when he tried to blame the ball-girl for giving the ball to a Liverpool player too quickly.

We were well beaten in the replay three days later at Anfield, but this was the start of the cup run which eventually led to Kenny resigning as Liverpool manager after that dramatic fifth-round 4-4 draw at Everton.

In the league it was getting desperate. We had a terrible run of injuries and Don was scrabbling around the loan market for players to do a short-term job, but it wasn't working out. After three years in the play-offs and the Full Members Cup win at Wembley, we were looking ripe for relegation. And then up stepped Jack Walker, like a knight in blue and white armour, to take control of the club. He'd seen enough.

The story goes that he was in the car on his way back from some dismal game or other and decided it was time to do something with his money. Jack was from Blackburn and had made his fortune from the steel stockholding business he ran with his brother, Fred. When Walkersteel sold it raised more than £300million and was the biggest private sale in British industrial history. He invested in property, an airline and Blackburn Rovers.

The big money was some way off, but a flash of Jack's cheque book brought in Bobby Mimms from Spurs for £250,000, which was a club record. Bobby was an honest lad who tried his best and liked a pint but the problem for any goalkeeper was living in the shadow of some of the great keepers we'd had, and he was trying to replace Terry Gennoe, who had been magnificent.

Regardless of the injuries, it was difficult to see why we were doing so badly. We had a decent side on paper that had been much further up the table in previous seasons. I suppose our collective confidence must have slipped, but I always felt we would come good sooner or later. It helped that Jack's cash also brought us Steve Livingstone and Tony Dobson from Coventry for £750,000 – it was a sign as to how things were changing.

The money was there, it was obvious to everyone at the club. As a group of players we just got on with it. There's nothing else you can do. I used to think if the manager is going to replace me it's going to cost him a lot of money. I thought I got on well enough with Don and I thought I deserved my place in the team so I wasn't too worried about it. I felt confident enough in myself that I had proved what I could do.

But those outside wanted a little more reassurance. They didn't realise the scale of Jack's passion and Don's name wasn't strong enough to bring in the players he really wanted. Teddy Sheringham was on the shopping list and turned Don down, but Mike Newell was the classic example. Don tried his best to sign Mike with no luck. As soon as Kenny Dalglish was in charge, Mike was wearing blue and white.

But the players he did get did enough to help us limp to safety and we finished four points clear of the Second Division relegation zone. Hardly an achievement but a big sigh of relief for everyone. It felt like things were improving on the pitch. In the last couple of months we beat Oldham and West Ham, who would go on to finish first and second in the league.

Steve Livingstone did well, even if he did keep me out of the team for a while, and both Bobby and Tony played their part. Times were changing, of that there was no doubt, and the impact for the club and for me was about to become clear.

Fitness is a constant worry for footballers. Without it we cannot play and ultimately that can mean no job. That's not to say players go out on to the pitch and deliberately avoid physical contact. Far from it. Pulling out of a challenge can often do you more harm than going in full blooded because you put your body into unfamiliar and vulnerable positions when you're trying to keep out of danger. When you go for it in one of those big 50-50 challenges, you're ready for it. I'd been lucky with injuries and the double hernia was the first real problem I'd had. I was getting sharper all the time, but it took me until the summer to approach full fitness. Don clearly didn't agree with the progress I had made and was stalling on my new deal at Ewood. So was I. From my standpoint I was trying to secure improved terms – I felt I'd done my bit to deserve them and I could see the new resources that were coming into the club. Don used the excuse that I wasn't fit and wouldn't agree to a new contract until I'd proved otherwise. We were playing cat and mouse with each other. He clearly felt I might be surplus to requirements if he could land the players he wanted, while I was honest enough to realise that if he didn't get them immediately then he wouldn't be waiting long. It looked like being my last season with the club and with no idea what might be around the corner I was seeking financial security.

Let's be honest, players are much less inclined now to stay with a club for life. With the increase in money comes an increase in mobility and at all levels players are calling more of the shots than they did even in the mid-1990s when I left the professional game.

But loyalty wasn't the only reason I wanted to stay. James and John were happy at school, Mandy and I were getting on well, we had lots of friends in the town and at last it looked like the club was gearing itself up for a big push to promotion. I wanted to be part of that, especially now, thanks to Jack Walker, the days of counting the tea bags into the urn were history. Blackburn Rovers had been my employer for fifteen years and I had drunk some weak tea in my time. Now I fancied a sip of Earl Grey.

Things were changing rapidly. Steve Agnew came in for £700,000 from Barnsley to become the club's record signing and Stuart Munro came from Glasgow Rangers for £400,000. This was huge money for a club like ours.

Steve and Stuart were both great lads. Agnew was a solid player, a hard-working midfielder who took the game very seriously. He was another of those players who you could see becoming a coach or a manager. None of us had heard of Stuart Munro so no one knew what to expect. He wasn't the best player in the world and was very quiet in the dressing room. He didn't really get involved in the nights out or anything like that, he just did his stuff and went home.

In the end poor Steve and Stuart never got going. Both of them picked up ankle injuries early on and by the time they were fit again, Don was gone and so were their places in the side.

The big signing was David Speedie, who Don picked up from Liverpool, also for £400,000.

It was an exciting time to play at Blackburn, mainly in terms of the names being linked with the club. As the signings were announced, three things were in my head: these guys were being paid well, the club was readying itself for a proper tilt at promotion and, more than at any time during my career, my job was well and truly under threat.

With the new money being injected, I was adamant I deserved better terms and any improvement to my £600 a week would provide increased security for my family. Don was very honest, or he certainly appeared to be, and offered what he said he could. But it was merely an extension on the same terms as before. I took advice from my former teammate Frank Stapleton, who by this time was working for Paul Stretford, one of the major players in the football agency world, and decided to bide my time. As a stopgap I took the offer of a monthly contract. If another club had come in then at least I'd have a bargaining position to work from. It didn't happen and, in true Garner style, football came first. I dropped my demands and got on with the job with a contract on exactly the same terms as before. Except my job was changing.

Speedie was clearly the first-choice striker and it was no surprise that I spent much of the early part of the season on the bench. Steve Livingstone and even Lenny Johnrose, who had come through the youth ranks, were getting the nod over me. Howard Gayle was also still in the squad. The competition up front was strong, though I didn't realise how much tougher it would get as the season progressed. There always tends to be a rivalry between strikers. We all want to be playing every week and we all think we deserve to be on the team sheet. If you're scoring goals and doing all right you certainly don't want to be dropped. It's not like in today's game where the top teams in the Premier League tend to rotate their players regardless of whether they are scoring goals or not. But if I was banging them in it would really annoy me if I wasn't in for the next game. Thankfully it didn't happen too often, certainly not up to this point.

The spotlight was focussed squarely on Blackburn Rovers. The media was quick to pick up the scent of a club starting to throw cash around and we were one of the bookies' early favourites for the title. The fans, starved of success for so long and witnesses to so many false dawns, were more reticent and the expected big crowds never materialised. Not yet. Their hopes, like those of the players, had been smashed too often before and the cynicism was understandable. It was also well founded because we had a dismal start to the campaign. One point from three league games was bad enough, but to cap it all we were dumped out of the Rumbelows' League Cup by Hull City, who were in the division below us at the time. After the home defeat by Ipswich Town on the last day of August, a game I watched from the bench with fewer than 9,000 supporters for company, Don was given the order of the elbow. It had been coming.

I knew Don well. We'd spent a few years together at the club and had always got on even when I was out of favour, as I clearly was then. Before it was announced he called me into the boardroom and I assumed he was going to explain his thinking behind leaving me out of a losing team, but it was more serious than that.

"The board has asked me to resign, what do you think?"

I might never had had a full grasp of behind-the-scenes politics, but what he should do was obvious.

"I'm not trying to be funny Don, but what's the point in resigning? You've got time left on your contract so if you resign you'll walk away with nothing. If you hang on until they sack you they'll have to pay your contract up."

I reckon he still owes me a pint for that.

He had definitely been under pressure, and while the papers and the supporters were asking questions there was no suggestion he had lost the backing of the playing staff. There's a lot said, too much probably by people who should know better and, if they don't, should keep their thoughts to themselves, about players losing confidence in managers, but I've only seen it happen twice. The first was with Jim Iley at Blackburn and, at the end of my career, with Alan Smith at Wycombe after he replaced Martin O'Neill. Once you step over the white line you always give 100 per cent, you always want to win. It may not look like that sometimes, but the shirkers are few and far between. At a club like Blackburn where the supporters demanded graft, they were almost unheard of. The club motto is 'Arte et Labore' – through skill and hard work. It's a matter of professional and personal pride. But with these characters – Iley and Smith – it was different. You didn't want to lose but if you did it didn't hurt like it should and, at the back of your mind, you're thinking that you want a new manager. It wasn't like that with Don.

He was generally well liked by the players and that probably had something to do with the fact he was such a soft touch. Don couldn't bollock the players, it just wasn't his style to stand up and shout. Even if we were losing games he wouldn't tell us off but, at the same time, he wasn't that constructive either. Whether or not managers shout and scream, they will eventually work out that they need to talk and work on the training pitch when things are going wrong. We didn't get that with Don, he just didn't seem to have the nous to change our approach or tactics and I think that was part of his undoing. After three promotional near misses, we were nearly relegated, due in part to the fact the opposition knew what we were going to do next.

Don made his own problems at Blackburn, though, and not just with the players. From the start he interfered, trying to take control of the club from top to bottom. Even the most mundane things.

"How many tea bags in that pot?"

Seriously, he really did ask that of the tea lady. And he'd try to tell the groundsman his job, too, and whoever else was within earshot.

Don was the last of the great unknowns to manage Blackburn Rovers. And the Full Members Cup and play-off near-misses turned out to be the pinnacle of his managerial career. He went on to manage Fulham for a couple of years in the Third Division (which became the Second Division in 1992) but was sacked with the club on its way to relegation in 1994.

Perhaps he was already aware of the investment to come and was trying to confirm his own standing around the club. If he'd just concentrated on managing the team I think we may have had more success but he wanted his fingers in every pie. He lost focus towards the end because, while the tea tasted great and the pitch was perfect, we were playing crap.

Scott Sellars

Teammate at Blackburn from 1986 to 1992

Before I joined Blackburn I knew about Garns as a goal scorer and a player. I played against Blackburn quite a bit after making it in the first team at Leeds and they were a very experienced side. Simon, at about 27, was probably one of the youngest in the team. There were a lot of established and experienced players who had been there for a number of years. They were very difficult to play against, very well coached and organised. You never felt like you could get near the goal but you knew given half a chance, Simon Garner would score against you.

It can be intimidating going to a new club, especially when you are young. It's like the first day of school. You want to make a good impression. You never know how people are going to take to you and some might be wary that you're coming in and maybe taking a shirt from another player. But it wasn't like that at Blackburn. It was a great group to join. I was only 20 when I went and I grew up a lot. At Leeds we were a very young team. There were a lot of kids who had come through and so it was quite a difference when I got to Blackburn. But they really welcomed me and I felt really well looked after by all the lads, including Garns.

I could see straight away Simon was a character. He was really friendly and didn't take life too seriously. A really funny guy as well. He was never the hardest trainer. He was always at the back if there was any running going on. He never took anything too seriously. He took each day at a time and enjoyed life. He loved his football. Loved scoring goals and he certainly loved winning. He liked having a smoke and a drink, loved spending time with his family, loved being in Blackburn. I never felt he had a desire to go anywhere else. He was very content and settled and he was left to be who he was because it worked. So why change him? You were never going to get him to stop smoking or to get fitter. He enjoyed being the way he was and was still a really good player.

We used to train at Pleasington and I didn't drive back then. As we became good mates over time I used to get a lift from Ewood to training and back with Garns. The first thing he would do when we got in the car was put the lighter on and have a fag. After training he would always take a huge first drag - you could tell just how much he enjoyed that first cigarette.

I played with a lot of great players in my career but I would say there weren't many who were as two-footed as Simon. Peter Beardsley is probably the only other player who was as good with both feet. I never knew if Simon was right or left-footed. I could play it on either side of him and he would smash it. I was the total opposite, I could only use the one foot. Garns would score fantastic goals. We used to call him 'no back lift'. He could hit a ball and it looked as though his leg hadn't moved. It never went back but somehow he could generate so much power.

He wasn't very big but his movement was outstanding and he had a great first touch. He would always try to get that first touch away so he could score, or at least get a shot in. His first thought was always scoring. He didn't like the rest of it. He didn't like the running around, he didn't like the pressing, he didn't like trying to get the ball back, he didn't like making runs. But he did like getting the ball in and around the box and shooting - and he was very good at it.

I shared a room with him on many occasions, which wasn't great as he smoked and I was asthmatic. We would go to the hotel before an away game and I would hear the clink of his cans for the Friday night - he was always well prepared. This would have been frowned upon by the management but there was an element of 'well that's just Garns, that's what he does'. Everyone knew he liked a fag and a couple of cans. That was just him and his persona. It was part of who he was and it was accepted.

We both had hernias at the same time and we were in the same hospital. I remember going to see him in his room and he was in there with his head sticking out the window having a fag. We did our rehab together and I was trying to do everything right and Garns took his time and did things at his own pace, but in the end he got back playing before me because I ended up getting injured again.

If we were having a bad time, the manager would take us away for a night to somewhere like Lytham for a few drinks. We would have a good time but then on Saturday the lads would be saying: "Listen, we need to win today. If we don't, we'll never go away again."

It was always a good way of getting everyone together. We would go away, take the Mickey out of each other, cheat at a few card games and get drunk.

On my first trip with the team we went to the Isle of Man, which they had done every year for quite a while. I had just come from Leeds who had just come out of a successful period with those great teams of the 60s and 70s and so had everything, the facilities were superb. We had a gym, a sauna, a kitchen where we used to get fed. In pre-season we would go away on fancy trips. And then I came to Blackburn and off we went to the Isle of Man and it was just an absolute piss-up. I was shocked at first but it was just the way it was. It was acceptable and we were out every night. We trained really hard, played a game and then went out. Those days with Garns and that group, they were very hard-working players but they certainly liked a good time.

I saw Simon at a dinner we had at the club to celebrate the Full Members Cup win and he hadn't changed at all. He is still the same lad he was when I met him in 1986. He is still revered in Blackburn and at the club, and rightly so. He was there for a number of years and I am sure if he had wanted to, and he had pushed it, he could have got away and played in a higher league. But he was happy where he was. He is a fantastic lad and I really enjoyed his company.

CHAPTER 11

Uncle Jack's Rovers revolution

1991 to 1992

Tony Parkes was again employed to steady the ship in preparation for the new boss. This time it was trickier working under Tony because even he wasn't picking me. That might sound odd but because I had so much respect for him – and he was a pal – I didn't feel it was appropriate for me to go into his office and demand to play even though I was performing well in the reserves and in training. It was a tough enough assignment for him as it was and it didn't help that the fans were chanting my name while I was on the bench. That really put him in a quandary – if he was to bring me on was it simply for me to snatch a goal or was it to get the fans off the players' backs?

Tony changed the system as soon as he stepped up and our fortunes changed instantly. We won at Derby in his first game and David Speedie started finding the net on a regular basis. I kept a low profile and did what I could to help the team. My patience paid off because I came back in late September without anyone losing face.

I got my first goal of the season – and it felt like a hell of a wait – away at Millwall early in October. The abuse we received for winning 3-1 at the Den was horrendous but after a couple of dodgy results I'd have been happy taking three points from the lions at the Colosseum.

It was a good time to start finding the net because by the following Saturday Kenny Dalglish had arrived. Kenny's arrival was a huge surprise to us all. We had no inkling at all that he would be coming in. This was the days before the internet and social media of course, though there was some speculation in the press. Peter White of the Lancashire Evening Telegraph stuck his neck out on Kenny being tempted in and that should have given the game away – Peter tended to be cautious and avoided speculation – but the players didn't have a clue and we weren't told until a couple of days before we played Plymouth in the second week of October, and we didn't actually meet him until the day of the game.

Tony picked the team, I think that's the way Kenny wanted to do it and, besides, under Tony we had lifted ourselves from the bottom of the table to a more stable 15th position. I also guessed – wrongly as it turns out – that Kenny didn't really know much about the players.

He came into the dressing room with Ray Harford an hour before kick-off and introduced himself. We all shook hands – it was a brilliant moment, an unforgettable experience. Here he was, one of my heroes, the player I'd tried to model my game on and now we were going to be on the same side. I was like a schoolkid – totally gobsmacked. I'd played against him a few times in cup matches and just to be on the same pitch as him was a thrill. I used to watch him work the ball and think 'bloody hell, what a wonderful player'.

Those first few minutes of meeting Kenny and Ray had a lasting impact. Kenny can make an impression just by walking into a room because of who he is and what he has achieved. As for Ray Harford, to be honest I'd never heard of him. He knew me, though, and knew a lot about how I played. That level of homework was impressive. Ray's contribution gets overshadowed but he was massively important to Blackburn's success under Kenny and had a real pedigree – he'd been a top flight manager with Luton and Wimbledon for the previous five years.

I had felt a bit sorry for Don, but I don't think they made the change too early. It became clear at this point that Jack Walker had decided he wanted Kenny and that was that. There were certain players they wanted to bring in and Don was struggling to get them. They needed the big name to get the players in. It would be interesting to know what would have happened if we had started better that season and how long Don would have been given. But they were bringing in Dalglish one way or another because Jack had a plan. I got on well with Jack. He was brilliant for the club. He had a vision and it worked out well. And as soon as Kenny came in, players who were not interested suddenly turned round and said, 'I'm in'.

All the players were on a high. The money was there, that was apparent, now it looked like we had signed the manager who would be able to make the best use of it and give the club what it had been chasing for so long. I definitely raised my game. I wanted to be picked for the next one. I scored a goal in each half – a low one across the keeper into the far corner in the first and one into the top corner from the edge of the box in front of the Blackburn End in the second – and we won the game 5-2. Great, I thought. That should see me picked next week. But I wasn't, I was on the bench. And we lost away at Swindon. I learned a lesson – never assume anything with Kenny Dalglish.

I made a few calls within the game to discover more about Ray and all I kept hearing was about the quality of his coaching. Within a couple of days it was obvious the reputation was deserved – he was first class. He really knew what he was doing. Training was varied so no one was ever left on the sidelines twiddling their thumbs, and he kept the players interested – which isn't always that easy. What really gave him the edge over others I've worked with was his ability to explain what he was trying to achieve. With some managers and coaches you can stand around in the freezing rain for 20 minutes while a point is discussed and still be none the wiser. With Ray, he'd talk for two minutes and the concept became crystal clear, then he would move on to something else.

At the time we were doing most of our training on the public playing fields at Pleasington, which is on the road to Blackburn crematorium – hardly what Kenny and Ray were used to – and the pitches were terrible which, considering they'd been hammered by God knows how many pub teams over the weekend, was hardly surprising. They must have known what they'd be working with before they arrived and I guess they would have also known about the club's plans to develop new facilities in the Ribble Valley a few miles out of town, but I doubt if they realised the first job each day was to clear away the dog shit.

The early changes to the club were probably more noticeable on the training ground than they were during the games. The players definitely started to give an ounce more effort and the crowds suddenly started to flock down to watch us training. Previously it would be one man and his dog, a shitting dog at that. Now even the odd cortege would stop for a look on the way back from seeing off their dearly departed.

This sudden upsurge in interest had nothing to do with me or my teammates, or even what we were doing on a Saturday afternoon. Fans just wanted to watch Kenny Dalglish playing five-a-side. That in itself was a boost for the players. Kenny set standards during his career that all footballers should aspire to and training was given a new spirit – it became very competitive. Who wouldn't want to impress the new boss?

One of the weirdest ideas he had – at least it seemed weird at first – was to stop us wearing tracksuit bottoms. He even instructed that we had the pockets in our shorts sewn up. The thinking was that you can't play a match in your tracksuit bottoms and there ain't no pockets in match shorts. The more cynical members of the squad reckoned it was to just keep us moving, a fitness-by-necessity regime, because when the wind's up at Pleasington you may as well be north of the Arctic Circle. I've not trained in tracksuit bottoms since. Good habits die hard.

The new management team certainly suited me. I was pretty much a regular first-team choice until Christmas, though that had as much to do with Speedie's suspensions and injuries as anything else. I was back in the side after the Swindon game and scored my fourth goal of the season – a right-footed volley into the left-hand corner – in a 3-1 win against Grimsby. It was a good feeling knowing Kenny was watching on. I'd been itching to get off the bench while we were struggling to get goals and now, for a while at least, I was given the opportunity to do just that.

Save for that loss at Swindon in Kenny's first match in charge, we would only lose one game from then until just after Christmas. Within a few weeks we were closing in on the teams at the top after sorting out a lot of problems in training. Ray had got through to us the patterns of play and we started to get that little bit better in terms of organisation. The training procedure was that Tony would usually take the warm-up before Ray took the bulk of the session – he was definitely in charge – with Kenny standing on the sidelines. He'd only really join in for the five-a-side at the end. Ray was coach, he took training. Kenny was manager, he picked the team.

An example. We were due to play away at Charlton on 9 November, which was a big test for us because as it turned out we sneaked into the play-offs just ahead of them at the end of the season. We had lost our last game, a 3-0 stuffing at Southend, and Ray told us on the Friday that, as a one-off, we were going to play in the style of Wimbledon, where Ray had worked before, with a long ball pressing game. We were working on the tactics and Ray sent three players, including midfielder Lee Richardson, to train with the reserves leaving just 11 of us, which we assumed was the starting line-up. Almost the minute we arrived at Upton Park, where Charlton were playing at the time, Nicky Reid stripped off and put on his jockstrap, shorts and number four shirt and started going through his stretching routine. Kenny walked into the dressing room at about two o'clock and looked straight at Nicky.

"What are you doing, Nicky?"

"I'm warming up."

"Oh, so you're playing are you?"

Silence.

"Bobby, Keith, Alan, Lee, Colin, Kevin, Jason, Mark, David, Simon, Scott. Craig, you're on the bench with Nicky."

He picked Lee, who had trained with the reserves the day before and had no idea what we had been doing while working on this new style of play. We won 2-0. Kenny wasn't trying to prove a point, it was just the way he worked. Just about every other manager I've played under would name his team on the Friday but Kenny would pick a squad of about 16 – this was in the days when you only had two substitutes – and not announce his selection until an hour before kick-off. I can't say exactly why he did it this way but we reckoned part of it was that you couldn't fall out with the manager at two o'clock on a Saturday if you weren't picked. As soon as the team was named, Kenny would slope into the background while Ray talked us through the set pieces and tactics. Jack Walker had started to sit in on team talks too by this point. He was like a dutiful child sitting quietly in the corner, hanging on every word. Despite the millions, despite all his success, I genuinely believe he would have swapped the lot for a single game in a blue and white shirt.

I was under no illusion about my situation at Blackburn that season. The money was available and now we had a manager who was going to be able to attract the top talent. Kenny had already signed Alan Wright from Blackpool to play at left back and Colin Hendry had just returned from Manchester City.

There was a rumour going round through the dressing room while Don was still in charge that Colin might be coming back and that some kind of deal had been struck, but nothing happened until Kenny came – surprise, surprise. It was good to have him back and his game had improved massively. Defensively Colin had learned a great deal and under Kenny and Ray he went from being a very good player to a genuine great.

But I was more concerned with the strikers. We already had depth in my position but it was only a matter of time before Kenny started to look at bolstering the forward line. Mike Newell, who had worked under Ray at Luton, was signed in the week following the Charlton match for £1.1million from Everton. It was the club's first seven-figure signing and while the figure didn't make any particular impression on me I thought, hang on a minute, now we've got Newell, Speedie, Livingstone, Johnrose and Gayle. And me. I knew I was being pushed down the pecking order.

If I'd thought it before, I knew it now. I was only going to get the odd game from this point on. But I wasn't about to knock on Kenny's door and wave a transfer request in his face. I'd been at Blackburn since 1976 and now, finally, it looked like we might achieve what we had threatened for so many of those years – and I wanted to be a part of it. I wanted to be there when it happened.

Kenny was very astute with his signings during that period. He came to understand the culture of the club quickly and I think he was impressed from the start by the atmosphere. It was probably one of the reasons he came to Blackburn after the pressures he had faced at Liverpool. It had always been a friendly place with a real family atmosphere. Everyone knew each other well and whether you were a player, in the management team or working behind the scenes, people got on. To Kenny's credit, he didn't make wholesale changes to the club when he came in. He improved the squad and brought in Ray, but the philosophy and ethos of the club didn't change. He kept Tony on the staff and that was really important as he was part of the furniture by now – even more so than I was – and that said it all about the way Kenny wanted to run the club. And he was bringing in the right players. Mike – and most of the others – fitted into the spirit.

Gordon Cowans arrived around the same time from Aston Villa and he added a whole new dimension to our style of place. If he wasn't the final piece in the jigsaw, he was the one that linked most of the others. He had played for Villa and Bari and was an England international. His reputation was massive. Franco Baresi, the AC Milan legend, would call him from Italy after a game to see how he'd got on – now that's impressive. On the pitch his passing and vision was the best I had ever seen in a Blackburn shirt but there was more to him than that. He was constructive in training and after games he could dissect the way the match had gone with real clarity. He had it all – thoughtful, intelligent, great player, fine reader of the game. And a great bloke who loved a drink.

Newell's arrival might have been a boon for the team but for me it meant I was back on the bench for the next match against Barnsley, which we won 3-0, and I was dropped completely for the first time in the season for the 0-0 draw at Newcastle. Speedie was out for the next three games, he was having a bad time with injuries and suspensions, and so I partnered Mike and we went top of the table. Then Speedie was back and I was out of the 13 that lost at Ipswich, who went on to win the league.

Mike was great to play with. He worked very hard and did a lot of running off the ball, which opened spaces for me and the midfielders to get into, and he never stopped talking – a great team player. Off the pitch he was unassuming, quiet even. He'd turn up and train, have a laugh with the players – he had a wicked dry sense of humour – and got on with everybody.

Speedie on the other hand was incredibly selfish and temperamental as a player. That said, he would take weight off partners because defenders would concentrate so much on him that it wasn't unusual for two defenders to sit on him throughout a game. He was also a great header of the ball and a fantastic goal scorer even if he didn't contribute much to the team as a whole.

In training he was fiery and obnoxious and never minced his words. He'd tell anybody – including Kenny – if he felt something wasn't right. And he didn't mix that well with the other players. Socially he could be a nightmare. There was always a dark side lurking and once he'd had a few drinks it came out as angry, pathetic nonsense and he'd start picking fights with anybody.

I was glad Mike was involved in my last goal for Blackburn Rovers. He crossed the ball and I slid in to score in front of our fans at Oxford in a game we won 3-1. By now, every game I played was a bonus. Even if I'd gone out and scored a hattrick I knew there'd be no guarantee of getting picked for the next match. Under previous managers it would be expected, under Dalglish it was very different and he wanted to use Speedie and Newell together when they were both available. It was 7 December, 1991. Thirteen years and a month after goal number one at Craven Cottage back in 1978. I'd like to say it was a memorable event, my last and 168th league goal for Blackburn. Number 194 in total, but it wasn't. After all, I wasn't to know there wouldn't be another. It's a club record and one I doubt will be broken in my lifetime, if at all, which is something I am very proud of.

We had now made it into the top three in the league, which was some achievement considering the start we'd had.

The day after that final goal, Bill Fox, the Rovers chairman, died. It cast a shadow over the whole club. Bill had been chairman since 1982 and steered the club through hard times. He was never the most popular figure with the fans because he was forthright and outspoken. And as chairman the supporters would turn on him if things were going badly. But you only had to look at the rest of the clubs in Lancashire to see what he achieved. None of the others, at that time, had enjoyed the kind of stability we had. Burnley, bless 'em, were within a game of joining the Conference and Preston had to apply for re-election to the league. Even Bolton dropped down to the Fourth Division.

Things have changed of course, and the county's clubs have enjoyed relative success compared to how it was back then, but for Rovers to have been so close to the top flight on so many occasions during the eighties, when the club could barely afford to turn the floodlights on, was some achievement.

Bill was a fruit and vegetable merchant and used to have a number of potato suppliers in Boston. He knew my home town well and that created common ground between us. He built the base for Jack Walker to develop and I regret enormously that he never saw the crowning achievement of promotion and, after I'd left, winning the Premiership title. He was Blackburn Rovers through and through and I was devastated when he died. My dad used to go to most of our away games and Bill would personally ensure he had a ticket.

They say bad news comes in threes. While football's only a game, it was my game, and I was soon on the extreme fringes of the team. That's two. The third was at the shop. I'd never really had any hobbies since my snooker-playing days before I got married. I liked a drink, of course, but it was very much family and football. But I did move into the fashion trade for a while.

Rococco was supposed to be my pension fund. I worked there every day after training – it was midway between home and Pleasington, about two minutes from each. As a sideline to my real job of kicking a lump of leather round the park it was okay, but as time passed it was obvious it wasn't going to provide for my family just on its own. But I had partners and felt responsible for the business.

My investment was £7,000, which came from my testimonial fund, and my partners were Andy McKie and Ian Battersby. We'd socialised as families and were pretty close and I think it was one drunken night that we decided to go for it. Well, you're only young once.

Initially we considered a sports shop but we felt for that to succeed we would have to go into the town centre where the rent and rates were out of our reach. There was also a lot of competition, but there weren't many quality clothes shops.

I knew I was hardly in George Best's league – and even his shops folded – but I had a good team and I wanted something to fall back on. So we bought a shop on Preston Old Road at Cherry Tree and opened Rococco by Simon Garner.

My name was attached to the signage purely for marketing purposes, to try and get people in knowing there was a good chance I'd be about. And business, to begin with, was brisk. Obviously you have your ups and downs but I was getting good advice from my mum who had been a partner in a high class ladieswear shop back home.

"Be patient, Simon. It'll take you three years to get that business going."

And she was right. We weren't making any real money, but we weren't losing either, which was the main thing.

Ian's wife, Sue, and Mandy put most of the hours in. Yvonne, Andy's wife, rented some space at the back of the shop for ladies' clothes while Mandy and Sue dealt with the men's. I enjoyed the work and it was the closest I'd ever come to having a proper job. Some punters would come in just to talk to me about football without any intention of buying anything, but that was fine. I've always been happy to talk football with fans. I did have one or two problems from Burnley fans, though. There was an infamous incident when some of the 100 Club crew clubbed together to send a plane over Turf Moor after another disappointing season with a banner flying from the tail. The message read, "Staying down forever. Love Rovers. Ha ha ha." Now don't get me wrong, that was very, very funny. But, contrary to popular belief, I had nothing to do with it and I didn't even know it had been planned. One of the first things Blackburn fans every ask me is about the aeroplane and none of them ever believe it wasn't my work. I even said so in the Lancashire Evening Telegraph at the time but it made no difference.

Anyway, back to the shop. I think it was some time after the plane incident that we got a call saying a Burnley fan had been in and left a bomb. Well ho bloody ho. I can only assume the call came from the same headcases at Burnley who, rumour had it, had devised a method of bringing down the roof of the Blackburn End terrace by removing a single brick, because I knew for a fact there was no bomb in the shop.

I'd been behind the counter since we'd opened and we hadn't had a single customer in the shop. And while that's nothing to be proud of, it meant the stock was safe for another day.

After the ram-raid it was a different story and it was difficult to raise a smile then.

I was at home in the evening and got a call from the police saying the shop had been ransacked. The stock had been completely stripped out. The fella who owned the sweet shop next door told me four or five lads in balaclavas pulled up in a car, rammed through the shutters, nicked the stuff and sped off. It wasn't the first time the shop had been turned over, but ram-raiding seemed a bit excessive. There was nothing I could do other than board up the windows and get back to Mandy and the kids.

The next morning, I got another call from the police saying the car had been found about a mile from the shop, and I later learned the car belonged to Gordon Cowans. Unbelievable! It had been taken from outside the Trafalgar Hotel near Preston, where he was staying.

"All right Gordon, found your car yet?"

"How do you know it's gone?"

"Because you drove it through my shop window last night you thieving bastard!"

"I don't suppose my golf clubs are still there?"

It became even less amusing when it came to convincing the insurance company that it wasn't an inside job. We closed the shop shortly afterwards. After four serious thefts and dwindling profits, you start to question why you're bothering.

Meanwhile, all was well at Ewood Park, even if I was only getting the occasional appearance as a substitute. When 1992 rolled around we went eight games unbeaten, winning six of them. Speedie was on fire and attendances at Ewood were consistently around the 15,000 mark – more than double what we were used to just a couple of years earlier.

It was party time and at Christmas the club put on a do at the Dunkenhalgh in Clayton-le-Moors, a hotel just outside Blackburn where a lot of the newer players like Speedie and Cowans would live for part of the week. It was a great night – it always was once the drinks started to flow – but all night there was an empty seat next to mine. I just assumed someone hadn't turned up on the night. At around midnight, in walked Kenny and he came over and sat down next to me. By this time I was pissed as a fart, he just looked at me and laughed. In fairness to him, like most of the managers I had during my career, he was happy for the players to have a drink and a laugh as long as it didn't get in the way of the performance on a Saturday.

But in mid-February, for the first time, we started to feel the pressure. The expectation was getting higher by the week and the fans thought we were going to walk to the new Premiership. But it doesn't happen like that and we were brought back down to earth when Notts County knocked us out of the FA Cup. That shocked us because we had become so used to winning and it knocked some reality into us. Thankfully we regained our form in the league and had a three-match winning run culminating in a 3-1 victory over Newcastle. Speedie scored a great hattrick that day, but the main talking point was the fact Mike Newell broke his leg.

That opened the door for me again, particularly as Speedie was missing for the next three games as well, but the loss of Mike was a terrible blow. People remember Speedie as being the main man that season because he scored 24 and made the headlines, but Mike's role shouldn't be overlooked. After the Newcastle game we only got 14 more points from the next 17 games, and eight of those came from the last four matches – when Mike was back in the starting line-up. Mike made the difference when it mattered.

I was definitely out of favour now. I played three games in which we only picked up two points, but only had a recognised striker to partner me in one of them. Inevitably the chequebook was out again. Chris Price was now back at the club having re-signed from Villa for £100,000. Bobby Saxton originally brought Chris from Hereford for £25,000 not long before he was sacked and he proved an excellent buy, which wasn't lost on Aston Villa, who paid £125,000 for him two years later. I don't think we every satisfactorily replaced Chris who could happily operate at right back or right midfield and he was just the kind of player to bolster the squad at a tricky time. I was surprised when he came back, though, because he left under something of a cloud. I don't know the full story, but there was definitely some bad blood there. There was a feeling he may get a rough ride from the fans but they took to him straight away. Scoring a goal in each of his first games back helped.

Tim Sherwood also joined and was an unknown quantity to everyone having come from Watford via Norwich. Kenny paid £500,000 for him and in his first season, when he barely got a game, it didn't look the best buy in the world. Three years later as captain and with the Premier League trophy in his hands, it was a different story. Oh, and another striker was introduced – Roy Wegerle from QPR, another £1.1million man.

This was an unusual signing and didn't seem to fit Kenny's other buys. Roy was a very skilful player, a magician with the ball, but he gave the impression he'd rather be anywhere other than in an English climate.

"It's cold. I'd rather be surfing."

And he meant it. Not surprisingly, he ended his career in America. The problem was that Roy was an individualist and we needed team players who would graft to get us out of the division. We were never a flair side and if you think about the teams Kenny played in and managed it was always the case that the whole was more important than the component parts. Still, I was the guy who favoured Hill over May and Skinner over Wilcox, so what did I know?

March was a tough month for the team and for me. The wins dried up immediately after Mike got his injury. We drew 0-0 at Middlesbrough, which doesn't sound a bad result in isolation, but it was the first in a series of games we just could not win. We lost at Cambridge in the next one and the rot was well and truly setting in.

I completely dropped out of the starting 13 and we really were struggling. The tabloid vultures were out and after a 3-0 win at Brighton we managed to lose six on the trot. My final appearance in a Blackburn shirt was in the first of that sequence. On 21 March 1992 I came on as a substitute as Charlton beat us 2-0 at home. It was the end of an era, for me. Not that I knew it at the time.

The club remained calm and Kenny and Ray carried on as if it was a mild cold, not the full-blown pneumonia everyone else – particularly the very twitchy fans – considered it to be. The supporters, like me, had seen it all before. Great promise and then bugger all to show for it. Given I was fit at this point and that we'd only lost one league game all season when I'd been on from the kick-off, I thought I might be due a recall. Speedie was off the boil, Wegerle was struggling to get goals and fit in with the style of play and Newell was still being treated for his injury. But no – Kenny went and paid Swindon Town, who were still in with a shout of the play-offs, £700,000 for their top scorer Duncan Shearer just before the transfer deadline.

Duncan had built a reputation for being a big, powerful lad who scored a lot of goals, which was exactly what we needed at the time. Though I felt Kenny could have done a lot worse than to take a chance on me instead. Luck was at a premium for us then and even Duncan, who had scored 30 for Swindon, couldn't make a difference. I saw his debut at Barnsley – I'd gone with some mates and sat in the stand – where he scored his only goal for Blackburn. We still lost 2-1. It has been suggested that Kenny only signed Shearer to cock things up for Swindon who were becoming a promotion rival, but I'm not sure that's Kenny's style.

The next game, midweek at Port Vale, was even worse. They were bottom of the league and gave us a 2-0 hiding. It's at times like these you just need to get away and get your head together. Or in Kenny's case, grab a bag of golf clubs and hitch a ride out of town. He took us to his homeland for a breather and we had a 10-day break before our next game at Watford. It was time to get down to some serious bonding. And golfing. And drinking. We were staying at the Dalmahoy Hotel and Country Club, which has a really nice golf course, apparently. I wouldn't know because I have as much interest in golf as I have in National No Smoking Day. Most of the players played solidly for the two days we were there. I did a bit of swimming.

Events like these tend to fall at a time when there's a few glum faces appearing at a club. Just to get away for a couple of days in a fresh environment can help break any staleness and improve morale, especially when you get a couple of good nights out thrown into the bargain. Invigorated and ready for the challenge ahead – we were still second and in an automatic promotion position – we headed back down the M6. Then we lost to Watford. And to Wolves. And to Leicester. So much for a refreshing break.

By the end of the losing streak in mid-April when Leicester, one of our promotion rivals, beat us 1-0 at home, the unthinkable had happened. We had even dropped out of the play-off zone. In just a few months we had turned from a club seen as a quaint, loveable outfit, a club the press and fans from outside the area had a real soft spot for because of how friendly it was and how close we had come to having success, to one people wanted to see fail. It was jealousy I suppose. Jealousy at the resources that were being pumped in. That and the fact the media loves nothing more than a falling star.

This wasn't lost on our opponents. While we weren't playing particularly well we had become a prized scalp. Big crowds were watching us wherever we went and opposition players raised their games to take us on. It was only natural. In the big cup games against First Division sides, we always wanted to prove a point, too. Now we were on the receiving end. We were the moneybags boys. We were football enemy number one.

Despite everything there were no panic buttons being pressed within the camp. Training didn't change and we didn't alter the game plan. Visibly Kenny didn't seem to be under pressure at all. The dressing room feeling was still good, we were still up for the challenge and genuinely believed we'd still be promoted even if it was through the back door of the play-offs.

It is impossible to put a finger on what was going wrong. It was just one of those things. We had got to the top very quickly and Kenny and Ray wouldn't let us get complacent. It wasn't in their vocabulary and our feet were kept firmly on the ground. We started the season badly, then had a great run – and like all clubs we hit a rocky patch. Only ours didn't seem to stop and it was made worse because we were expected to win every match. They kept us motivated during that run and made sure we didn't lose belief in ourselves. Even though I wasn't playing I still felt it all applied to me. That was an indicator of the qualities of Kenny and Ray – no one was excluded from the team effort.

We scraped our first point in a month with a 2-2 draw at Tranmere on Easter Monday, which was Newell's first start since the Newcastle match in February. He scored from the spot but there was still a lot of work to be done. We beat Millwall 2-1 the following Saturday in front of 12,820 fans – our lowest gate since before Christmas – and then we were at home to Sunderland when Scott Sellars brought us level with a great shot near the end. We had one league game left at Plymouth.

I wasn't on the trip, but the nerves were still intense for me. It would have been easier being with the squad. Being so distant from it was horrendous. We were confident we had the talent to take us up through the play-offs, but we were still sweating on making it over the final hurdle.

Plymouth were just outside the relegation zone and needed to win to make sure they avoided the drop. We were sixth and needed to win to cement our place in the play-offs. Speedie came up trumps with a hattrick and we won 3-1. Plymouth were down. Play-offs again, then. Our record so far – played in three, lost in three.

We scraped through the semi-final against Derby after a backs-against-the-wall performance of real grit at the Baseball Ground. We were 2-0 down inside 15 minutes of the first leg at Ewood. There were real fears of 'here we go again'. But the lads turned it round. Scott bundled a free kick home to pull one back and then Newell scored a screamer from outside the box to draw us level. There was no way we were going to let this one slip and Speedie scored two in the second half to give us a 4-2 lead.

I was at both games and went in the crowd. For the home game I was in the main stand and I can still see David Speedie's winning goal. The place went mad when that went in. I had been there a long time and of course I wanted to be playing, but I was a fan that day and I went just as mad as anyone.

In the return leg just three days later things got hairy when Derby took the lead, but thanks to Kevin Moran, who risked his life (and not for the first time) to equalise from a corner, we managed to squeeze through, despite Derby scoring a second towards the end of the game.

And so it was Wembley for the final against Leicester City. And while I knew there was no way I'd ever be playing, or that I would be considered for the bench, it was still one of my best days in football.

I had played my part that season and had been proud of my achievements, despite the limited opportunities. And I've Kenny Dalglish to thank for the memories because he made sure I was among the three non-playing squad members assigned a seat on the bench that day, even though my bum barely touched it all afternoon, and he took me down for the whole trip rather than have me just turn up for the game. While I felt I deserved to be part of what turned out to be such a historic day, I was no less grateful to Kenny for making it happen.

I was only with Kenny for one season – and not even a full season – but I could see he was an incredible manager. And that wasn't just because he was my hero growing up. When I was a kid I idolised Kenny Dalglish. I would watch him play at Liverpool and think, "I wish I could be half as good as him". And when he came he taught me things that stayed with me, even at this late stage of my career.

"You don't need to run around like a blue-arsed fly. Your job is to score goals."

I had been playing professional football for 12 or 13 years but he improved my game and prolonged my career. I was 28, 29, and his impact was massive.

Even in the best circumstances, that play-off final was going to be a difficult game to watch. I had been to Wembley before, of course, for the Full Members Cup final, but this was such a one-off game, such a massive game, that my experience didn't count for much and there was little I could offer my teammates in terms of how to prepare for the experience.

The Second Division play-off final was always a big game. Getting to the First Division was what every club, player and fan wanted. But there had been so much talk about the new 'super league' that was to be created that getting promoted that season took on extra significance.

Wembley that day was baking hot. Tony Parkes was asked to lead the team out. That was another great touch by Kenny. Tony had been at the club since 1970 and this was the biggest day for Blackburn and for any of us as players. He had contributed so much in so many ways and he deserved this moment in the spotlight.

You used to hear players talking about playing in the shadow of the Twin Towers and people who have played in these occasions often say they remember little of the game. It was the same for me that day, just as it had been for the Full Members Cup. No matter how hard you try, the occasion gets the better of you.

We didn't play particularly well – I remember that much – and there wasn't much between the teams in the first half and precious few chances. Then, just before half-time, Speedie was decked by Steve Walsh in the box.

The referee was George Courtney in his last senior game. Courtney, not that anyone needed reminding of it, was the guy who gave Palace the so-called penalty which meant we missed promotion in 1989 and since then the fans had given him terrible stick every time he was involved in our games. As Speedie went down it was like slow motion, and it felt an age until Courtney awarded the penalty. Newell held his nerve and sent Carl Muggleton the wrong way. It was mayhem on the pitch, the bench, and in the crowd.

After the break, the game livened up but Leicester were in control and we cleared the ball off the line more than once. Kevin Moran and Colin Hendry performed heroics. We even got another penalty which Mike struck well but Muggleton made the right choice this time and stopped it.

If my description of this game, the most important in my 16 years at Blackburn, is sketchy, that's for two reasons. Firstly, as I mentioned, the occasion gets the better of you. Secondly, I didn't actually watch much of the second half, I was too busy smoking myself to an early grave.

It would be wrong to say I was nervous. I wasn't. A shuddering wreck would be a more appropriate description. And thank God for the Portaloo. There, half way up the tunnel, was my very own smoker's corner. I don't know if it was there for the Queen's private use or something but I was in there every 10 minutes.

We won, we were up. And so was my time at Blackburn.

The celebrations were, of course, incredible. On the pitch and off it. The journey home was a blur, though I still have a memory fixed in my brain of seeing Kenny swigging from a Champagne bottle on the coach and waving to fans as we headed up the motorway.

And I'll certainly never forget seeing him force that ample rear through a window at the Woodlands pub on Preston New Road because we couldn't get in through the front door.

The reception we were given at the Town Hall was another brilliant occasion, though one tinged with a touch of poignancy for me. The crowd launched into a lengthy refrain of 'There's Only One Simon Garner' and, drunk on a combination of beer and emotion, I conducted it from the balcony.

I knew it was the last time I would hear it as an employee of Blackburn Rovers and I milked it for all it was worth.

David Speedie
Teammate at Blackburn from 1991 to 1992

It was a breath of fresh air to come to Blackburn. I needed to get away from Graeme Souness at Liverpool so I was absolutely delighted when Blackburn came in for me. I had played with Souness for Scotland against England on my debut at Hampden Park and he had slaughtered me all the way through the game, even though we won 1-0. When he walked through the door at Anfield it was never going to work and I knew my days were numbered.

Mind you, it was a bit different leaving Liverpool and going to train at dog shit park! I was covered in the stuff on my first training session. And it was right below the crematorium so had to stand to attention every time a funeral car went by.

Simon Garner was an absolute gentleman. He was one of the quietest men I've ever met, but what a goal scorer. He was one of the best I've ever played with finishing-wise.

Before I joined Blackburn I knew very little about him. I don't think I'd ever played against him. He was a really nice guy. Simon and I were similar in that we both came from a working-class background. I spent 10 months working down the pit, I certainly wasn't born with a silver spoon in my mouth. And because of that background Simon, like me, appreciated life and what he had and his ability.

As a goal scorer he was in the Ian Rush and Kerry Dixon mould, and those are the only two players I'd put ahead of him. He was a great finisher. He just knew where to be on the pitch to get the goals.

In training he was funny. A bit like me, he didn't want to train, he wanted to play. So if we were doing any running exercises I'd be at the back moaning. Simon might not have moaned so much, but he was certainly at the back alongside me.

At the start of the season I wasn't fit because I hadn't played any games. I'd gone away with Liverpool for pre-season training and we had been to Ireland, Denmark and Germany. I was disappointed in myself in those early games of that season because I just wasn't prepared. I was doing a fair amount of moaning because I wanted perfection and

I knew that, at first, my game wasn't as it should have been.

Simon wasn't a moaner. He was quiet and reserved. He never said anything, and he never criticised me in those first few games when I wasn't playing well. We were very different in that respect because I was always very vocal, but I felt that we got on really well as a partnership.

I did have a few disagreements with Don Mackay and the way he wanted me to play. He was asking us to drop off whereas I thought we needed to close the opposition down higher up the pitch. And then when Tony Parkes took over he really got us playing. He was brilliant.

When Kenny Dalglish came in and started to build his team, Simon didn't get to play as much. I'd known Kenny for a lot of years, I played with him for my country and then played under him twice. He brought in Mike Newell from Everton and he obviously did really well, but when Simon did play he often played well and scored.

Off the field we did a fair amount of drinking as a group. Win or lose, have a booze, if you draw, have some more. That was the motto I brought with me from my days at Coventry. To get that great team spirit you have to socialise as a group, and we did that at Blackburn. Simon lived in Blackburn and he had his family but he always had time for a beer with the lads.

I lived in Merseyside when I signed and then moved back to Warwickshire, so I used to travel in with Gordon Cowans and Chris Price. We spent half the week at the Dunkenhalgh Hotel where we were all put up by Jack Walker and enjoyed many good nights. Jack paid for everything – I don't think I ever bought a drink in that hotel!

One of the best nights of my life was after we won promotion to the Premier League. On the way back, Kenny stopped the bus at an off licence because we had drunk all the ale before we had even got out of London. We emptied the place. Everyone was drunk before we even got to the pub. And Simon was right in the middle of all that. Even though he didn't play, he was as happy as everyone else was.

He was always upbeat and never complained. If I was ever not playing I would be knocking on the manager's door, or if I was coming back from an injury or suspension and I was put on the bench I would be moaning constantly to the manager to get me on the pitch. Simon was never like that. He just got on with it.

On the day of the play-off final Simon wasn't in the squad but he wanted to be there. He wanted to support the team and for us to go and get the promotion. And that was Simon. He always gave everything, whether he was playing or not. He never complained he just got on with it and enjoyed being in the dressing room and having a laugh and a craic.

After we got promoted, Simon would want to be playing. He wouldn't want to stay at a club where he wasn't going to play. So I understand why he moved on at the end of that season.

Simon Garner was a great player, an excellent teammate and a real gentleman, one of the nicest guys you could hope to meet.

Mike Newell
Teammate at Blackburn from 1991 to 1992

It's not always a nice feeling to walk into a dressing room and feel like you're pushing another player out. You can feel like that player is looking at you and thinking their time's up. Thankfully, because of the way Kenny Dalglish managed the team, it wasn't like that. Everyone had a chance.

Blackburn had already come in for me in the summer. I went to meet Don Mackay and he was a lovely bloke. We never even spoke about money or a contract, we just talked about football. Jack Walker had just come in and was obviously very wealthy but I just didn't see Don getting them going.

When Kenny came in it was a different story. Going to Blackburn was exciting. Kenny Dalglish had been my idol since I was 11 when he signed for Liverpool. He was the best I had ever seen. Growing up and playing against Liverpool for Luton and Everton was amazing. And then when he came to sign me it was a no-brainer.

Simon obviously knew his time at Blackburn was coming to an end. But when he was asked to play he was still well capable of scoring goals. He was such a great finisher as everyone knows, and with the quality of players coming in he was getting even more chances.

He was a proper centre forward. A worker and a grafter. He was the type of player you don't tend to get these days. I enjoyed playing with him. He was a bright lad who was able to put himself about. I played with lots of good players but I also played with some who you just couldn't connect with and that is difficult – but with Simon it was easy. He was very much a team player.

I spent plenty of time with him before he moved on at the end of the season and he was a great character. There was no edge about him. For somebody who scored lots of goals and was a Blackburn legend there was no 'big time Charlie' about him. There was no attitude.

I roomed with him when I first signed and I remember going on a team bonding trip to the Dalmahoy golf course in Scotland. It was the year Liverpool beat Sunderland in the FA Cup Final – I remember that because we stopped on the way up to Scotland from Blackburn to watch them play Portsmouth in the semi-final.

There was no game coming up so it was just good to get away as a group and have a laugh and a joke. I was still out injured with my broken leg, but I must have been on the mend because I played golf with Kenny against David Speedie and Gordon Cowans. Simon hated golf so he just stayed in the hotel playing snooker and relaxing in his own way.

We shared a room on that trip and I remember him asking me if I minded him having a smoke. And then he went over to the window to blow the smoke out of the window. When you are a younger player and you are surrounded by players who have been in the game for years and scored lots of goals and had good careers, you look up to those guys. So for me, Simon was the elder statesman. He was someone I looked up to in that dressing room. And here he is asking me if I minded him having a fag. I couldn't believe it.

"You can do whatever you want Simon. You're a bloody Blackburn legend."

But that was just the type of bloke he was. He didn't have an ego and didn't think of himself as the superstar all-time leading goal scorer for Blackburn Rovers.

I think, like me, he felt lucky that he was able to do a job that wasn't really a job. Going to training every day and playing football and getting paid for it. He just loved playing football. I think we both would have done it for free if you could look after your family and pay the bills. It was never about the money or the wages, it was always about playing football. We were blessed. It was about winning games and scoring goals. Simon epitomised that.

We were flying for a lot of that season but we almost didn't get there. That breakdown in February and March felt like it would never end. And with my broken leg I couldn't do anything. But we did get there and it was just in time because I don't think we would have got Shearer if we hadn't made it to the Premiership when we did.

The best thing Kenny did that season was to keep all the players involved. He could have come in and decided he needed a whole new team but he gave everybody a chance.

This gave people like Jason Wilcox and Mark Atkins the opportunity to really break into the team and make a name for themselves. And he had people like Simon and David Speedie who were already there who he knew could play. And even though Simon was coming towards the end of his career, by working with Kenny and the players he brought in, he was able to improve his game and he became a better player.

The facilities at Blackburn were, it has to be said, a far cry from what I had been used to. At Everton we had probably the best facilities in the country at the time, with a dedicated training ground with indoor and outdoor facilities. Blackburn was a long way behind but there was a real buzz about the place with Kenny and Jack Walker, and an anticipation that good things were coming. But just like Simon, both Kenny and Jack were down-to-earth normal people. You could talk to them and get on with them and it really helped everyone to come together.

There were new players signing every week and we had an in-joke about Thursdays as that's when players used to come in. Back then there was no 24-hour news like there is today, it was all on Teletext and so every Thursday night you'd go on Teletext and there was a new player coming to Blackburn. It was weird. Gordon Cowans, Alan Wright, Colin Hendry, me, Tim Sherwood. It was great. But at the same time he kept people like Simon on board and gave them a chance, which made everyone feel more comfortable.

It was a great time to be there. A few of the lads had been there for years and knew where the club had come from. Especially Simon, who was probably one of the happiest of all of us to see the club finally make it to the top flight.

When it came to the play-off final we went down to Wembley for about three or four days. Kenny wouldn't have taken anyone who could have disrupted our preparation for the day. Simon knew he wasn't going to be playing, but Kenny knew Simon just wanted to be there to support the team. He was still on our side as a fan and that makes a massive difference to players who have taken his place. On the day he was as happy as anyone else that we won. And he partied just as hard as those of us who had been on the pitch. Not that you'd expect anything different.

It is a massive shame Simon was never able to quite make it to the First

Division when he was younger and he came so close with Blackburn in the 80s.

Football was starting to change and modernise by 1991, but in fairness to Kenny he made gradual changes, he didn't try to do it all at once. Things like bringing in a couple of fitness coaches and changing the training schedules. We were still allowed to have a pint on a Tuesday night or a Saturday night but there was more of an input into what we should be eating and more of a focus on being healthy, and this was probably a shock to Simon who was still puffing away on his fags before and after training.

But Kenny didn't try to change Simon's habits. He knew by that time there was no point. Simon was from the old school. I'd played with loads of them during my time at Wigan, Luton and Leicester – players who would finish a game and go straight for a pint and a smoke. As a young player you couldn't believe there were players who were smokers – I didn't even drink until I was 24. It was incredible to think these blokes could drink and smoke and then turn up and perform.

Simon will always be a Blackburn legend. To play so many games and score so many goals for one club is unheard of in today's game, and even back then it was still some achievement. And it is right that even after all these years and the success Blackburn have had since going up to the Premiership that Simon is still such a hero for the fans.

CHAPTER 12

The end of an era

1992 to 1994

Kenny brought in Alan Shearer for three and a half million pounds in the following pre-season. David Speedie went to Southampton as part of the deal – a British record. Kenny and Jack Walker meant business.

Speedie was gone but now he had Shearer, Newell and Wegerle. I was at least fourth in the pecking order so I knew I wasn't going to get a game. I was 31 now and I knew Kenny didn't want me in the team. It was obvious from the start. I'd scored twice against Plymouth in the first game he and Ray Harford came to watch and I still didn't get picked the next game. He had put his marker down early and I knew my time was up.

I did train with Shearer for a couple of sessions after we all joined back up for pre-season and he was a really nice lad. But what a lazy trainer. Bloody hell, I thought I was bad. He was like a younger version of me. Crap trainer, but a goal scorer.

You could tell Shearer was a special talent even then, before a ball of the new season had been kicked. He was young and enthusiastic and had such an eye for goal. On top of that, he had that extra bit of pace back then before he got the cruciate ligament injury that forced him to alter his game.

I had Kenny to thank for ensuring I remained a first team footballer, although sadly in pastures new. Ossie Ardiles was now manager at West Bromwich Albion. He had remained a good friend since his brief spell at Ewood and I knew he was keen to sign me.

I was playing in a reserve game at Barrow and later drove down to a hotel in Stoke to meet with Ossie. This was before anyone at Blackburn knew about it. We sorted things out and he explained that I would be getting first-team football, which I knew I wouldn't get at Blackburn, and he would match my wages. But he didn't have a lot of money to spend.

"Simon, the most we can afford is £30,000. If they let you go on a free, the money's yours. If they want £20,000, you can have the difference."

I really wanted a free transfer and felt, after all the loyalty I had shown the club, I deserved it.

Blackburn had stuck a £100,000 price tag on me, which felt a bit ridiculous. I knew I had to speak to Kenny or I was stuck playing in the reserves.

"Ossie can't afford more than £30,000, boss, which is a long way short of what the board wants."

"Sorry Simon, can you just move to your left a bit?"

Typical Kenny. He was watching the golf and I was blocking his view of the telly.

"What was that?"

I explained the situation and asked if he could help. Kenny had nothing to do with transfers in those days. He would go to the board and tell them what or who he wanted and it was up to them to go out and make it happen.

"Leave it with me."

Kenny knew how important it was for me, now in my 30s, to be playing. He was honest enough to say I would be a fringe player and the best I could really hope for was a few starts on the bench.

Kenny was true to his word and delivered a compromise that kept the board reasonably happy and, while I didn't make a bean on the deal, at least I had what I really wanted – a starting position in a decent club. The fee was £30,000 and I packed my bags. As part of my exit deal, the club and I shook hands on a second testimonial match, but it would be a decade before that happened.

I sorted my own financial package with Ossie, which is unheard of in the modern game. Agents were only just coming into football. I had used Paul Stretford while sorting out one of my new contracts with Blackburn a couple of years before. Paul – who went on to represent Wayne Rooney – had acted for Frank Stapleton when Blackburn signed him from Le Havre and he signed a few of the Rovers players to his books. I had told

Paul about the West Brom deal and he said he would sort it out for me, but I was good friends with Ossie and so did the deal myself. Paul wasn't best pleased he hadn't been involved. I guess he missed out on a few quid there. I didn't use an agent again.

So as Blackburn moved up to the top flight, I went the other way, dropping down to the third tier (although confusingly now called the Second Division). West Brom had been relegated in 1991 when they finished just four points below us at the end of Don's final full season. And having just missed out on the play-offs in their last season, the fans were keen for a genuine promotion push.

Moving to a new club was an odd sensation. There are plenty of players who have moved clubs six or more times in a career but for me it was something I don't think I was prepared for. I had been at Blackburn since I was 16. I had settled both in the club and in the town and my whole life was there. My wife was there and so were the kids. And I couldn't ask them to leave work and school and join me in the Midlands. If I'm being honest, I didn't want to. I was going to have to get used to a new lifestyle, a new club and a lot of new names. It was like being a teenager again. In all respects.

A couple of years before signing for West Brom I had been sent off after a scuffle with their centre half, Martyn Bennett. So of course the first time I walked into the dressing room at The Hawthorns, the only other person in there could only be Martyn sodding Bennett. I couldn't believe it. We looked at each other.

"I remember you!"

We were teammates now and we had already moved on.

An agreement was reached that I would train in Blackburn for the first part of the week, then travel to the Midlands on the Thursday and stay until the match on a Saturday before heading back home again. So it was nice in a way because I still got to train with Kenny and Ray and his team of Premier League stars and, in theory, that should benefit my new teammates when I joined up with them on Thursdays. This meant that, on paper, I would only be away from home for a couple of nights a week and that suited Mandy and meant I could still see the boys regularly.

I knew Ossie and didn't think I needed to prove myself to him, but that still left the players, officials, fans and media. My first duty was to try and match the most expensive player in history with, incredibly, a friendly match against Blackburn Rovers. It was Shearer's second game for Blackburn and all eyes were on him.

It was a very weird feeling lining up across from the Blackburn players – my teammates just' a week or so ago. The crowd was small but I got a great reception from the West Brom fans and there were a few Blackburn fans there and they were singing my name as well.

I scored first – my only goal against Blackburn in my career, until that testimonial penalty at Ewood in 2003.

That was another weird feeling. It was in front of the West Brom end which was great as they took to me straight away. And then Shearer grabbed two. Show off.

The end of the game was the hardest bit. I went over and clapped the West Brom fans but the Blackburn fans were still singing my name so I went across and clapped them as well. That choked me up a bit. Because of the way the previous season played out, I didn't get the chance to say a proper farewell to the Rovers fans who had been so great with me for all those years, so to have the opportunity then was welcome, but upsetting. Blackburn always had a good following away from home and a lot turned up for that game. I'd like to think they came to see me, but Mr Shearer may have had something to do with it as well.

I went in the away dressing room after the game to see the lads and to say a proper goodbye, although of course I was still seeing them at training at the start of the week. Or at least that was the plan.

We were playing a lot of midweek games and that meant I would end up away for the best part of a week. The cracks in my marriage were starting to emerge. I didn't help matters either. I could be in a hotel room for five nights a week or I would stay over at our goalkeeper Stuart Naylor's place, an arrangement that became more or less permanent after a while, and we would do a lot of drinking. It was a new lease of life for me and though I know it was selfish and I missed the boys, I couldn't get enough of it.

There was a good team spirit and some serious drinkers to keep up with. The squad was brilliant and I got on really well with them from day one. They were a down-to-earth bunch. It was very much like it had been at Blackburn under Bobby Saxton.

Ossie's training was brilliant and in complete contrast to the way I had worked before. It was a simple approach – play football all day. The way that converted on to the pitch was in an all-out attacking style. There was no doubt I had lost a bit of pace since the hernia operation so that suited me down to the ground because I wasn't expected to do much tracking back. Just concentrate on getting forward. 'Pass, pass, pass' was Ossie's motto. Keith Burkinshaw – who managed Spurs to two FA Cups and a UEFA Cup in the Eighties – was there as his coach and he would work out set-piece routines but Ossie wouldn't let it drag on. He didn't want the players bored.

My full debut – the first debut I'd had in 14 years – came in the opening game of the season. We were playing Blackpool at the Hawthorns and won 3-1. I didn't score but I set up the second and won a penalty (that Craig Shakespeare bloody missed). It felt good to be back playing. To be part of a first 11 again and not a bit part player. And there were more than 16,000 in the ground and a fantastic atmosphere. I may have moved down the leagues, but this was a big club with a big following. And I didn't have to wait long to get on the scoresheet.

August 22, 1992. Leeds Road, Huddersfield, Second Division. Garner scores the only goal in a 1-0 win for West Bromwich Albion. Off the mark. Get in.

The good start continued and we won six out of the first seven games before losing 4-3 at Stoke, although I did smash one in to the top corner from the edge of the box. Stoke went on to win the league that year. After a win against Exeter at the Hawthorns we lost three on the bounce. The first of that run of defeats came at Turf Moor. It was a disappointing result but I did get a goal in that happy hunting ground, much to the annoyance of the locals who had, as you would expect, brought out the welcome mat and given me the full treatment.

There was certainly no love lost between me and the Burnley fans thanks to my years at Blackburn. I didn't travel with the team that day as I was still living in Blackburn so I met them part of the way there and followed the coach to the ground. In those days people said my teammate Craig Shakespeare and I looked quite similar. And yes, he always was a handsome lad. He was sitting at the back of the coach and I was following behind in my car. The Burnley fans were shouting all sorts of obscenities at him. They thought he was me. I made sure I was wearing sunglasses and got to the car park as quickly as possible. At one point it looked like they might start throwing bricks.

We were already 2-0 down when I scored near the end of the game, right in front of our fans. I saluted them before making the obligatory gestures to the Burnley supporters as well. You could get away with that in those days.

That season we were top scorers in the league, though unsurprisingly our defensive record wasn't great. We were pushing for promotion and the supporters loved the way we were playing. If we conceded a goal it didn't matter because we had the confidence to get another ourselves. The fans were fantastic – crowds were regularly 16,000 at home and 4,000 would travel to the away games.

I had been doing well, too. Until I picked up another serious injury. It was just before Christmas and we were playing Swansea. I went up for a header at the far post and landed funnily on my leg. Not that I was laughing about it. I ended up being stretchered off while being given dog's abuse by the Swansea fans. I was able to sit up to give them a bit back.

I thought I had twisted my ankle and I ended up missing a few games with it. Danny Thomas was the physio at the time – a former Tottenham left back who could have played for England but he injured his knee and could never straighten his leg properly after that and so switched careers. Danny didn't like putting strappings on players' legs but having missed four or five games over the Christmas period and with a cup game against West Ham coming up, Ossie told Danny to get my leg strapped. He wanted me to play in that game.

I did a fitness test and it was still a bit sore but I could play through it. Not long after the game kicked off I went to volley the ball and I went down in absolute agony. My God it hurt. An MRI scan showed I had cracked a bone in my ankle, which hadn't shown up on the x-ray. I ended up in plaster for about two or three weeks. Merry bloody Christmas.

It was a strange one that year. I was hobbling round on a bad ankle for starters, but it was the first time in my career I was away from home at

Christmas. We had a home game against Chester City on Boxing Day and we always had to train on Christmas Day, so I didn't have time to travel back to Blackburn, though Mandy and the boys did come down to see me.

When I did come back, it couldn't have been in a better fashion. Against Burnley I needed one more goal to hit my career 200 mark. The chairman had words with me on the day before the game.

"If you score and it's in front of the Burnley fans, you are not allowed to celebrate."

Well. With two minutes on the clock and with my first touch of the game I scored right in front of their fans. It was a crisp hit from the left-hand side of the box into the far corner. A temporary bout of amnesia meant I was back in the chairman's office on the Monday. It's another of those incidents that seems to have found its way into Blackburn folklore and people still ask me about taking my West Brom shirt off to reveal a Blackburn shirt underneath. Yes, I made a meal of the goal in front of their fans but the two-shirts story has absolutely no truth in it. I wish I'd thought of it, though.

We won the game 2-0, which was sweet revenge for the defeat at Turf Moor earlier in the season.

I struggled to get a regular place in the side, though. Partly because I was picking up niggling injuries and also because Ossie signed Andy Hunt, who was a great goal scorer. Andy was a player Ossie had while he was at Newcastle and clearly admired him. He brought him in on loan at first and he was scoring goals for fun. And so I spent some time on the bench watching him and Bob Taylor.

Bob was adored at West Brom. In a lot of ways he kept the pressure off me because he was a hero to the fans. And he was great to play with. He wasn't one of the boys who came out drinking with us, but he was a really great lad. A proper down-to-earth Geordie and we got on really well. Playing with Bob reminded me a great deal of playing with Chris Thompson at Blackburn. We both just knew what the other was going to do. We clicked on the pitch and formed a really good partnership.

For me, it was nice to walk into the club realising there was someone else to shoulder the burden of goalscoring expectation. But I knew I'd have to work hard to convince the fans of my own value because I had seen the treatment given to new strikers by Blackburn fans.

After the Burnley win we went on a great run, only losing twice, and finished the season fourth and went into the play-offs. We beat Swansea in the semi-final, although much like my previous season with Blackburn we did it the hard way, going two goals down in the first leg before pulling it back to 2-1, and then winning the second leg at home 2-0.

In the final we met Port Vale at Wembley. I was on the bench again, but not in a suit this time, and Ossie threw me on for Andy Hunt in the 89th-minute so I could soak up a bit of the atmosphere. We were already 2-0 up thanks to Andy and Nicky Reid, who also came from Blackburn that season, and I had the best seat in the house when Kevin Donovan smashed it home to make it three in the last minute. I was screaming for the ball just a few yards to his left but he didn't need me.

While we won the game I still feel the play-offs are wrong, regardless of the fact it spins the season out for more clubs. This was my fifth play-offs and in none of those cases had my team finished in the top three, which should be the real dividing line between success and failure. Still, it was a fantastic drinking session when we won. And the crowd was deafening. Out of the 52,000 at the game there were 40,000 Baggies fans.

We had an open-top bus trip round West Bromwich and Birmingham and the bottles never dried up. For two or three days we just didn't stop drinking. And that's just about my last happy memory of West Brom.

Ossie left for Tottenham – a dream job for him which sadly did not work out – and Keith Burkinshaw was appointed manager, a nightmare for me. I had never really seen eye-to-eye with Keith. The first time we crossed swords, while Ossie was still around, was when I said I didn't go on to the pitch to warm up until the teams were led out by the referee. He called me a lazy bastard.

"Yes, he is a lazy bastard, Keith, but this lazy bastard will score goals."

Keith didn't like Ossie undermining him – after all it was Keith who brought Ossie to Spurs back in 1978. I spent most of the time in Division One on the bench and in the reserves. That meant I was rarely home for more than a day or two each week because the reserves played midweek and I was on call each weekend. The strain was starting to show on the marriage. Mandy and I weren't communicating through anything much more than small talk about the kids and there were too many arguments for sanity's sake. And I was still enjoying my bachelor lifestyle in Birmingham. I was drinking plenty and generally reliving my childhood. Mandy wasn't impressed and neither was Keith. He didn't like his players drinking, a sentiment not shared by many in the dressing room.

The core drinking squad was me, Gary Robson, Stuart Naylor and Darren Bradley. Keith would come into training and slyly try to smell our breath for booze. Stuart and I got wise to it and invested in extra strong mints and aftershave, but Keith was quite happy to send Gary home if he got a whiff. The writing was clearly on the wall for me and it came to a head on a trip to Halifax, of all places, for a cup match. We took a squad of 17 players and I didn't even get on the bench. They were a non-league team and beat us 2-1. The next day we were off to Italy to play an Anglo-Italian Cup game against Fiorentina and get a bit of a break in what was proving to be a tricky season. When we got back to Birmingham from Halifax, Keith turned to me and told me, without offering a reason, that I wasn't on the trip. That was harsh and I eventually submitted a transfer request.

It dragged on and on and it was embarrassing because no one was interested in me. Eventually, I got a call from somebody at Wycombe Wanderers saying they were interested. A few days later, Martin O'Neill, who was their manager at the time, called me himself and said he wanted to sign me. I was really excited to move somewhere and play again. And then I spent 10 weeks sat next to the phone, waiting.

Everything was settled at West Brom, they were letting me go on a free transfer, but it still took an age for the deal to go through. It was a nightmare. I could never get past Martin's secretary to speak to him and Keith wouldn't even talk to me at West Brom. I couldn't work him out because I don't think I'd been disruptive at all. Bloody hell, David Speedie had come on loan during Ossie's time – now that was disruptive. He was dropped for one game and we never saw him again!

The daft thing was the West Brom team was battling against a relegation straight back into the Second Division and Keith wouldn't let me have a kick. I didn't score a single goal for West Brom that season but would have given anything to be given the chance. In the end, they scraped through and stayed up on goals scored. I was happy for the fans, even happier when Keith was shown the door. He treated me poorly and I wasn't sorry in the slightest.

It was depressing that Wycombe were the only club to come in for me, because I still felt I had a lot to offer. And this was a drop of two divisions into the basement of the Football League. It wasn't how I had planned the end of my career. But it kept me in a living and my wages stayed the same.

Finally, in February 1994, the move to Wycombe happened. I really felt Keith had treated me poorly in the end and I was glad to get a move to a club where I might get some games. Mandy wasn't happy, though. She had wanted me to go back north. I had just signed for Wycombe, another hundred miles down the motorway.

When I realised how desperate I was to go, I realised the marriage was over. I didn't want to go back home.

I tried to persuade myself it was for the best, particularly for the boys. I didn't want them living in a home when I was resentful of having to be there. And because I had no choice about where I worked, I didn't want them uprooting from school.

But in reality it was much simpler and much more self-motivated. Despite missing the kids, I loved being on my own. The boys were devastated when I told them – even though they knew things weren't right between me and their mum. The worst thing was the distance. I spoke to them every night but it's just not the same as being there.

Ossie Ardiles
Teammate at Blackburn in 1988
Manager at West Brom 1992 to 1993

When I first met Simon, immediately we were on the same wavelength. We became very good friends. In a lot of ways I think this happened because we are very different characters. I am much more reserved and Simon was quite flamboyant. He liked to talk to people.

Out of nothing he could score goals. He was a very good player. A goal scorer. If the ball was there he could put it in the net and it is a very special skill to be able to do that. For that reason it was great to play with him. He was a very clever player. He could find the spaces behind the defenders and he was always there in the right place.

I think he could have played at a higher level. To do that he may have had to sort out certain issues. We all have issues, including myself. I could have played at a bigger level as well but I was happy with the level I played at and I know Simon was happy as well.

In training Simon and I were quite similar in that we didn't enjoy the fitness side of sessions. I was naturally fit so I didn't need to train a lot. When it was five-a-sides or working with the ball and movement and so on then yes, we would be very much involved. But if not, if they were asking us to run or do gym things, we were not so keen. But Simon did what he had to do. At the end of training he would often be working with the goalkeeper practising his finishing. That was his job and that's what concentrated on.

When I was managing at West Bromwich Albion and I found out he was available I went in to sign him immediately. We needed someone who could score. We were playing some wonderful football at the time but for all the beautiful play and creativity this was not being translated into goals. I jumped at the possibility of Simon coming to us.

When I went into management I didn't change the way I was. I wanted everyone to enjoy themselves. I made training a happy place. I didn't tell the players to arrive early, they did that on their own. And when Simon arrived he was able to slot straight in and I believe he enjoyed that season playing for me very much.

He was someone who could play football and had a powerful shot and you had to utilise him in the right way. It was no good asking him to be running all the time. He had to do as little as possible and just be ready for when the ball was in that final third or when we were ready for the counter attack because you knew if he was in the right place he would score goals.

We became very close friends over the years. Simon was great company. A great person to spend time with. He was never serious, he was always taking the Mickey out of somebody. Sometimes we would talk seriously about football, but he had a great sense of humour.

CHAPTER 13

Back in business

1994 to 1996

I don't think Martin felt he was taking a gamble when he signed me. He had watched me enough and had sent scouts out to see me.

With Wycombe new to the league I think he felt he needed someone with experience. The club had just sold Keith Scott to Swindon for £300,000 and I was seen as a solid replacement.

I went down to meet Martin and he was a lot like Ossie – a very down to earth guy. He made me an offer. Take it or leave it. I was desperate to play first-team football again so I signed the deal. I never asked for anything more than what was on offer and it was a little bit less than what I was on at West Brom, but I was sick of travelling miles to play in reserve games in front of crowds of about 50. I'd had enough of it. I knew I was at the back end of my career but I knew I had a couple of years left in me so I wanted more than reserve team football.

Wycombe were flying and had surprised everyone. The season before, while I had been enjoying my first season at West Brom, they had won the Conference by a clear 15 points. When I joined they were fourth in the Third Division and well and truly challenging for a second straight promotion. It was a nice change from the relegation battle I was watching from the sidelines at West Brom.

I was straight into the first team, which after a period of rotting away on the bench and in the reserves was a welcome boost. I made my third debut in a career that had by now lasted 16 years on 12 February 1994 at Craven Cottage. Fulham v Wycombe Wanderers in the southern area semi-final of the Autoglass Trophy. It was a 2-2 draw that we won on penalties. Now I have played with some interesting striking partners over the years – Speedie, Newell and Stapleton among them – but my experience at Wycombe was something new. Before Wycombe were promoted to the Football League, Tim Langford had been a postman. But like the others who packed in their former jobs to turn fully professional, he was ambitious, determined and a decent player.

I wasn't finding the net in the league games but I did finally get my first goal for Wycombe in the next round of the Autoglass Trophy, which was the southern area final. A two-legged affair with the winner getting a big day out at Wembley for the national final. We had just gone 2-0 down when Tim found me on the left of the area to slot home. We went on to lose 3-1 and could only win the return leg 1-0 and so missed out on the final, which Swansea went on to win.

I was off the mark after a bit of a slow start, and in the next game it took just 50 seconds for me to score my second, this time with a header in a 2-1 home win against Bury. It was a welcome relief for Martin as we had just lost three games on the bounce and desperately needed to turn that form around. I was in my stride but frustratingly I came off in the next game after my hamstring went. I missed the next few games, but the team continued to do well.

The injury didn't get me down. Far from it. I was back playing first team football, the club was pushing for promotion and I was having the time of my life. It was like starting all over again, except this time I was the experienced pro. My age apart, it was like being at Blackburn in the early days. It was a family club with a great manager and the players were a fantastic bunch who lived and breathed football without any sense of ego playing a part.

And when you combine that with the fact these lads had just realised their life's ambition of becoming professional football players, some of them at a very late age for football, then the sense of excitement that was around the place every day was understandable.

As a club, Wycombe had a rich non-league history and had recently celebrated its centenary. Under Martin, they had finally reached the Football League and the club really was riding the crest of a wave, pushing for a second successive promotion. In terms of footballing achievements, what Martin did with Wycombe probably ranks up there with Kenny and

Jack Walker taking Blackburn up to the Premiership.

The standard of football was much higher than I had expected. Martin's philosophy was to play to our strengths and not to worry about our deficiencies. A dream to a player like me. So long as we scored more than the opposition, he didn't care how many we conceded. We rarely practised set pieces, rather we'd play by instinct. Anyone would take a corner or throw-in and we weren't assigned positions to defend or attack at particular points in the game. Martin was much keener that we use our heads and take responsibility for situations ourselves. It made us an attractive attacking side.

The training facilities weren't ideal, but Adams Park Stadium was – and is – a great place to play. They used to have a ground that was renowned in the game for having a nasty slope, but Adams Park was purpose-built and has been improved over the years to hold about 10,000 people.

The proceeds from the sale of the old ground had been put to good use – and not just by developing the new stadium. Money was earmarked for Martin to make his players feel good about life in the league and we had hotel stop-overs for most away games. Martin was a god at Wycombe and if he had asked for gold-plated goalposts I think he would have been given them.

If tactics were never part of his make-up in those days, motivation certainly was. He had an uncanny ability to understand the needs of individuals and slot them into the requirements of the team.

He was perfectly happy for us to have a drink in the bar on the night before a game and, because he treated the players like grown-ups, they didn't abuse his generosity. This stemmed from having managed the team in non-league. You couldn't treat part-time footballers the same way you would a professional. But now these lads had turned pro, he couldn't change everything. In all honesty I couldn't believe we were allowed a drink on the Friday night before a game. I was used to sneaking a couple of cans to my room the night before a game – it was contraband – and now I didn't have to.

Martin trusted us not to be silly with it. We knew when to stop. Some players would have one or two and then go to bed. Some didn't drink at all. And there would be other players who would have four or five pints.

Glyn Creaser, our centre back, had only just turned pro at 34 or 35. He had worked for John Lewis for 20-odd years but he resigned from there just to get the chance to be a professional footballer. He was the sort of fella who could go in the bar, have a few pints, and then be absolutely fine the day after. He was a legend at Wycombe and a good drinking buddy.

Every away game with Wycombe was an overnight stop, so we had a lot of those nights in the bar. The boys all got on really well but we didn't tend to meet up after training and go out. Even after a match on a Saturday most of the boys would go their separate ways. Most had families to get back to and a lot of players didn't live locally. I was still living in Birmingham when I first signed and there were three or four of us who would share a lift.

We had fun and games at Wycombe and the lads could be as daft as any group of blokes can be, but you could only take it so far with Martin. He knew when to turn around and put a stop to something.

He was absolutely brilliant at motivating players. After a good win on a Saturday players might typically be given a day off on a Monday, but sometimes Martin would get us in when we weren't expecting it. And vice-versa, if we lost on a Saturday he might say, 'Don't come in until Thursday'. He was very good at things like that. He kept us on our toes.

During our time together at Wycombe I got to know Martin very well. There isn't much between us in terms of age – he's only seven years older than me – and I think it was useful for him to be able to speak to someone who had recently played at a high level with some of the best managers in the game. Alan Parry, the television commentator and a big Wycombe fan, was also someone I got to know well and the three of us and our partners would often share a drink. Alan later helped me get some work as a pundit for Sky Sports.

For the club and for me it was a great season. I was enjoying my game again and Martin's magic was working well.

After missing a month with my injury, I scored a last-minute equaliser at Rochdale and then, in the next game, I got the first in a 3-0 win over Walsall. Our form dipped and we didn't win any of the final five games, and I only scored once more, again against Rochdale in a 1-1 draw.

We finished the season fourth, a remarkable achievement, and though I know it sounds big-headed, I made it into Wycombe folklore.

Once again I was in the play-offs and once again I put my prejudices about the end-of-season lottery to one side. Carlisle was our first opponent and I scored in both legs. We did ourselves a huge favour winning the first 2-0 at Brunton Park, taking a two-goal cushion into the home tie. We were already 1-0 up, 3-0 on aggregate, when a long ball over the top dropped beautifully just in front of me. I had the beating of the Carlisle defenders and there was no way they were stopping me. I took a couple of touches and then slotted it under their keeper to put us 4-0 up. We were on our way. Carlisle got one but they had no way back.

What a feeling. I knew I was coming towards the end of my career, but what a way to do it – back to Wembley. Again. And back in another team with my old Blackburn room-mate Nicky Reid, who had now followed me to Wycombe after we had been together at West Brom.

Our opponent for the final was Preston who, under John Beck, were a nightmare to play against. Beck was at the opposite end of the managerial spectrum to Martin. There was a routine for everything and the style of play made Wimbledon at their worst look pretty. Long balls into the corners, long balls over the midfield, long balls to force throw-ins. It wasn't football as I knew it, but it was bloody effective.

There was some speculation that Beck had wanted to sign me before I joined the Wycombe revolution, but there were too many reasons I could never had done that. Firstly, I wasn't big enough and, more importantly, I would have hated playing that style of football.

What we did have on our side, though, was the knowledge of exactly how they would approach the game. We, on the other hand, didn't have routines, so god knows how anyone prepared to play against us.

Everyone was desperate to play their part in what could be the biggest moment in the history of the club. Paul Hyde, our keeper, was in a terrible state. His guts were mangled, he was being sick and had dreadful diarrhoea. He lost half a stone in the days leading up to the final and I would say he was about 20 per cent fit, but there was no way on earth he was going to miss this game.

Martin's team talk was one of the easiest he's ever given.

"Look, you know how to play them. We know what's coming. Get it on the ground, play football and let the ball do the work. Preston will get knackered."

And they did get knackered.

The first 20 minutes were incredible. The ball fizzed from end to end and we had the opportunities to make the game safe before the break but we went behind – a long throw, surprisingly enough, which led to an overhead kick.

We were level within a minute when I played a neat ball through the channel for Steve Thompson, who had been in the RAF, to score. But the joy was short-lived and we conceded again.

I couldn't believe we were losing at half-time – none of us could. But we stuck to our game plan and played the only way we knew. And then it happened.

A looping ball came from Dave Titterton in midfield. I was eight yards out with a defender on my back, I controlled it with my right foot and stuck a beauty away with my left. I'd scored at Wembley. After nearly 20 years in the professional game I had achieved something I had only previously dreamed of. Even at the time I understood how important it was to me on a personal level.

Even before we had equalised a second time, I never felt we could lose the game. We were just too good for them and we had a team with spirit and skill. And so it proved.

Our third was a great move. Steve Guppy played through to Thompson and he put a great ball through the defenders to me. I could have turned and struck but I saw Dave Carroll on the right and he was unmarked. I swivelled and passed into his path for a sweet finish.

I thought he might have returned the favour for our fourth but he beat three defenders, then turned two of them again to get the ball on his right foot before finishing a brilliant solo goal.

I even had time to 'score' one of the goals of my career from just inside their half. I was given offside. It was the wrong decision.

But what a day, what a season.

I was interviewed straight after the final whistle.

"You didn't want to play in the Third Division for very long did you, Simon?"

He was spot on. No, I didn't, and I was glad to have played a part in getting Wycombe into the Second. It was one of the best seasons of my career, even if it had only started with my transfer in February.

We went back to the ground and hosted a serious party.

It wasn't long before I was back at Wembley, this time for the 1994 Charity Shield to see my old club Blackburn take on champions Manchester United. The game is usually between the league champions and the winners of the FA Cup, but on this occasion United had won both, and so Rovers were the opposition as they had finished second in the league. Incredible considering we had come so close to blowing our promotion chances just two years before.

I never imagined life in the Second Division was going to be easy. And it wasn't. But Martin worked more miracles. He signed Cyrille Regis and he made me feel very good – not only was he an excellent player, but at 36 he was a year older than me!

We were, by some measure, the oldest strike force in the league. A combined age of 71. But while I was in pretty good nick, Cyrille was ridiculously fit and, if I'm honest, was more useful to Wycombe that season than I was. But as a partnership we were great.

Cyrille lived in Birmingham and, as the elder statesmen of the team, Martin told us we just had to come in from Thursday and gave us the first half of the week off. We would meet up and have a couple of drinks during the week and a chat – nothing over the top as Cyrille wasn't a big drinker. We would socialise more during the day than at night.

He was a really nice man who had time for everybody and would talk to anybody, including the fans. He was an absolute gentleman – but a beast on the pitch. He would wipe out a centre half and then apologise to them.

Cyrille was definitely one of the best I ever played with, even at the ripe old age of 36, and it really shook me when he died.

In many ways what we achieved in the 1994-95 season was more remarkable than the promotion campaign. A personal highlight was scoring the first ever goal at Huddersfield's McAlpine Stadium in the second league game of the season. We won 1-0. That gave us two wins from two after a comfortable 3-0 win over Cambridge at home on the first day of the season – a game I also scored in.

That season there was a restructuring taking place and five clubs were being relegated. I think we all felt we had to keep our noses clean to keep away from that pack, but Martin refused to even consider a season of consolidation. What was the point? He had always wanted us to play to our abilities, so there was no way we were going to be able to change that now and start trying to close games down. And anyway, our fans were used to real football and that approach would have bored them rigid.

At the top of the table there was only guaranteed promotion for the league champions and a play-off lottery for the teams from second to fifth. By new year we were third and had only lost four. We were out of the Coca Cola Cup and the Auto Windscreens Trophy, so there were no distractions.

And then we hit a run of rotten form to rival even the darkest days at Blackburn. In the run up to Easter we won just eight games. In true Garner style, I had my post-Christmas dry spell, but this one was the worst I ever went through. I didn't score in 14 league games. When I did finally break my duck, in a home game against Peterborough, we finally got the win we had been craving. But the damage had been done and we were down to seventh – two points off the play-offs.

Our form turned around and Martin's gamble almost came off. We finished sixth which, in most years, would have seen us into the play-offs, but we missed out by just three points. Huddersfield finished fifth and went on to win the play-offs to go up with Birmingham City. I scored 14 goals throughout the season and was the club's leading scorer. An honour for me in what would become, although I didn't know it at the time, my final season of playing regular professional football.

A week after the end of our season, Blackburn Rovers were crowned champions of England. I'd spent the day in Windsor having lunch and an extended drinking session with some friends and only learned the results when I got home late in the evening. I'd like to have celebrated. The only trouble was that I was already pissed and crashed into bed wearing a big smile.

There had been a lot more investment into that Blackburn team that won the Premiership title but a lot of my old mates were still there. And I was really happy for Kenny. I hadn't featured in his plans but he helped me get a move so I could keep playing. I'd played with Mark Atkins and Jason Wilcox back in the Second Division so to see them holding that trophy was wonderful. They really deserved it. And of course Mike Newell and

Bobby Mimms were still there, although thanks to Flowers, Sutton and Shearer they didn't get to play a great deal that season.

Later in the summer it was back to Wembley for the Charity Shield to summarise for BBC Radio Lancashire.

I cut a deal with the commentator that I'd watch the game in the bar, which was pretty close to the press box, and pop back to the microphone when something interesting happened.

No problem. For the first half anyway. I stuck to the brief and came back every few minutes to talk about the game. But it was a free bar and by the second half I could hardly get a word out. I got through it somehow and they have invited me back many times so I can't have been that bad.

After the game I went to talk with some of my old friends in the bar when I saw Jack Walker chatting to Terry Venables. I had no hesitation in going over to offer my congratulations to Jack on the title-winning season.

"Erm, Mr Walker ..."

I got halfway through the sentence and he immediately broke off from speaking to Venables and we nattered like long-lost buddies. We might not have had much else in common, but we were both Blackburn through and through.

Away from football that summer I did get the rare pleasure of going to the opening night of a new restaurant in Bray with my mate Paddy. I've no idea how it came about apart from the fact Paddy lived there and was a local businessman. The Fat Duck has gone on to become famous as the owner, Heston Blumenthal, has made a name for himself on TV making all sorts of weird and wonderful stuff. Back then it wasn't so fancy and I remember having steak and chips which was no better than average.

Martin left Wycombe to take over at Norwich City, who had just been relegated from the Premiership, and nobody I knew could fault his decision. He had served the club admirably. He took them from the semi-professional ranks to the brink of Division One, the highest level I played at. I owe him so much for rescuing my career, for giving me a chance to play the kind of football I had always wanted to play in an atmosphere that just couldn't be beaten.

As for the other players, you have to remember that two years earlier most of them had proper jobs in the real world. Thanks to Martin and the vision of the club, dreams had come true.

When Martin left for Norwich it was a sad day but one which brought back some of the best memories I'd had in the game.

So why did Alan Smith have to go and fuck it all up?

I'm not just saying that because he didn't fancy me much, though he obviously didn't. The whole place just lost its momentum from the minute he arrived. As managerial appointments go, the only one to rival it in my life in the game was that of Jim Iley at Blackburn.

So before I'm accused of whingeing and whining because he ended my professional career, let's lay a few facts on the line.

Under Martin we finished sixth in Division Two. Under Smith, we dropped to 12th. He dumped Steve Thompson, Paul Hyde and Terry Howard into non-league football. He changed the first team kit to resemble that of Crystal Palace, the club that had just sacked him after being relegated from the Premiership. He made us train at Bisham Abbey where the facilities were good, expensive and, coincidentally I'm sure, where he had his tennis lessons. And he wore very short shorts. On one occasion it was raining as we were walking on to the training pitch and we could see fake tan running down the back of his legs. One of the lads laughed and he never played for the club again. He presided over the worst attendance in the league history of the club and looked on as the Wycombe board announced record losses of £300,000 for the season.

Cyrille's contract was up and he went to Chester. Alan didn't want us older players. Some managers don't like having older players around as they don't want anyone to have an opinion, and this was certainly true of Alan. Perhaps he thought we would undermine his authority. He wanted younger players who would just do as they were told. He signed Miguel de Souza from Birmingham who went on to score a lot of goals for Wycombe. He was a chirpy lad who was popular with the supporters.

I was in and out of the side, starting a few games early on and getting a few appearances on the bench, but often not included in the squad at all, which I found frustrating having been the previous season's top scorer. Burnley had just been relegated into our division and I always had a good game against them, but Alan didn't even put me on the bench. I grabbed three goals for Wycombe that season. I thought I was playing quite well and was in good shape, but at the first whiff of loaning me out I was off to Torquay. They obviously wanted me pretty badly because they organised a chauffeur-driven car to get me there. I accepted the offer on the condition I wouldn't have to live in Devon. It was just too far from home.

And, in all honesty, that was the problem with Torquay in general and why they are always going to struggle – just about every game involves a million-mile round-trip. I trained at Wycombe from Monday to Wednesday, although that was tough because I didn't get on with the manager. And then I would drive down to Torquay on a Wednesday night to train Thursday and Friday and play on the Saturday.

They put me up in a hotel but it was a real pensioner hotel. Indoor bowls was about as lively as it got and everyone was in bed for 9pm. There was me and another lad from Doncaster who used to stay in the same hotel so we would go out and have a drink together to avoid going stir crazy or being dragged into the bingo hall.

I signed for Torquay at the back end of January and I enjoyed myself even though they were a poor side and finished the season at the very bottom of the league, only surviving because Conference champions Stevenage were refused entry to the League because their ground didn't measure up. Eddie May was the manager and doing his best in the most difficult of circumstances imaginable. Rodney Jack was playing and he was a great guy to have in the side because he was fast as lightning. And I wasn't. Rodney was a real talent and got a good move a few years later when Crewe paid a club-record £650,000 to sign him. Even though results weren't great, the team spirit in the dressing room was brilliant. It was such a good bunch of lads which made my time there really enjoyable, especially seeing as I wasn't getting anywhere near the Wycombe first team.

It was clear I wasn't wanted by Smith, who wanted me as far from Wycombe as possible. Back then our boots were provided by the club and the pair of Asics boots I had were dropping to bits. I called the kitman at Wycombe and asked him to get me some new ones.

"Sorry Simon, the gaffer says you can't have any."

"Tell him if he doesn't send me a new pair of boots I'm cancelling this loan and coming back to Wycombe."

Lo and behold, a new pair of boots was with me in Torquay the next day.

The chairman was a good laugh, too. Mike Bateson had this great habit of inviting players into the boardroom for a few bevvies after the game. He enjoyed a spot of ventriloquism, although he wasn't particularly good at it. One Friday before the derby game against Exeter City I was bored and convinced Ian Gore to go out for a few beers. We drew 2-2 and I missed a sitter. I was summoned to Mike's office on the Monday morning. I thought it was to sign off my expenses. All of a sudden the dummy emerged on the end of his right arm.

"I'm fining you two weeks' wages."

I can't believe I did it, but I replied to the dummy.

"Erm, why?"

"Because you were out on Friday night."

I was fined. By a bloody dummy. It was possibly the most bizarre experience of my footballing career.

And I also got to know the television presenter Helen Chamberlain pretty well, too. She really is a mad Torquay fan and used to drive from London to the game after presenting Soccer AM on Sky Sports. She would join us in the boardroom after games, although she didn't drink.

I played nine matches and got one goal for Torquay, my last in professional football. Obviously at the time I didn't realise the significance when I volleyed the ball past Fulham keeper Tony Lange on 3 February 1996. It wasn't a bad strike and it won me a bet. I knew Tony from my West Brom days and we had agreed that it was a pint on him if I scored and a pint on me if I didn't. I think buying the pint hurt more for Tony than picking the ball out of the net because he was never known for being the first to the bar.

When I got back to Adams Park I didn't get another game under Smith and I was starting to get a bit concerned for my future. My contract was up at the end of the season and I knew I had no chance of being offered anything with Smith, even though, at 36, I thought there was still a job I could do.

But nothing could prepare me for the way I left the full-time ranks.

Over the years, lots of people have asked me about moving into the coaching or management side of the game. And my answer has always been the same, that it's not for me. I don't want to be the guy who has to tell kids who have their hearts set on a career in the game that they're not up to scratch. I don't want to be the guy who has to show the door to an experienced player at a club he's served for most of his adult life.

Decisions have to be taken but those who do take the management route need to understand the responsibility they have for the careers and lives of others.

And Smith didn't.

After 20 years as a professional footballer I was told by letter that I was out of work. He didn't even have the decency to tell me face-to-face. I received a letter from the club secretary and that was that.

Alan was finally dismissed at the start of his second season after the club was humiliated 6-3 by Peterborough after leading 3-1. It took years for the club to recover and while I'm not a bitter person by nature, his treatment of me left an enduring bad taste in my mouth.

Martin O'Neill
Manager at Wycombe Wanderers from 1994 to 1995

A late sunny afternoon at Wembley Stadium. 1994. The second half of a Football League Fourth Division play-off game has started. Wycombe Wanderers, in its first season as Football League members, are trailing Preston North End by two goals to one, despite monopolising play in the first half of the game.

Some supporters haven't yet taken their seats for the resumption when a deafening roar reverberates all around the hallowed stadium. A wonderful equalising goal has been scored by the Wanderers' centre forward.

Never taking his eye off a cross-field lob he deftly controls the ball with his right foot and doesn't break stride as he glides past two Preston defenders and, with consummate ease, strikes a left-footed shot beyond the goalkeeper and into the net.

A goal of sublime beauty scored by a thirty-four-year-old footballer in the autumn of his career.

The scorer, Simon Garner, wheels away in delight, acknowledging the approval of both the Wanderers supporters and his admiring teammates. The goal inspires a magnificent second-half performance and when the referee blows the final whistle Wycombe Wanderers has beaten Preston North End 4-2 and clinched promotion into the Third Division at the first time of asking. Simon accepts the plaudits with almost immodest humility.

A few weeks earlier, his displays and goals against Carlisle in the two-legged play-offs semi-final had paved the way for this historic afternoon at Wembley. In a few months at Adams Park he had not only excelled himself he had been a major contributor to the club's promotion success. I could not ask any more from the little magician.

In truth, Simon had been doing all his career what the legendary manager Brian Clough once said was the most difficult art in football – scoring goals.

I had watched Simon's career from afar, blossoming with Blackburn Rovers where he remains a cult figure.

Not the tallest, Simon's low centre of gravity and wonderful ball control gave him an innate ability to swivel either side of his marker and shoot at goal. His proud goalscoring record at Ewood Park bears testimony to this.

By early January 1994, Simon was playing for West Bromwich Albion. We had sold our centre forward, Keith Scott, to Premiership club Swindon Town. Keith's departure left a large void in our team and filling it was not going to be easy. I turned my attention to Simon who although not playing regularly at the Hawthorns may not have wanted to drop down the Football league ladder, Albion being a vastly bigger club than newly promoted Wycombe Wanderers.

But, in conversations with him, he expressed a strong interest in coming to Adams Park, giving me the hope that a deal could be done. And so it happened.

Simon's arrival at the Buckinghamshire club was an absolute game-changer. He became an instant success on the field and proved to be a very popular figure not only on the terraces but in the dressing room as well. More than a little set in his ways, Simon enjoyed a cigarette and the occasional drink. I did not have a problem with that, having played myself with some teammates who also enjoyed a smoke and a pint, but who proved themselves to be top class footballers on the field of play.

Simon's performances on the pitch were my concern – and didn't he perform for the club.

Simon's footballing career has come to an end. He is this very day revered at Blackburn where he was inducted into the club's Hall of Fame some years ago. He is also extremely well regarded by all at Adams Park. A really fine career envied by many a footballer.

But in my opinion Simon had the talent to have been a top-quality player plying his trade in the biggest league in football for at least a decade. And I'm sure, when he sits down in the corner of his local pub reminiscing with some old friends, he probably thinks the same as I do.

CHAPTER 14

Dropping into non-league

1996

The treatment I received from Alan Smith was shoddy to say the least. I had been a professional for two decades and whatever he thought of me as a player or person, I deserved better.

And so did Wycombe. They spent a few years struggling in the lower midtable of the Second Division before being relegated in 2004. I was really pleased to see their fortunes changing in recent years and when Gareth Ainsworth took them to the Championship that really was the fairy tale the club and the fans deserved.

I remember Gareth coming through at Blackburn, just about. He was just starting out in the youth team when I was reaching the back end of my Ewood career. But what a great lad he is. Whenever I saw him down at Wycombe he was all over me. It was embarrassing sometimes because he did such a good job as a manager of that club and yet whenever we were together he told me I was his hero. He was and still is a Rovers fan and saw me scoring the goals in the 80s, so it was nice to get that recognition from someone doing so well in the game.

When Wycombe were in the Championship I summarised with BBC Radio Lancashire's Andy Bayes when they played against Blackburn at Adams Park. I said to Andy that I would go and ask Gareth if he would come and do an interview. Andy couldn't believe it. At 2.15pm, 45 minutes before kick-off, he came up to talk to us and left his coaches to do the warm-up. And then all he wanted to talk about was me. Needless to say, I get on very well with him.

I was asked to present him with a special shirt when he played his 600th game for Wycombe. It was before a game against Port Vale and he loved it. I think it meant a lot to him that it was me handing it over, and it meant a lot to me, too. He played for Port Vale as well so both sets of fans gave him a standing ovation. He will admit himself, he wasn't the most gifted footballer, but he gave everything in every game he played. He never stopped running – and was as fit as a fiddle – and he's taken that dedication and hard work into management.

I was out of work now for the first time in my life. I had been gainfully employed as a footballer since Blackburn offered me the chance to sign back when I was 16 years old and my two club moves since then had been relatively smooth. Now I was without a club, although I was confident that I would be soon, though I was realistic enough to know that it was unlikely to be in the full-time professional ranks.

When I was shipped out to Torquay I was approached by Woking, who were then one of the leading lights in the Conference. Their assistant manager came to see me play a number of times for Wycombe reserves when my loan period ran out in Devon and I was assured they would be interested in signing me when I became available.

Sure enough, within a few days of me being release by Wycombe, Geoff Chapple, Woking's manager, gave me a call.

"Still interested, Simon?"

I really didn't need much persuading. I had only been playing in Wycombe's reserves so there weren't any league clubs knocking on the door to sign me. And I was no longer interested in trying to find a club up north as Mandy and I had split up and I now had a partner who lived and worked in the south.

Woking was a first-class set-up. It was one of the top clubs outside the League, boasting a number of England semi-professional internationals and Clive Walker, who was even older than me, was their star striker. From a playing perspective, I was unlikely to get a better offer. Woking had just finished second in the Conference to Stevenage and so were knocking on the door of the Football League. Could they be another Wycombe?

The deal wasn't bad. They were prepared to pay me £300 a week and with no other skills to my name I was hardly in a position to turn down the money. It wasn't a fortune but it was better than signing on and I could live on that amount.

All seemed fine to start with. I felt fit and strong and I was performing well in training. The only trouble was that I was only making the bench. Clive had played for Chelsea and was still a great player. I got on with him and we had a laugh together, but Geoff preferred him to me. A few weeks earlier they had been desperate to sign me. Now I was being called into the manager's office. I was fairly confident it wasn't going to be the offer of a pay rise of an invitation to dinner. And I was right.

"I want to pay you off."

I had to think quickly. They owed me around £9,000 on the balance of my contract and if I took it I would be free to find another club. Given that I hadn't kicked a ball for Woking it would make good sense for me to take the money.

"I understand."

"We're prepared to pay you £4,500."

Now hold on a minute. This wasn't right. Woking had approached me and I had done all I could to prove myself. I was convinced I could have done a job if only Geoff would give me a chance. If they had got their sums wrong and couldn't afford me than that wasn't my fault. I was having none of it and I told him so.

Eventually a deal was worked out and I was loaned to Walton and Hersham, who were then in Division One of the Ryman League, two steps down the ladder from Woking. Woking would pay half my wages with Walton and Hersham making up the difference.

I can't deny that my pride was hurt. Just over a year previously there had been the possibility, if we had achieved promotion again, of playing out my days in the First Division with Wycombe. Still, I trained with Dave Russell's side and thoroughly enjoyed it. On my debut in November I played well and scored. The standard might not have been great, but I was back in the game.

In the bar afterwards I requested permission to miss training the following week because I had to visit Blackburn to discuss my ongoing divorce proceedings.

"No problem, Simon. I'll see you on Saturday for the game."

If only.

Gareth Ainsworth
Apprentice at Blackburn Rovers, 1989 to 1991

I've been a Blackburn Rovers fan since I was a lad. And a Simon Garner fan for just as long. I was six when I got my first season ticket and started watching the Rovers with my dad, Bill. It was the early 80s and Simon Garner was the main man. He immediately became my hero and has been ever since.

I knew I wanted to be a footballer and I based my whole game around what I saw from Simon. I watched him avidly every game and I just wanted to be like him. He was so quick in and around the box and was always in the right position. I ended up as a winger, but I was a goal-scoring winger, and that was down to Garns. I saw him banging in the goals and heard the fans singing his name and that was just what I wanted to be.

I grew up in an area of Blackburn called Pleckgate and my brother Liam and I would play on the local fields and pretend to be Rovers players. I was always Simon Garner. That was the impact he had on me from such an early age and continues to have to this day. Kids these days look at players like Messi and Ronaldo, or Harry Kane, or if you go back a bit players like Paul Gascoigne. For me it was Simon and it always will be.

I went to an open day down at Ewood Park when I was about to meet him. I had a picture taken sitting on his knee and it found its way into the papers a few years later when I signed for Blackburn.

One thing I always remember about Garns was that every time we got a corner he would just stroll about and walk around the box, it was as if he wasn't interested, almost to stay a bit incognito. He would lean on the back post and even put his hands on it. He would just hover there. And he scored so many goals by doing that. The number of times it flies over to that back stick, and Simon had a habit of just being there. He's the record goal scorer but a good percentage of those must have been tap-ins at that back post.

Years later, I played for John Beck at Preston and Lincoln and he was massive on set pieces. He always told me the back post was the POMO – the position of most opportunity – at any set piece, so Garns really was ahead of his time there. He just knew where to be to get the goals and I think the Rovers team at that time played to that strength brilliantly.

When I signed as a YTS I made a massive point of being around Garns as much as possible. When I watched him as a kid I didn't realise he was such a big smoker and drinker. We used to get changed at Ewood Park and then drive up to Pleasington to train. I was amazed just how many fags he would manage to get in at the ground and then up at the park before and after training.

He absolutely hated pre-season training. We used to do this run under Don Mackay called the Pleasy Run. Tony Parkes would be leading the way – he was a real fit bloke – and we had players like Mark Atkins who were really fit as well. Proper runners. And then you had Garns who was the superstar top scorer and he just could not run long distance. He was so bad at it. And so was I in my early days.

These experienced pros would be coming past me and saying, 'Come on Ainsworth, get to the front, you're only a lad'.

And in the end I could only beat one person and it was Simon Garner. I was okay with that. Simon was my hero and he was banging the goals in every week. If I was one in front of him that must be okay.

He told me that it didn't matter what you did on the runs, it's what you do on the pitch that counts. If you're at the front of the running but you're not a good footballer it counts for nothing. And he was right. These days everyone has to be ridiculously fit but, back then, hearing those words from someone like him, really gave me some comfort.

As a striker, Simon used to love crosses into the box and as I became a winger I tried to model myself on Ian Miller.

Simon told me: "Look at Dusty. Whenever there's a chance to cross it in, he does. He doesn't check back, doesn't mess about with it, he just gets it in the box."

The worst thing a winger can do in the eyes of a centre forward like Garns is pretend to cross it and not cross it. He was an absolute poacher and he knew where that ball was going to go before anyone else did.

"I'm going to make my run based on that cross and if you don't cross it, I've wasted my run. And the more times I waste my run, the more pissed off I'm going to get."

And that was a really good bit of advice. I was lucky enough to play in the Premiership with Wimbledon and my game never really changed. Beat the full back and get the cross in. The target was John Hartson. I would have loved to have played with Simon and got a cross in for him. I may have played a reserve game with him but I never made it to the first team which was a shame.

I played against him twice in 1994 for Preston when he was with Wycombe. The second time was in the play-off final at Wembley which was absolutely heart-breaking for me. We lost the game 4-2 and Wycombe went up. I was only 21 so it was really tough to take. I remember Garns scoring in that game. He came up to me at full time and put his arm around me. He was in tears - it was obviously a massive game for him and it meant a lot for him to score and win at Wembley. He told me he was sorry and that I had played well. He told me I was going to have a great career. And coming from my hero that meant a great deal.

Simon had been so close with Blackburn so was no stranger to play-off heartache. I was at Crystal Palace in 1989 and that was a really tough one to take. Garns had been there all through the 80s and seen Blackburn through all the tough times and all those years when they had no money and managed to survive in the Second Division. It was Garns's goals that kept them up. When the money came in from Jack Walker the club was able to sign the likes of Speedie and then Shearer, but without Simon Garner that club would never have won the Premiership. It would probably have fallen down into the Third Division long before.

I retired from playing after my 600th game while I was at Wycombe and Garns was there to present me with a Wycombe shirt with 600 on the back. I still have the shirt in a big frame with and a photo of me and Simon - the person who, apart from my dad, was probably the most important in terms of shaping my footballing career. That photo is in my office and everyone who comes in can see it and I am really proud of that because not only was it a nice recognition for my career and to have played so many games at every level of English football, but I also had my hero there as well.

What's great for me is that Simon finished his career down in this part of the world so I still see a lot of him. We've done radio together and we'll get together for the odd glass of wine. We often share a text message whenever the Blackburn v Burnley game is on. And whenever the Blackburn job comes up he's always texting me because I tend to get linked with it.

A great player for Blackburn, and for Wycombe, and a great man. There's only one Simon Garner.

CHAPTER 15

Going down

1996

The minute I moved to West Brom my marriage was doomed. A great drinking crowd and a couple of nights a week away from home – life was good. Then when Keith Burkinshaw made it clear I wasn't going to figure in his first team plans, it really started to crumble.

The reserves played mid-week, usually Wednesdays, but I still had to be around in case I got called up for the Saturday. Two nights away turned into two nights at home. Mandy asked me to find another club, preferably one closer to home. And by home I mean Blackburn, not Birmingham.

I remember the conversation well.

"I've been offered a new club."

"Where?"

"Wycombe."

"Where's that?"

"About 100 miles south of Birmingham."

Silence. Then the look. Then the words. Then the screams. Then there was no turning back. Then there was no marriage. Then the divorce started.

The writing had been on the wall for some time. Living away was tough at times and, yes, I missed the boys, but I had a bloody good time living with Stuart in Birmingham. And at the end of the day, I didn't really have a choice in the matter, my football career could have flatlined if I hadn't signed for a new club, and Wycombe was the only option I had, so I had to take it.

I guess signing for them was the proverbial straw that broke the camel's back. Or something like that.

Everything was fine to start with, genuinely fine. It was for the best – for us, for the boys. It was over.

She had a solicitor, I had a solicitor, and I was told it would take at least five years to sort the divorce out. I thought that was ridiculous but what could I do?

After a couple of years we didn't appear to be getting anywhere and I knew something had to change. I had to meet with Mandy and her solicitor once every two or three months in Blackburn at the county court, which is right in the shopping centre in the middle of town. A bugger to get to, especially when you're driving up from miles away. Mercifully the court is very close to the big multi-storey car park and so I didn't have to make my way across town trying to avoid attention. I've no doubt people would be well-meaning, but it's hardly what you want when you're on your way to a courtroom to discuss dissolving a marriage.

We'd sit there – me and Mandy, our respective legal advisers and a district judge – in a small upstairs room around a table for an hour and talk about sod all. It was costing me a fortune so I decided to look after my own affairs which, in hindsight, probably wasn't the most brilliant idea I ever had.

Now I was on my own and I really couldn't see any difference in the proceedings, except my pocket wasn't quite so light every time I left Blackburn. Another five or six times we went through the process. I'd drive the four hours to Blackburn from Berkshire, park on the multi-storey car park near the court, pass the time of day with the security guard, head up the stairs to the room with the table, talk for an hour, go home. Everything was fine, if you count wasting time, effort and money as fine. We'd talk about the kinds of thing you'd expect. How much maintenance I was going to pay, what I'd pay for on top of that. The kinds of things, in fact, two adults who have known each other for a decade and a half should be able to discuss without a bunch of strangers helping you out. But that's divorce for you.

When we first split up I was paying all Mandy's bills at the house in Blackburn and, while we weren't getting on, I didn't mind. Mandy stayed at home and looked after our boys, so it was important I saw her right. Money has never been the greatest motivator for me. I've always been happy to get by with the basic essentials – bed, food, beer, fags. Perhaps that's why I didn't make more money out of the game. Mind you if I had, then the divorce would have ended up costing me even more.

I was paying about £500 a month in bills, plus the mortgage and whatever the kids wanted. And that was before my own living expenses in Birmingham which, given the amount of partying, were quite substantial. While I was at the peak of my earnings at this time, it was only £600 a week. I use the word 'only' with some trepidation because I think anyone would swap their job, however much they were earning, for mine at that point – playing football with some great players in a very exciting team was magnificent. At the same time, just three or four years later, players in my position were being paid five or 10 times that amount.

And so it went on – and I never missed a payment. I had no reason to suspect that my visit north in November 1996 would be any different. I stayed at a friend's the night before but otherwise followed the usual routine. Parked on the multi-storey, walked down the steps on to King William Street, took a look in the window at Marks and Spencer, then slipped round the side of BHS and into the court building.

"All right Simon?"

"Fine, thanks."

And I was. It had been a good drive up. I was getting a decent run-out with Walton and Hersham – on a decent whack – and I only had to train twice a week. All was well with the world.

Then the security guard said something I'll never forget. Not that it was anything special, far from it. It was mundane, but it was unexpected, though it didn't register until much later that it had any significance at all.

"You're downstairs today."

No big deal. I'd been going to the court every couple of months for just over two years, every time in the same room, and I thought nothing of the change of location. But as soon as I walked through the door I knew something was going on.

Instead of walking into a small room, maybe 12ft square, with just a single table in it, I was confronted by a whole mass of new faces. There was a woman sitting at a desk with her fingers hovering over a machine like she was on Judge Judy or something. Another was doing something or other, I don't know what. Mandy was sitting with her solicitor but now she had a barrister as well. This was new. At the back of the court was Mandy's mum and two smartly dressed blokes. Smartly dressed and identically dressed – definitely not police, definitely not security – though I didn't give them a second thought. Why should I? I didn't know how courts worked. My only experiences with court were the visits to the small upstairs room with the table. But I had this feeling and it started nagging me.

In reality, the feeling probably came later when I'd had the chance to think about the day. The security guard telling me about the room change, the new faces in court, the smartly, identically dressed men.

"All rise."

This was also new. This isn't right. We're not sitting round doing the usual.

Mandy's barrister called me into the witness box.

"Are you Simon Garner of 7 Bridge Court, Maidenhead."

"No. It's Simon Garner of 1 The High Street, Bray."

Maybe with hindsight I could have been a bit more honest here. Technically I was based at my car dealer mate Paddy McClure's house in Bray. But I had been spending a lot of time at my girlfriend Heather's in Maidenhead. But for obvious reasons I didn't want this to be widely known at the time.

I probably should have seen all this coming as Mandy had put a private detective on my trail while I was living in the south. There had been a knock at the door one day and this bloke handed me a brown envelope and cleared off. When I looked inside it was full of pictures he had taken of us. It led to some difficult questions about where I was living and the standard of accommodation I could afford.

A pause.

"Have you disposed of certain monies?"

Back then, when a footballer turned 35 they were given a lump sum of cash by the PFA, which was based on a percentage of your salary at a certain point in time. I don't know if they still do this, although I doubt it as most players earn a bloody fortune and the whole system would probably go bankrupt. I think the idea was that it would help players as they came to the end of their career who could easily get very skint very quickly. So in 1994 I got £25,000. Mandy had asked for – and got – an injunction on me spending the money. Fair enough, it was going to form part of the divorce settlement.

A year after I received the money I rang the court at Blackburn. I had a simple request. I wanted to know if the injunction still stood and could I spend any of the money yet. I was told, quite clearly, that the injunction was spent and, yes, I could now access the cash. I've never been one for tidying up the details and I know now I should have had this in writing, but there was a shiny Vauxhall Calibra sitting on the forecourt of Bob Dickinson's garage in Walton-le-Dale near Preston begging me to buy it. So I did. It was the first new car I'd had in years. When I say new, I don't exactly mean brand new – the Walker revolution came too late for me to properly benefit. I'd asked Bob, a mate, to keep his eyes open for a car for me and he found the Calibra. It cost me nine and a half grand and I had it for years – it was knackered by the time I got rid of it.

I also paid off some debts, but these weren't gambling debts like one of the papers said, just credit cards. Gambling was never really my scene – beer and cigarettes were my vices. Playing a few hands of cards on the team bus was about as far as it ever got for me and I'd never lose more than £20 in a session.

The answer was yes. I had disposed of certain monies.

The barrister carried on with his questions. The judge asked a few more. All connected with money. Basically they were asking, "What have you done with the money?" I told them what I had done, what I had spent the money on and about my understanding of the injunction. But it transpired I'd been given the wrong information. The injunction still stood. Why I had been told differently, I just can't say.

"Please stand, Mr Garner."

The judge looked up.

"On the evidence presented, Mr Garner, I find you in contempt of court."

I'm not entirely sure what he meant by that. But it was a damned sight easier to understand than what he said next.

"I am, therefore, sentencing you to nine months in prison."

The words echoed around my head. I felt dizzy and sick. My knees went weak. The judge walked out of the room. Mandy ran out of the room. Her mother chased her. I lost all sense of time and space. The room was hazy. I needed a fag.

I had absolutely no idea it was coming. All I expected was to go to the room at the top of the building and have the usual chat. Now I was being sent to prison. By the time my head stopped spinning, probably no more than a minute at most, the room was empty except for the woman who had been typing and the two guys in the uniforms, which I now recognised for what they were. I sipped on some water – my mouth was so dry. I was shattered.

And then a thought hit me. How much is my bloody car park bill going to be in nine months?

As far as I knew I'd done nothing wrong. I'd never missed any payments, I'd always arrived at court on time. The contempt was based on the private detective's report saying I lied about where I lived, which I hadn't, and breaking the injunction on spending the money, which I had. Whatever the whys and wherefores, I was now in big trouble. Big, big trouble.

But all that would come into focus was the bloody car. That's what landed me in this mess in the first place and, if I didn't do something quickly, it would land me with a bloody great parking fine. So I thought I'd better nip out and move it.

"Okay if I nip out and move the car? It's on the multi-storey and I don't want nine months' worth of parking tickets on it when I get out."

Not surprisingly, the question was ignored.

"If you'll come with us downstairs, Mr Garner."

Well, I've seen it on the telly. From Kojak to The Bill. I know you can at least make a phone call.

"Can I make a phone call?"

"No."

This was getting silly. I've spent my whole adult life being kicked from every angle and relishing the challenge of getting back up and back to it, but this was different. The rules had changed. I couldn't kick back. So I asked nicely.

"Look, please, I've got my mobile with me. Do you mind if I just make a couple of calls?"

In all my time as a footballer I'd had one freebie. It was the night I scored five against Derby and I accepted a meal on the house at the Bull's Head in Wilpshire with a mix of embarrassment, pride and genuine appreciation.

"Simon, it's on me – great game today."

This, the second freebie, was a long time coming but I was no less grateful.

"We really aren't supposed to do this, Simon, but we know who you are. Go on, make your calls."

First on my list was Heather, who I'd left the night before saying I'd be back for tea. I got through first time.

"I've got us lasagne, what time will you be home?"

She didn't find it funny when I said August. Those were not tears of joy.

Bob Dickinson was next. I'd stayed with him the previous night and we had a great time.

"Enjoy that pint, Simon, you might be going to prison tomorrow!"

We laughed.

"Piss off!"

We laughed some more. Ho ho.

It was Bob, you'll remember, who sold me the bloody car which started all this.

"Look, Bob, my car's on the car park, can you come and get it?"

"Why"

"Because I'm going to prison."

"Yeah, right."

I wanted to flatten him.

"Bob, this is serious. I'm going down for nine months. The battery's running out on my mobile and I am not joking. My car's on the car park. It's on level one. I'll leave the keys here. Go and get the car. I can't afford a nine-month parking ticket."

He got the message and just in time because the phone went dead. I sat drinking coffee – I needed something a lot bloody stronger – and smoking my last fag of freedom and tried to get my head round what was happening. Shit, I didn't even have a lawyer.

"Ready?"

"What for?"

"We're going now."

"Going where?"

"We're going to Preston jail."

It really hadn't sunk in. Having a pair of handcuffs clamped round my wrists soon sorted that out. But it was still difficult to comprehend. I'd never been in trouble with the police, never broken the law. I didn't have some Swiss bank account where I'd stashed my millions from football. I wasn't exactly what you would call a rich man. Never have been. Never will be. But I doubt if that's the way people at that time were viewing footballers.

Blackburn Rovers had recently won the Premiership with a team including two British record signings – Alan Shearer and Chris Sutton – who were earning a fortune. By association, and as a former fans' favourite, people probably thought I earned a fortune as well and that I was up to something devious. I know some thought I was being done for not looking after the kids properly or evading tax – but it was much simpler than that. I had made a mistake and didn't even know I'd made it. And my sentence was harsher than for most burglars. That's justice for you.

In the room below the court the two prison officers told me not to worry, that I would be out in four months. Some comfort. It was the 18th of November, less than a week to my birthday. My kids had birthdays coming up and it was just five weeks to Christmas. I was going to be in jail at Christmas. And I was wearing handcuffs.

The handcuffs really didn't feel necessary. I mean, I had always hated running and I wasn't about to start now. The lads had obviously never watched a training session down at Pleasington.

I got into the back of a Volvo with absolutely no idea what was going on. We drove to Preston nick – about a 20-minute journey – and ended up in a waiting room at the prison. There were bars on the windows.

CHAPTER 16

At Her Majesty's pleasure

A guard looked at me.

"What are you doing here Simon?"

"I don't bloody know. I haven't a clue."

I was in a state of shock with just six fags in my pocket. I knew I should have asked them to stop at a shop on the way.

I waited for an hour on my own. It was the pits, like sitting in a toilet without the smell – or at least the smell of a toilet. The smell of 'institution' was there, though – stale bodies, stale food, stale cheap tobacco.

Now I'm quite happy getting naked in the company of men. It went with the job as a footballer. I had bathed alongside hundreds of different burly blokes during my almost two decades in the game. But I did not feel so comfortable doing it in a prison. I stripped off and was given a set of prison overalls – very fetching. They took everything off me – keys, wallet, basically all my possessions – except the cigarettes. The lighter went, though.

Another waiting room, this one with a grubby bunch of blokes, and I sat there for two hours. It was eerie, the conversation revolving only around whether anyone had any fags. I kept quiet, I only had half a dozen – certainly not enough to share with the twenty or so blokes who, quite frankly, looked like criminals. I wondered which one of these gentlemen I'd be sharing a cell with.

Eventually a warder arrived and started directing these guys, whose only discernible physical attributes ranged from mean-looking to tough-looking. They seemed perfectly at ease in their surroundings.

The only exceptions were me and a bloke in the corner who was in for drink driving. We looked as mean and tough as laboratory mice.

People kept walking in, prisoners who had just been sent down.

"All right mate, what are you in for this time?"

It was like a youth club for hard nuts. I shared a cell with a bloke called Alan, from Blackpool. It was his third conviction for drink driving. Pillock. Although it was something of a relief as I had been terrified about who I was about to be put in a cell with. A drink-driver was probably not going to be the dangerous mad man I had been worried about.

Bunk bed, toilet (flushable), sink, table, barred window, cream walls, six by ten. It's amazing the detail you can pick up when there are so few distractions. Within a minute of me stepping into the room there was a knock at the door.

"You all right in there? Do you want anything?"

I thought it was a warder. It wasn't. It was Dunc. I don't know who Dunc was, but I was glad to hear from him. I assumed he was a Blackburn fan who had heard I was on the wing.

"Are you all right, son?"

"No, not really."

"What do you need?"

"I need a pillow and I could do with some matches."

Five minutes later I had a pillow and a box of matches. Another half an hour passed and this time it was a warder at the door.

"Garner?"

"Yes, that's me."

"If you're thinking of appealing you need to fill in this form."

Appeal? Of course I'm going to bloody appeal. He also told me there had been a call from a firm in Manchester, George Davis and Co, which worked on behalf of the PFA and had promised a solicitor would be with me the next day.

I hardly slept at all. It just kept running round my head – what the hell am I doing here? This isn't right. Looking back I wondered why I wasn't more scared, but Dunc's visit made me feel quite strong. I was known, I was a personality of sorts. I'd be all right.

The next morning, after breakfast, I got the message I was moving on to Kirkham open prison. Cuffs on again – as if I was going to do a runner, the warders clearly didn't know my current state of fitness – and into the back of a Black Mariah.

"You get your kit from over there and then they'll tell you which hut you're going in."

Kirkham's an old RAF camp – long huts, flat landscape and about as inviting as cold porridge. Which is appropriate.

The regime, as well as the surroundings, was very different to my brief experience of Preston. There were eight or ten rooms to a hut – cells would be the wrong word because you weren't locked in – a television room, showers, and a bath.

"You're in B2. Find a bed."

Out of all the rooms in B2 hut there were just two beds left. In one I could see all manner of pictures and paraphernalia about Liverpool Football Club. In the other room, all I could see were pictures of topless women. And I didn't want to see his paraphernalia.

So went for the scouse football fan. At least we'd have something to talk about. I made my bed up. Then started to feel isolated. Something will happen, I was thinking. I'm going home in a minute. All of a sudden this huge geezer walked into the room. Huge he was. Built like a breezeblock shithouse, mid-twenties. Scary.

"All right?" I said. He looked at me then turned round and blanked me completely, never said a word. Double scary.

"Hello, I'm Simon. How are you?"

He was silent. Then I saw the scar on his face – from chin to forehead. Scary no longer seemed a strong enough word. My life would probably have flashed in front of my eyes if I wasn't too busy shitting bricks.

He was messing about in a drawer at the end of his bed then stopped abruptly. He turned, stood up, and stared down at me.

"You're Simon Garner, aren't you?"

I looked at his pictures of Liverpool and I thought, shit, I hope he doesn't remember the goals I scored against them!

"Er, yeah."

"You nearly knocked us out of the FA Cup."

Oh dear.

"Nice one, man. I'm Pete, pleased to meet you."

Phew.

And as this great shovel of a hand crushed my fingers, I could feel the weight fall off my shoulders in that split second of relief. And so we talked about football, about me scoring against Liverpool, which he thankfully didn't hold against me. But the conversation took an odd turn.

"I've enjoyed talking with you, Simon, but being in here is a bit like playing for a football team."

Eh?

"You can't do it on your own. You need people to help you out."

Erm.

"And I'm going to look after you."

Which I have to say, if only for a few seconds as I recalled a couple of jokes about prisons and showers, caused me some concern.

"Whenever you're in this hut, I'm your minder. We have tea at 5.30pm, we get locked up at…"

I breathed a sigh of relief. What a grand lad!

Over tea the prison routine was explained more fully and, if I'm being honest, it wasn't as bad as I had imagined. There was a lot of freedom of movement and the food was okay.

I do worry about people's perceptions of this more relaxed approach to treating prisoners, and you have to remember that Kirkham was for low-risk inmates only. I know there are many who believe a prison regime should be tough, aggressive even, that prisoners deserve punishment in its bluntest terms. But can you imagine not having easy access to your loved ones, not being able to meet your mates, not being able to go to the match on Saturday or work on Monday? That's the punishment: being, as lawyers like to say, deprived of one's liberty.

A case in point.

"Do you need anything?"

I had cigarettes for now – priority number one sorted, but I needed a phone card. Pete, God bless him, lent me one. And then I went to use it. There was, naturally, a queue, as there was every evening. The phones were turned on at 6pm and lock-up was at 8.30pm. With queues of up to 90 minutes to use the phone the only way to guarantee making a call was by missing tea. Even if people do hold that prisoners should be punished as well as being kept out of society for a while, does it serve anyone's interests that a dad can't say good night to a child because there aren't enough telephones?

We're still, by the way, on my first day at Kirkham, my second of incarceration, and I was really starting to regret my decision to dispense with my lawyer despite the assurance of an imminent visit by a PFA representative.

Pete and I were nattering in the room after tea when – at last – there was a knock on the door at 7.30pm. But the little lad in the prison garb who poked his head round the door didn't look much of a brief.

"Simon Garner?"

"Yeah."

"Somebody wants to see you in C2."

"Who?"

"John wants to see you in C2."

The distant tinkle of alarm bells could be heard.

"I don't know any John."

"He wants to see you in C2."

This was now an instruction, not a request. I lit a cigarette, as much to look hard as to try to calm down, and pointed to Pete.

"Mind if my mate comes along?"

"He's not coming."

"What do you mean?"

"He's not coming."

Then he ran off. And Pete and I carried on talking. Half an hour later he was back.

"Simon, for your own good, come to C2."

The tone was now urgent-approaching-desperate.

"Right. He'll come, but I'm coming, too."

Thank you again Pete.

On the end of a bed in a well-turned-out room in C2, John was relaxing. I learned immediately that he came from Blackburn and was a big Rovers fan. Thank God for that! Seconds later I knew he 'ran' HMP Kirkham. I knew it because he told me. Any suspicions he might be winding me up were dismissed almost instantly because he was certainly well connected.

"I knew you were coming today."

"How did you know?"

"I had a message from Preston nick. They let me know."

I didn't ask, but I'd still like to know who 'they' were. Then he took me by surprise, because up until this point, what with all the trouble it had taken to get me there, it felt like an interrogation or, at best, a job interview.

"What do you need?"

My preconceptions about prison daddies – based only on having seen Ray Winstone wielding a snooker ball-filled sock in the film Scum – were beginning to feel heavy handed.

"I've got a phone card now but I could do with some tobacco."

"Okay."

The lackey produced some.

"You're in B2 aren't you?"

"Yeah."

"Who's looking after you?"

Pete was just out of vision by the door.

"Well, Pete. He's here now. He's looking after me well."

"Good. But from now on Andy is looking after you when you go for a meal. If you're going to the gym, Dave looks after you. When you're at work, Steve looks after you, and when you've got your spare time, if you go to the library or anywhere else, Tony looks after you."

Everywhere I went after that, my team of minders would pop up with a "Hello Simon, everything all right?" I'd never experienced anything like this level of celebrity in football, and it was a weird feeling.

"Hi Simon, I'm Keith. Dave's ill. I'll be with you in the gym."

Bloody hell. A real star at last! All I needed now was a pair of shades and a stretch limo. Looking back I was really quite lucky. If I hadn't been a footballer and John hadn't been a Blackburn fan I might not have been quite so well looked after. In that situation, you have to use whatever means you can to give yourself an advantage and stay safe.

I got a real cushy job in the laundry. It helped that the guy who ran it was from Darwen and was a big Blackburn fan. The work was okay but the money was terrible: £4.50 a week. A packet of fags and a £2 phone card and you're into overdraft. And you didn't even get paid in cash, it was credited to your account at the tuck shop. Like everyone else, I latched on to the fact you could get two-and-a-half ounces of baccy, a phone card and a few teabags for that, so it was bye bye Silk Cut. All things considered it wasn't turning out to be a bad day. I even got to meet my new solicitor.

Roger Davies was a great bloke and a straight-talker and I immediately felt things were getting sorted out. He was already working on an appeal and suggested I get a barrister. Now I know it was important and I was in jail and desperately needed to get out, but I knew I wouldn't be able to afford the £750-an-hour or whatever. Shit, I was on Legal Aid. So I asked Roger to contact a barrister I knew, Stephen Dodds – a mad Blackburn Rovers fan. Stephen's uncle was a really keen fan as well. He died at a game away at Carlisle and his widow presented a trophy to the club, The Arthur Todd Memorial Cup. I was the first winner for the five I scored against Derby and Stephen presented it to me. The first time I met him we talked about football for 45 minutes and my case for 15. We also smoked a pack of 20 fags between us.

Roger made a number of visits and with each one I felt we were making progress. A couple of weeks into the sentence I bumped into my old mate, the solicitor Paul Schofield who had been on my first testimonial committee and helped out on the second, in the visiting room. He was seeing a client and Roger had just left. It was good to see a friendly face.

With what was a strong team working for me, it became easier to settle into the prison routine. No question it was miserable, boring and I missed my children and friends, but I made the best of it and it helped to have people watching out for me, people who'd bring something back from the canteen while I was standing in the phone queue. Having said that, you could never let your guard down and relax. I felt as though I was on constant alert and looking over my shoulder just in case something was to happen. The food wasn't bad, though. Three meals a day, all hot and freshly cooked. Not bad considering where we were.

And, of course, I got asked to play for the prison football team. I forget who the opposition was, but they were a local team who fancied getting stuck into the lags. We murdered them (not literally – it wasn't that kind of prison) and I got a double hattrick. But this central defender just kept taking lumps out of me, partly because I was in prison and with some added venom because of my Blackburn connections. I asked him as nicely as possible to stop kicking me. No, I threatened him. And it worked to a point. A minute later he flattened one of my teammates who, not having had the benefit of my grammar school education, took a more direct course of action to prevent further hassle and punched him square in the face. This was not handbags at ten paces – it was more pistols at dawn – and a few more ended up getting involved.

At right back we had one of three warders in the team. He came running across and I thought there might be some trouble. There was. He twatted the opposition defender who started it.

My professional income might have dried up, but I got an ounce of baccy for being man of the match which, in prison, is more useful than a substantial win bonus on the outside.

There was an inter-block five-a-side competition that I was advised not to take part in as I could have been targeted for a bit of off-the-ball antics. I stood behind our keeper to watch our block team. He looked like he could barely move. After receiving a pass back he waddled out, a bit like a penguin, and inexplicably gave the ball to an opposition player who duly put it in the back of the net. When he waddled back I asked him what the matter was. It turned out he had a load of drugs stuffed up his backside and was worried they would fall out if he ran too fast. I nearly fell over laughing. Crack up the crack. Cracked me up.

It was the done thing to call the warders 'screws', but I tried not to. It wasn't me at all and, with one exception, I got on well with them. He was just a tiresome dickhead and I did wonder for a while if he was a Burnley fan. I was treated well by inmates and staff everywhere, but this guy seemed to go out of his way to wind people up. If you got a visit on a Sunday, you had to wait in the recreation room for your name to be shouted.

"Garner, you little shit, your visit's here."

Okay, so it was hardly grand-scale abuse, but it was unnecessary and provocative.

Some days later, after more legal discussions, I was chatting to Pete in our room. There was a calendar behind him.

"That's when I'm going – 17 December."

I think I had to tell myself that to keep going. It was wishful thinking more than anything else.

"No way. You got nine months, you'll be here until April."

We were both wrong, but I was less wrong. On the afternoon of the 17th one of the warders came in.

"Garner?"

"Yes."

"2136?"

"Yes."

"Be ready at half past nine tomorrow morning. You're going back to Preston."

I'd been given no notice at all, but it looked like the appeal was moving ahead. A miserable night was spent on the drugs wing at Preston. I have no idea why the drugs wing was chosen. Perhaps because there wasn't a six pints and 20 fags wing. I was in the company of space cadet Mick and a father-and-son burglary team from Darwen who, through a relative who worked at a law firm in Blackburn, heard I was being transferred back to Preston. They'd come to look after me. What a friendly place prison is.

Handcuffs back on and another ride in a Black Mariah for the journey back to Blackburn. It was slow and bumpy and I needed a wee. I saw Stephen in an upstairs room but I was still wearing the cuffs. At least now I wasn't handcuffed to one of the prison officers like I had been in the van. Stephen got his cigarettes out straight away – not only was he a fine lawyer, but he was also a mind reader, too. I couldn't light the cigarette because of the cuffs and Stephen asked if they could be removed. They couldn't. But I still needed the loo and they still refused to uncuff me. They let me have a little privacy, by tying a chain to the cuffs so I couldn't run off. Public enemy number one, Mr Simon Garner.

Stephen and I talked through the proceedings and then we were back into the same courtroom I'd last seen a month before. And – unbelievable – in front of the same judge. My hands were still cuffed and now I was chained to each of the prison officers who flanked me. No defender had ever been so close.

It seemed like an eternity, but it probably only took 15 minutes for Stephen to do his bit.

"Mr Garner would like the court to know who much he regrets his actions and his contempt of court."

That was the gist of it.

Five minutes later – a bloody long five minutes, mind you – the judge set me free after serving four weeks of a nine-month sentence. I sat back down. I couldn't take it in. Only when the prison officers took the cuffs off did I feel like it was happening to me and not someone else.

I was straight on the phone.

"Bob, I need my car back!"

To this day I don't know why I received such a harsh sentence. I can only assume they wanted to make an example of me, and perhaps I was a relatively high-profile case for them. I don't think Mandy expected it, either. Of course, by this time we were hardly best friends, but I don't believe she would have wanted to force me and the kids apart.

One of the lads in the nick had told me that when you leave the prison they give you some money – I think it was £40 – to help you out in case were broke. I'm still waiting for mine. They must have thought I had loads of money.

Stephen and I went back to the room upstairs and that's when I realised the press were there. I really didn't want to do it, but Stephen persuaded me to give an interview to the Lancashire Evening Telegraph so I could say thank you to people in Blackburn for their good wishes and letters. I was glad he made me go through with it.

While this was going on Heather had gone to fetch the car and I came out of court with her sister, Elizabeth. Unfortunately for Elizabeth, she was pictured in the Telegraph next to a picture of Mandy and was wrongly billed as one of 'the two women in Simon Garner's life'.

I hadn't seen the kids in over a month. We had written but it's not the same. Our first stop was St Bede's school. To them it was like nothing had happened. For me it was like everything had. We were together for about 15 minutes, but they had to get back to lessons. We drove back home, back to Berkshire, stopping only for 40 Silk Cut. And then I got gloriously pissed on two pints of lager.

I was home for Christmas, which a few weeks earlier I had been worried I was going to miss, and while it was a strange one, it was definitely merry.

CHAPTER 17

Life as a part-time footballer

1997 to 2002

Once the hangover had subsided I had some serious thinking to do. I was now unemployed and, having spent a month in prison with only limited opportunities to keep myself fit, I was hardly going to be at the top of any potential manager's shopping list. I had also just turned 37, so I wasn't exactly in my prime.

My contract with Woking was terminated during my stay at Her Majesty's pleasure. They wrote and said that since I was unavailable for training I was in breach of my contract. It added insult to the injury of incarceration. I argued that I was hardly in a position to fulfil my duties but it didn't get me far. The PFA, once again, gave me a leg up when it was needed and at least managed to secure two weeks' wages. But that wasn't going to last long.

Another letter I received while at Kirkham was from Steve Hayes, a Wycombe fan. It was more positive.

"If you're stuck for work when you get out, give me a call."

I was on the blower within a couple of days and landed myself my first proper job – selling mortgages to people who wanted to buy their council house. The gesture from Steve was much appreciated, though I didn't really enjoy the work. The travelling was dreadful and my area essentially covered the whole of the south – from Birmingham downwards.

There were days when I would have to drive to Cornwall for an evening appointment and I wouldn't get home until two or three in the morning but still have to be ready for the next day for another assignment. On one occasion I drove to Bournemouth which was two hours away and when I got there they had cancelled the appointment and nobody had told me, so it was just a huge waste of time.

It was odd having to wear a suit and tie to work. And I certainly had responsibilities that just didn't exist in sport. As a footballer much of your life is managed for you. You turn up when you are told to and someone else takes care of the details. At training there are always balls ready to kick and cones to run around. On away trips you arrive at the allotted time and someone takes you to a hotel where the rooms have already been booked and a table reserved for dinner. On match days you get presented with a clean kit and told to get on with the job. Football has its stresses, of course, but on balance they are fairly inconsequential. All you really do is play the game. And once the game is over you have time to prepare for the next one. Real jobs aren't like that.

But what was really tough was going into people's houses to sell them a mortgage that I knew, deep down, they couldn't afford. But I was working on commission so I really needed to sell these bloody mortgages. I grew up in a council house so I knew what it was like for people, and to tell them they could buy their house but it would cost them three times what they are currently paying in rent, and knowing what they were bringing in, and knowing that if they missed a payment in the first three years they could have their house taken off them, it was just not right. Not for me.

I didn't take to it very well at all. I went to a house in London one day to see a man who was a bus driver. The house was an absolute tip. He had two dogs walking around, beer cans all over the floor, dog shit here and there.

"How are you going to be able to afford this?"

I already knew the answer. We had to go in with a Polaroid camera and photocopier and get them to sign there and then. They could be effectively signing their house away. And I just couldn't do it, I felt too guilty. To be successful in that game you needed to sacrifice your morals and just think about your own commission.

While Steve was still with the company I could cope because he made sure my diary didn't clash with football training. But when he left, the writing was on the wall. He sold the firm and it relocated from Watford to Wolverhampton and I was expected to travel to the Black Country three times a week and the new boss wanted me to do at least three appointments a day. No chance, not on the money I was being paid. Don't get me wrong, it was better than being on the dole, but it became a choice between football and the job. Football and secure money, if you like. No contest.

On getting out of prison I decided the only way I was going to get another club was by touting myself around. I contacted the local paper and they printed a story saying I was available. Gordon Bartlett, who was manager at Wealdstone, contacted me and asked if I would meet him. There was no way on earth I was going to say no.

We met in the Marriott in Slough and he offered me £70 a game and the promise that the club was going places. Gordon really sold it to me. He sounded like a manager who should have been in the game full-time. He had big ambitions for the club and knew what he wanted to do – and had the backing of the owner. It was an easy decision for me.

Wealdstone was about 30 miles from where I lived and was at that time playing in the Ryman League Third Division – it's called the Isthmian League now – four promotions from the Conference. Both Stuart Pearce and Vinnie Jones had started their careers with the club, so if it was good enough for them, it was good enough for me.

They had a team bus that most of the players would travel to games on, but as I lived in Maidenhead it was easier for me to drive there, or at least drive part of the way and meet them somewhere around Watford.

The chairman had a bit of money behind him who was able to pay a decent wage for that level of football and Gordon was able to build a good team. They were really good lads and the team spirit was great. We had some proper nights out.

The Wealdstone fans seemed to like me and I had a good rapport with them. It was a big club for that level. They didn't have their own ground and we played our home games at Edgware Town, another non-league club in the area. But at away games we used to take hundreds of fans – it was such a well-supported team.

I joined the side halfway through the 1996/97 season and it was a very solid outfit that went on to win the league and was promoted to the Second Division. I scored four goals for Wealdstone that season, including a brace when we hammered Braintree Town 6-0. They finished just a point behind us in second place in the league.

Winning the league was brilliant and I was so happy for the rest of the lads. Most of them had played non-league all their lives, so it doesn't get any better really. I was pushing 38 and I had just won the first league title of my career. It meant a lot to the supporters and the team after so many years of struggle. And it meant a lot to me. It still does.

Part way through the season I signed briefly for Dagenham and Redbridge who were in the Ryman Premier – just one league below the Conference. It was a move I couldn't turn down because it meant playing at a higher level and my money shot up to £150 a game. The only trouble was, that after just seven days, a couple of training sessions and half a game, I was told that I wasn't really the type of player they wanted after all.

It wasn't a big deal. I rang Gordon and he immediately offered me the chance to go back to Wealdstone. I was happy to go back if truth be told. The boys at Wealdstone were a great bunch and I really enjoyed playing for Gordon. At Dagenham it just wasn't the same. It didn't feel like a happy camp.

Just before we went up I handed my notice in with the mortgage company and went straight into a job as a postman, pounding the streets of Maidenhead. The early starts suited my wish to keep playing – I was finished for lunchtime so there was no problem with two nights a week of training. Unless we were training on a plastic pitch, and I'd have to tell Gordon I couldn't train because my knees were buggered. He'd tell me to just do a couple of laps of the pitch and get off. Fantastic – back to the pub.

The only difficulty was the fact I had to work on Saturday mornings and by the time it came to kick-off I was already feeling knackered. Add in a few pints after the game and Sundays became totally dedicated to recovery. Mind you, all the walking kept me fit.

I stayed for another season at Wealdstone and it was another great time for the club. We were promoted for the second season in a row, finishing third, and the club went up to the Ryman League First Division. It was a good season for me – I scored 14 – and Wealdstone has never looked back. The club has continued to move up through the leagues and is only a promotion away from the Football League which is incredible.

That eighteen months were pretty turbulent for me. If you tot it all up I had three clubs, three jobs, three homes and two girlfriends. Still, it kept me from being bored.

Heather and I split up at the end of the season and the only number Gordon had for me was Heather's. I'm not the best at keeping in touch and when Windsor and Eton found me I took them up on the offer of playing for them in Ryman League Division Two.

Less satisfactory was the fact I was living in a bedsit after moving out of Heather's. I hated it, but I wasn't there long. I went to a party with my mate Paddy McClure. That's where I met Suzy.

We clicked instantly and I soon moved into her house at Cookham in Berkshire. We married the following year, in April 1999.

I gave up the post when another pal, Billy Simmons, offered me a job as a painter and decorator. I kept that up initially until 2001. That August, Suzy gave birth to Thomas and after her maternity leave was finished she went back to work and I became a house husband. It made sense for a number of reasons, the main one being that Suzy's earning potential in the marketing world was a damn sight better than mine in the home decoration business.

I didn't mind the decorating and always had a laugh with the lads I worked with. We once had a job at the Chelsea goalkeeper Ed de Goey's house near Windsor. He had no idea who I was, of course, so I told him. I don't think he was particularly impressed.

I had a good year at Windsor and Eton and we weren't far off promotion to the First Division of the Ryman League. Despite being 39 I played 44 games that season and chipped in with 13 goals. In one game we battered Northwood 7-0 and I scored four goals. It was absolutely pissing it down that day and I came off with about 20 minutes to go.

I got on great with the lads at Windsor, another club with the right spirit. I played up front much of the time with Dennis Greene and between us we scored quite a lot of goals. We also supped quite a few pints – the craic was great at that level.

Just before Thomas was born Windsor and Eton's manager Alan Davies moved on. He had been with the club for a few years and really helped to turn around their fortunes. And he had been good to me in my season with the club. However the new boss – to follow the pattern – didn't like the look of me and so I moved to Flackwell Heath, back in the Ryman

League Third Division, for the 1999/2000 season.

Playing for fun and expenses I had a great time. The club was just five minutes' drive from home and the lads were enthusiastic about the game. I couldn't have asked for more in my final season.

The years were catching up with me. I was 40 now and my ankles and knees were starting to cause me real problems. They'd had enough and, frankly, so had the rest of me. I couldn't train any more because my body wouldn't allow more than one rigorous workout each week. The morning after a game I was aching all over. Ultimately it wasn't a difficult decision.

Towards the end of the season we played Hertford Town. It was a meaningless game between two sides in midtable. Former England international Graham Roberts – who played more than 200 games for Tottenham as well as playing for Rangers and Chelsea – was the player-manager for the opposition and in this game he was in goal, but I didn't beat him. I wasn't the only ex-pro ending my days at this level.

Also in attendance were a couple of Blackburn fans who had come to see what had happened to their former striker. Rovers had fallen into the First Division by then although Graeme Souness would lead them back to the promised land the following year.

One of the lads was Richard Slater, a journalist moving into a business career and he had some ideas for what I might be able to do next.

Gordon Bartlett
Manager at Wealdstone from 1996 to 1998

I had a phone call out of the blue one day from a supporter to tell me Simon Garner was coming out of prison and was looking for a club.

"We've got absolutely bloody no chance of signing Simon Garner."

That was my reaction at least.

Anyway, I was given Simon's phone number and I gave him a call. We met at the Marriott Hotel in Slough and it was obvious Simon wasn't bothered about the money or the level we were at. He was impressed with our ambition and just wanted to play. He said he couldn't train because he had a day job. That was fine by me.

We did the deal on the Friday and I kept it quiet. The following day we were playing away at Hertford Town. The players were arriving one by one and chatting on the pitch. I'd met Simon earlier and left him in the changing rooms when Steve Bircham walked out on to the pitch.

"Bloody hell, Simon Garner's in our dressing room."

There was a real buzz around the players that we had managed to sign him and he had a huge impact. The supporters loved him and bringing him in created a great deal of excitement.

I mean, Simon Garner wasn't the biggest name in football, but for a side in the Third Division of the Ryman League to bring in a player that a season before had been playing professionally at Wycombe in the Second Division was a big deal. To have a player of that calibre and proven experience was just enormous for us.

I was aware of what Simon had done, particularly at Blackburn and more recently at Wycombe, but what really struck me was his sharpness. He was probably the quickest player over the first yard that I saw throughout my career. His first touch was outstanding and his awareness and understanding of when to move the ball helped the team enormously. If he received the ball in certain areas he would almost slow it down to walking pace before one sharp movement and he got his shot away, got a cross into the box or found a teammate with a pass.

It wasn't all about scoring goals, although he probably managed about one in every three games he played for us. He had this knack of being able to take the ball on his chest, get it down and create a chance for a teammate.

It was early in my time at Wealdstone and it felt like we were in a hospice. We were dying as a club. We were just coming out of administration and the club had volunteered to move from the Southern League to the Ryman League in order to save money on travel costs, which was effectively a relegation down the leagues. We didn't have a proper ground and had really been through the mill. But it was my ambition to get the club back to the Conference.

With Simon's help – and he had a huge influence – we were able to secure two consecutive promotions. We were on our way and Wealdstone has not had a relegation since (at the time of writing). I took the club as far as the National League South and I was delighted to see it go back into the National League – or the Conference as it was. And the importance of those building blocks from 1996 onwards cannot be understated. Nobody at Wealdstone will want to see the club drop back to those levels again.

Simon's influence on the team didn't stay just on the pitch. He was a great help off it, but not in the most conventional of ways. While the players were all out warming up before a game, Simon would be having a fag or sitting in the changing rooms reading Sporting Life. He saved his energies for the pitch. At half-time he'd always have a fag and at full-time he'd have a fag and a pint with the lads.

He was a down-to-earth, cheeky chappy who was just a really nice lad to have around. His personality was infectious and he was popular throughout the club.

And I'll never forget that gummy smile when he took his bloody teeth out.

CHAPTER 18

Going home

2000 to 2003

Retirement can be a huge step for a lot of footballers. Suddenly the only thing you know is gone. It's more than just a job, it's a life. It's having everything prepared for you, being told where to go and how you are going to get there, what exercise you should do, what food you should eat. To go from that to suddenly having complete freedom and control over your own life is a big step and for many, especially in modern football, it can be difficult.

For me, it was a bit easier. I had been practically retired from the game since I left Wycombe. Yes, I was still playing, but when it's for expenses three or four leagues below the Conference, it's no longer your life. I'd had a 'proper' job since I came out of prison and was getting to grips with life outside the game.

Having said all that, not being able to play football any more was a big change for me. It didn't pay the bills by this time – it barely bought a pint – but I loved the game. I always had and I always will. I loved kicking a ball around, I loved seeing it hit the back of the net, I loved hearing the noise of the crowd – whether that's 20,000 in the Second Division or 25 in the Ryman League – and I loved being around the lads, having the craic and enjoying a beer or two (or three) in the bar at full-time.

But we don't stay young forever, and our bodies tell us at some point we can't do it anymore. Mine had been bollocking me for the past 12 months and I finally had to listen.

I was earning my living as a painter and decorator now, but I wasn't ready to give up on football entirely.

While I was still playing at Flackwell Heath, Richard Slater had called me to ask if I was interested in writing a book with him. The idea was I could waffle about the life and times of Simon Garner and he would put my words into some semblance of order. I'll talk to anyone about football and if there was a chance it could make a few quid then I was definitely up for it.

We agreed to meet up and Richard travelled down on the train so we could have a go at putting together one chapter and then see if we felt it could work. We went straight to the pub, Richard started recording the conversation and we got drunk.

What was taped was barely usable, but we hit it off straight away and from that point on we knew it was going to work.

He came and saw me a couple more times, including the day he watched that glamorous Ryman League Third Division game at Flackwell, and we had many hours of conversations over the phone and gradually the book began to take shape. We would be on the phone for ages at a time and I just loved doing it. It brought back memories that I wouldn't have thought about. Things you forget after so many years suddenly come flooding back and it is such a worthwhile experience.

Parrs Wood Press, now out of business, was a small publisher that had agreed to put the book out and that was really something. I wasn't a big name in the grand scheme of things. Yes, I might mean something to people of a certain generation in Blackburn, West Brom and Wycombe, but to the wider world I'm not especially known. It was an honour then to be told that a proper publisher, a company that made proper books about proper sportspeople, was interested in selling my story to the world.

We sold about 9,000 copies of There's Only One Simon Garner and that made me immensely proud. We didn't make much and I get bugger all for the copies that sell on Amazon now, but knowing my story was out there and was being read by all those people is still pretty special.

We got some really good reviews and coverage, including in The Times and one of the big football magazines, and I did BBC Radio Two with Adrian Chiles ahead of a game between Blackburn and West Brom. I upset him because he kept asking me for a score prediction and I just said it would be a draw, but when he pushed me I said Blackburn would win. As a West Brom fan he wasn't happy with that. The Paralympian Tanni

Grey-Thompson was also on the show that day and she was hilarious. You wouldn't expect it but she was effing and blinding and telling me all sorts of stories about how her daughter would leave her at the bottom of the stairs and take the Mickey out of her.

I don't want to sound too self-deprecating, but coverage on that level legitimised the book for me and gave me the confidence that I did have a story that had been worth telling and people had enjoyed reading.

We did some book signings and did really big business at WH Smiths in Blackburn where we sold hundreds of copies. I was signing copies of the book for hours – my hand was killing by the time we got out of there. The queue was immense and everybody wanted to come in and have a chat. Of course I didn't mind that at all. I loved talking to the supporters and I loved putting a smile on their faces. I was too old to do that by scoring goals, but if handing them a signed copy of my book and having a brief natter about the good old days made their day then it made mine as well. We had signings in Wycombe town centre as well which also went down a storm.

Book signings can be hazardous, though. I'd been in business with Ian Battersby and his wife brought a book for me to sign for him but I got his name wrong. I think I got away with it. We were mates.

Richard put me up when I travelled north for signings and promotional bits and pieces. We'd often combine work with pleasure and go for a few beers and usually a kebab to finish the night. Although there was one occasion when I had to cut a night short. He assured me his front door would be on the latch when I stumbled back. I spent the night asleep on his doorstep. It's all glamour.

Thanks to the book a few conversations started to take place with Blackburn Rovers, and I reminded them that I had been promised a testimonial back in 1992 which had so far never happened. I couldn't find anything in writing but Richard said he would make a couple of calls. Tom Finn was the managing director at Rovers and he could not have been more accommodating. The club also didn't have anything in writing about me being offered a testimonial, but people at Ewood knew the deal existed, and that was enough. And Tom and the rest of the management team at Blackburn offered us everything we could have wanted.

They gave us the stadium for free, including all the stewards and all the other behind-the-scenes stuff you need to put on a football match. We came up with the idea of setting up a game between the current team, which had recently won the League Cup and players from the team that won the Premier League a few years earlier. Between us, and with some help from Kevin Gallacher, Richard and I contacted most of the lads who played in that 1994/95 Rovers team.

Unfortunately Alan Shearer was unavailable, Chris Sutton had commitments at Celtic and David Batty couldn't have been nicer but said he had no interest in football – it was just a job to him – and he was going to be at his caravan.

But we did get Kenny Dalglish, Tim Flowers, Kevin Gallacher, Mike Newell, Stuart Ripley, Mark Atkins and Bobby Mimms who all gave up their time on a Saturday afternoon, which still gives me goosebumps today.

Mark Hughes, a hero of mine from his days smashing the ball home for Manchester United, was now manager of Wales having left Blackburn and retiring as a player the year before.

We put in what we thought was a cheeky request to the Welsh FA to see if he fancied managing one of the teams. We weren't sure if he was going to be there until he walked through the door an hour before kick-off.

"Of course I'm here. I've always been coming."

I really couldn't believe it. He was a top man, Hughesy. When he was managing and I was doing Radio Lancashire, I used to sit at the back of the press room and wait for the crowd to die down before heading home, and Sparky would always go out of his way to come over and say hello.

And then of course there were the players from the Blackburn first team. The season had only just finished – in which Rovers had qualified for Europe having finished sixth in the Premier League – and fresh from a 4-0 win at Spurs we had Alan Kelly, Tugay, Andy Todd, David Dunn, Nils-Eric Johansson, Craig Hignett, Dwight Yorke, Egil Ostenstad, Damien Duff, and a bunch of great kids from the youth team who all came and played their part.

Without Richard's involvement the testimonial probably wouldn't have happened. To be fair, a few days before kick-off there was some jeopardy when Mandy threatened an injunction if there wasn't a share of the takings for her. We came to an amicable agreement quickly and the game went ahead.

So we had Mark Hughes managing the current team and Kenny Dalglish in charge of the Premiership winners. Still pinching myself at that.

Into the dressing room walks Kenny.

"You're not starting the game."

Unbelievable. Bloody déjà vu. That was the first thing he said to me when he took over at Blackburn. He sat in the stand and watched me score two great goals in a great performance against Plymouth and then stuck me straight on the bench. And it was the same in the testimonial. I blame Richard. He'd forgotten to get GARNER printed on my shirt and Kenny gave him a proper bollocking for that.

"You can come on in the second half."

"Whose sodding game is this?"

We were laughing hard.

The 'Simon Garner XI' was 3-1 down at half-time thanks to Ostenstad, Yorke and Hignett. Alex Bruce – Steve Bruce's lad who was in the Rovers youth team at the time – had given us the lead early on but it didn't last.

I came on for the second 45 minutes, replacing Mark Hughes which was clearly an upgrade. And what an emotional moment that was. I had a lump in my throat. I was crossing that white line in front of 13,000 people, which was more than we were used to seeing at Ewood on a regular basis back in the 1980s, and despite the fact we had some big names on display, I liked to think those people were there to see me. And that felt really special.

Referee Eddie Wolstenholme had just retired from the game and graciously came to officiate the proceedings.

And then, would you believe it, a penalty was awarded. At the Blackburn End.

I always fancied my chances from the spot. And I had my chance. All that could stand in the way of a last slice of Ewood Park glory was if Alan Kelly, having been told exactly which way to dive, was to dive the other way.

Planned or not, it was a sublime moment. One last goal in front of the

Blackburn End. One last roar. It felt fantastic.

And then I pulled my calf and had to hobble off five minutes later. I really was injured.

The game, not that it matters, ended in a 6-3 win for the present-day team. Which sounds about right as they still had their legs. Mike Newell scored what was possibly the best goal of his career and Mark Atkins scored a penalty, while at the other end Ostenstad scored two more and Damien Duff scored one.

My appearance was short-lived, but it was enough to be named man of the match after a bit of haggling with the sponsor who, just because he had been brilliant, wanted to give the watch to Mike Newell. But I wasn't leaving without that thing on my wrist. And I didn't.

The night before the game the club had put me up at Northcote Manor, a fantastic hotel and restaurant close to the new state-of-the-art training complex at Brockhall in the Ribble Valley. Gordon Taylor, who was then the chief executive of the PFA, was in the private dining area and he sent through a bottle of Champagne. Gordon and I had always got on well, ever since I cleaned his boots as an apprentice during his playing days. The PFA was always great to me and if I ever had a problem, even after my playing days, I could call them up and ask for Gordon and he would try to help me out. Gordon has received a fair amount of stick over the years and he's left the PFA now, but for me he was great. Gordon made a sizeable contribution to the testimonial which was very generous.

After the game we went into the Jack Walker Suite and there was a dinner which was fun, with stand-up bingo and an auction. Duncan McKenzie came along to host the evening. And there was time for a little late drunken drama between two ex-players, who I won't name since one of them got smacked on the nose. I was more concerned about the bill to clean the blood from the carpet.

Going back to Ewood Park, after all those years, was a perfect way to wave a final farewell to my football career. But now was the big question … what next?

CHAPTER 19

Life after football

2003 to 2023
As it turned out, it wasn't long before I was getting my boots back on and heading back on to the pitch, this time for the Sky Sports Masters competition. This was a competition that ran from 2000 for about a decade until Sky cancelled it, probably because it was crap to watch. The idea was that retired footballers who were 35 and older came together to represent their former club in one last attempt at glory.

I played for Blackburn and we never got anywhere really, but it was good fun, and the best pay-days from football I ever had. One year they played it at the Metro Arena in Newcastle and getting there was a real palaver as I was living down south. The train was so expensive I ended up going on the plane.

A few years later I played in a competition in London that was on Sky and Ian Wright was there presenting. We played Manchester United in the first game and I scored the first goal. "There you go Wrighty!"

He laughed. We have always got on well ever since that Crystal Palace play-off game all those years before. The BBC presenter Mark 'Chappers' Chapman was on their team and he tried to kick the shit out of me. Ray Wilkins was also in their team – what a player he was! For this tournament each team had some ex-players and a couple of celebrities. This gave me the chance to renew acquaintances with Everton legend Neville Southall.

Neville was also with me for one of the toughest challenges of my life, which incidentally had nothing to do with football. For two years running I took part in a charity climb up Mount Kinabalu. It was an event called the PFA Borneo Challenge raising money for a charity in Chester called Children Today. The cash was going to buy some equipment for kids with disabilities.

As well as Neville there was Alan Kennedy from Liverpool, Brian Kilcline from Newcastle, Arthur Albiston from Manchester United and Peter Nicholson from Bolton. The second year I did it we had Lee Martin from United and David Oldfield from Manchester City. This was one of those charity events where it included footballers from teams all over the north west and fans of the teams had to raise a certain amount of cash to come with us.

For a guy who didn't like the more physical aspects of training and the cross country running we had to do every year, that was bloody hard work and it was a very long way up. It was unbelievable. But when you got to the top of that mountain it was just unreal and so worth it. It was one occasion when smoking helped because, as the air gets thinner, people start to struggle with the altitude. But as a smoker my lungs are used to getting less oxygen! I knew I was doing the right thing all those years.

You had to get to base camp and then we would set off in the middle of the night in order to get to the summit at dawn. There wasn't a bar or anything like that but there was a machine you could get cans of beer from, so I was drinking those while Neville – who it turned out was tee total – sat drinking cups of tea. We were out there for about 10 days in total and did all sorts of stuff as well as climbing the mountain, like white water rafting and mountain biking, but the main event was climbing the mountain by torchlight.

I carried on playing in the odd five-a-side. Whether it was with my mates in midweek or for charity whenever my legs and schedule would allow it, and I still like to get involved in events as they take place to this day. Although my playing time is much shorter and sometimes amounts to just the kick-off.

I said I would never do it but I did try my hand at coaching, although I lasted about three sessions. John Gorman – who was Glenn Hoddle's assistant when he was England manager – was at Wycombe and he asked me to go and do a bit of work with the strikers. But it soon became apparent that I wasn't going to get paid, so I told him to stick it. In all honesty I didn't enjoy it. I had never seen myself as a future coach or a manager and this experience just cemented that for me.

I tried after-dinner speaking and hated it. I was much happier doing a question-and-answer session and I could do those all day long, but after-dinner speaking is just horrible.

I did one at the Dunkenhalgh Hotel with the ex-West Ham and England international midfielder Trevor Brooking. Trevor had told us he was happy to do it but we couldn't have a dirty comedian. Unfortunately we had Wandering Walter, who was the East Lancashire equivalent of Roy Chubby Brown. Out he came effing and blinding. I thought Trevor was going to get up and walk out, but he didn't, he got through it although he kept giving me funny looks. Mind you when it came to him getting up and doing his speech everyone fell asleep. He was bloody boring.

I vowed never to do it again following an after-dinner event at Mitton Fold, another hotel just outside Blackburn. It was the third one I had done in quick succession and I had decided to change the script I had been using. Within minutes I could tell it just wasn't landing well and people were totally switched off. It was excruciating and after that I said I would only do Q&A sessions, and those can be great fun.

Like the time I did one at Accrington Stanley when they had just won promotion. The captain of the club was there and he was asking a question about bonuses and when they should be paid. I told him if it was in his contract then the bonus should be paid, and the Stanley chairman at the time was sitting next to me kicking me under the table.

With coaching and after-dinner speaking not being for me, one of the ways I have been able to stay in the game is by offering myself as a pundit. BBC local radio would often ask me to go and summarise alongside the main commentator for Blackburn games in and around the London area. I remember on one occasion they were playing at Watford. They were building a new stand so the press had been stuck in the corner at one end of the ground. The commentator, who obviously didn't have the best of views, was describing the play.

"Jason Roberts is heading down the wing. He's crossed it. And Jason Roberts has headed it in."

"What do you think about that then Simon?"

I didn't know what to say.

I have done Sky a couple of times as well. One of them must have been at Peterborough because Barry Fry was there. Going on TV is a bit weird because they make you wear make-up so you don't look haggard when the lights and the cameras are on you. After the game kicks off the make-up people come out to top you up before the half-time segment. On this occasion poor Barry was sweating that much it just kept running off his face as quick as they were putting it on. I saw him at QPR a few years later when I was commentating on a game. I said hello.

"I fackin' remember you from that Sky programme when I kept sweating!"

Sky also had me on for their coverage of the East Lancashire Derby game when Blackburn were back in the First Division and Burnley had got promoted. It was the first time the two clubs had played each other for years and Blackburn won 2-0 at Turf Moor, which I was obviously really pleased about. The presenter asked me again about the story of me playing for West Brom against Burnley with a Blackburn shirt under my top. And once again I had to deny it. The clip is on YouTube for all to see.

Perhaps my most bizarre television appearance was when I was asked to appear on the Frank Skinner and David Baddiel show Fantasy Football during Euro 2004. This was a live show and each week they had an ex-footballer come on and sing a song. They dressed me up as England assistant manager Tord Grip and, complete with a huge accordion, I had to sing a ridiculous song about Wayne Rooney while Baddiel and Skinner danced around watched on by pop star Brian McFadden and comedian Rhona Cameron. It sounds almost as ridiculous as it was.

The show went out live at about 10 o'clock at night and I had to be there from 10 in the morning to have singing lessons. The singing coach had me singing the words and then offering suggestions.

"For this bit you need to sing a bit higher. Try a bit quicker here."

After two hours of me nodding my head and then doing it exactly the same he just said: "Oh just get on with it."

"Rooney-oh, Rooney-oh…" That's all I can remember from the song.

Frank Skinner was a massive West Brom fan so we got on straight away. He was a great bloke and we had a good laugh. David Baddiel was a bit off. I was there all day at the studio in London thinking I could murder a pint but I very bravely refrained until I had done my bit. After that it was time to hit the bar.

By 2007 it was time to think about getting a 'proper job' and working out what I was going to do with my life. I had been enjoying the punditry and thought I would see if I could train to be a journalist. I found a course in Wimbledon and so I called up and applied for it. It wasn't cheap but when they discovered I was Simon Garner the ex-footballer they asked if I would agree to be questioned by the students on the course as part of their training. If I accepted they would let me do the course for free. Of course I jumped at the chance – I'll talk to people about football all day long and if it was saving me a load of money then even better.

I loved it. There I was, getting on for 40 alongside all these kids of 18 or 19, but we got on really well and I did enjoy the course. The one thing I remember that still sends shivers down my spine is shorthand. I just could not get my head around it. I enjoyed learning about media law, that was really interesting. Our tutor told us a story about a football manager who had been having it away with another player's wife and had taken out an injunction to stop it coming out in the press, I don't think it ever came out to this day.

In the end it all became a bit too much for me and I dropped out of the course after about a year.

I went back to painting and decorating and that's what I have done ever since. I enjoy it to an extent, it's a job. But I like working for myself as it means I am my own boss. I've been lucky and have never struggled to get work. When I first started out, everyone in the area knew I was an ex-footballer and I would spend a lot of time chatting about my career while on jobs. In all honesty my football career probably helped get me a lot of work, certainly in the early days, although now I like to think it's because I do a decent job.

Suzy gave birth to Martha, my fourth child and first daughter, in 2005, but sadly Suzy and I didn't make it and we went our separate ways a few years ago. I had quite a few years on my own after the break-up with Suzy and, if I'm honest, I had some dark times – but my best mate Alfie Lewis and his wife Billie were there for me and pulled me back.

I lived in Cookham for a number of years, which is a beautiful village in leafy Berkshire. Then in 2020 I met Jane, who I now live very happily with just up the road in Bourne End in Buckinghamshire. It's a lovely little place and the ideal place to spend my retirement. Between us we have seven children so life will always be pretty busy.

I still get back up to Blackburn when I can. It still feels like a second home having spent all those years up there. The council named a street after me on a local estate where the roads all bear the names of former Rovers players. Having Garner Avenue coming off Dalglish Drive is a real honour.

And that's not the only thing named after me. The Simon Garner bus can be found winding its way round the streets of Blackburn and Darwen every day. Funny, on occasions when I went through a barren spell people would say I couldn't hit the back of a bus, now my name's on the front of one.

And it's always nice to see a game at Ewood, sometimes doing the corporate hosting bit. I did get involved with the supporters trust for a while when they were trying to raise cash to gain a seat on the board. For a time under the new owners things looked a bit bleak for the club and I wanted to do my bit to help the supporters. It didn't happen and things have since calmed down.

My involvement in the game is minimal now, but football will always be a big part of my life. I still do BBC radio and get to a few games but I packed in the midweek five-a-side with the lads about four years ago as it was getting harder and harder to get up for work the next day. It was a tough decision as I wish I could still play. But head had to rule over heart and I had to think about the impact on my body.

I still get to Adams Park occasionally for the odd Wycombe match. It's a lot closer to home than my other clubs. Mind you, they once asked me to do the half-time draw and things got a bit heated. Someone obviously hadn't done their homework. They were playing Burnley, whose fans obviously still had fond memories of me. I gave them a nice wave and almost started a riot. I wanted to do it again the following season but the police said no. Spoilsports.

Every Saturday I meet up with the boys – Smithy, Jim, Luton, Snake and Peachy – in the local pub at 5.15pm for Final Score and we will discuss the game in great detail. They're cracking lads and we spend a lot of time together putting the world to rights.

Football gave me a great life and experiences that most people can only dream of. There have been challenges along the way, but I can honestly say I have no regrets and I would not change a thing.

When I look back on my playing career and think about those three ambitions I set for myself, I came very close to achieving all three. I broke records, I played at Wembley (more than once), and I was part of a side that won promotion to the top flight.

And I had a blast doing it all.

One Last Shot